The GUINNESS Book of
Seashore Life

The GUINNESS Book of
SEASHORE LIFE

Heather Angel

Illustrations by Vanessa Luff
Photographs by Heather Angel

GUINNESS SUPERLATIVES LIMITED
2 CECIL COURT, LONDON ROAD, ENFIELD, MIDDLESEX

© Guideway Publishing Ltd 1981

Designed and produced by Guideway Publishing Ltd,
Willow House, 27-49 Willow Way, London SE26

Published in 1981 by Guinness Superlatives Ltd,
2 Cecil Court, London Road, Enfield, Middlesex EN2 6DJ

Guinness is a registered trademark of
Guinness Superlatives Ltd

Angel, Heather
The Guinness book of seashore life.
(Britain's natural heritage).
1. Seashore biology - Great Britain
I. Title   II. Series
574.941   QH137
ISBN 0 85112 304 X

Printed by Morrison & Gibb Ltd, Edinburgh

Many people kindly provided information on the distribution of a particular group of life around Britain or supplied
information from local fauna lists. In particular, the
mollusc distribution maps were produced from information
provided from the Conchological Society marine census
data by the Recorder, D.R. Seaward. All other maps were
compiled from data supplied by the Nature Conservancy
Council from data collected as part of the intertidal survey
commissioned by the NCC and carried out by the Scottish
Marine Biological Association and the Marine Biological
Association of the United Kingdom; from Dr P.F.C. Cornelius, Dr Steven Knight, Professor M.S. Laverack, Dr J.R.
Lewis, Dr Roger Mitchell, Dr Eve Southward, Mr Alwyne
Wheeler, and from personal records. The oil pollution information was kindly supplied by the Advisory Committee
on Oil Pollution of the Sea and the Marine Pollution Control Unit, the Department of Trade. Thanks also to
Dorothy Herlihy who typed the complete manuscript.

Front Cover: Hermit Crab

Contents

Introduction

With a 2750-mile (4428-km) coastline around Britain, no one lives more than 80 miles (129 km) from the seashore. Yet most people visit the coast for only a week or two each year. Unlike terrestrial habitats, the seashore cannot be explored at any time of day or night. Only when the shore is exposed by the ebbing tide is this fascinating, and often little-known, habitat accessible from land. It is therefore essential to find out the time of low water prior to visiting the coast.

While anyone who is observant, and who is prepared to peer closely into rock pools or beneath rocky overhangs, will see a good variety of seashore life, it is true that, as with all branches of natural history, so much more will be seen if you know where and how to look. Although plenty of information is given in this book, it cannot compare with being guided around a shore by an enthusiastic marine biologist.

Walking from the land towards the sea, the extreme upper end of the shore, above the high water of the spring tides, is called the *splash zone*. The width of this zone is directly related to the degree of exposure: sheltered shores have a narrow splash zone, while exposed Cornish and south Wales shores which are buffeted by fierce gales may have salt spray carried up to 100 feet (30 m) or more above the high-tide level.

On any shore, whether it be rocky, sandy or muddy, the debris carried up the beach by the tide is deposited in a band known as the *tideline* or *strandline*. After winter gales, extensive mounds of brown seaweeds pile up on beaches, where resourceful farmers and horticulturists collect this valuable source of manure and minerals to feed their land. Sandhoppers are permanent inhabitants which scavenge beneath rotting seaweed in the strandline. Wading birds, especially turnstones, forage back and forth along it, and it is here that unusual animals can turn up, especially on our south-west coasts. Floating animals such as Portuguese man-o'-war (*Physalia physalis*), by-the-wind sailor (*Velella velella*) and the purple sea snails (*Janthina* spp), buoyed along by the North Atlantic Drift, can occasionally get beached in quite large numbers.

The part of the shore which is exposed by the ebbing tide—from high tide down to low tide—is known as the intertidal zone or *littoral* zone, whereas the shore which lies permanently submerged is the *sub-littoral* zone.

The temperature of the sea changes much more slowly than the air temperature, and this is why, on a hot sunny day early in summer, the sea feels very cold. It is not until September that the sea water has reached its maximum temperature, which varies in different parts of Britain. Along our south-west coasts, which are washed by the warm North Atlantic Drift, it can reach 63°F (17°C) or more; whereas in the North Sea it rarely rises above 59°F (15°C). In winter, the temperature off the south-west coast will drop to 39°F (4°C) or even lower in a severe winter. Even so, this temperature range is much less than the range on land. Animals which live between the tides, on rocky shores especially, are subjected to much greater extremes, not only of temperature, but also of salinity (the amount of salt in the water), than animals which live permanently submerged in the sub-littoral. On a hot summer's day, the sea-water temperature in a small shallow rock pool in the higher part of the shore can rise by as much as 50°F (10°C). This warming up is more gradual than the sudden drop which takes place as the incoming tide flushes out the warm water and replaces it with cold water. If rain falls on an exposed shore, this will dilute the sea water in a shallow rock pool.

The salinity of sea water is expressed as the total dry weight of all the chemical salts in a sea-water sample. If pure sea water is boiled so that all the water evaporates, white crystals will remain. These are chemical compounds or salts, which consist not only of common salt (sodium chloride) but many others as well. Around Britain, the salinity of open coast sea water is 35°/oo (parts per thousand) which means that 1000 grams of sea water contain 35 grams of total salts. In the Red Sea, where considerable evaporation takes place, the salts are concentrated so that the salinity rises to 40°/oo. In our estuaries where the sea is mixed with the freshwater moving down rivers, the salinity is much reduced, more so during the winter when the rivers are in flood.

A brief description of the fluctuation of tidal levels is given in the next chapter. Sea levels also fluctuate, not daily, but over long periods of time. Evidence of higher past sea levels can be seen today as raised beaches as at Port Appin in Argyllshire. Where submerged fossils and petrified forests are exposed at low water, these signify areas of land which have either become submerged by a rise in the sea level or by land subsidence. Fossil forests can be seen at low tide at Bexhill in Sussex, in Bridgwater Bay, Somerset and at Borth on the west Wales coast.

Parts of the coastline are constantly being eroded away or built up. On the east coast, the land is gradually sinking, hence the acute problems of coastal erosion and the urgent need for a tidal barrage on the Thames. On the west coast, however, the land is gradually rising.

The overall pattern of life on the seashore may be predictable from one year to the next, but the vagaries of tide, current and weather ensure that this environment, above all others, can show a dramatic variation from one day to the next. You may know what life to expect to find on a certain shore, but you can never predict what may turn up. It is this variation on a theme which excites young and old alike to renew their searches on well-trodden shores.

The Tides

For people who live on the coast and whose livelihood depends on fishing or on ferrying tourists from one island to another, knowing the state of the tide is essential for their way of life. Likewise, the marine biologist or anyone wishing to explore life on the shore must not only know the precise time of low water, but also the extent to which the shore will be exposed during a given tide. Tide tables are usually published in local papers for coastal ports or they can be bought from angling and boating shops.

Most places in Britain have semi-diurnal tides—two high and two low waters approximately every 24 hours. The tides are caused by the gravitational pulls on the earth by the moon and, to a lesser extent, by the sun. When the pull exerted by the moon acts on the oceans, it results in a piling up of the seas to form high water on the part of the earth closest to the moon. High water also occurs on the part of the earth furthest from the moon, where the moon's gravitational pull has least effect. At this time, sea water is drawn away from other parts of the earth which then experience low tides.

The tidal rhythm is maintained by the movement of the moon around the earth and the earth's own rotation and movement around the sun, so that the high-tide wave and the corresponding low-tide wave pass continuously round the earth. The earth takes 24 hours to rotate on its own axis, but it takes an additional 50 minutes for the moon and the earth to return to the same position relative to each other. For this reason, the actual time of low (or high) water is progressively later on each successive day. It takes approximately six hours for the build-up from low water to high water and another six hours for the fall from high water back to low water. The difference in height between low- and high-water levels is known as the 'tidal range'. This used to be measured in feet, but it is now quoted in metres in the Admiralty Tide Tables. The tidal range varies from day to day. The biggest range is during the *spring* tides (Old English *springan*: to rise) which are not restricted to the season of spring, but which occur once a fortnight throughout the year during the new and full phases of the moon. The moon and sun then lie roughly in line and so their gravitational pulls on the oceans are combined. At the time of the first and last quarters of the moon, the sun and the moon lie at right angles to each other, and so their pulls no longer combine but work against one another. This results in the low-ranging *neap* tides (Old English *népflód*). The transition from neap to spring tides and back to neaps is a gradual one, with each successive day showing an increase in the tidal range up to the springs and a decrease down to neaps.

Along much of the coastline of Britain, the average spring tidal range is 2-3 yards (2-3 m), but off the south-west coast of Scotland the range is a mere 1½ yards (1.5 m), while in the Bristol Channel, where the tidal flow is channelled by the funnel-shaped Severn

Shore levels and tidal changes

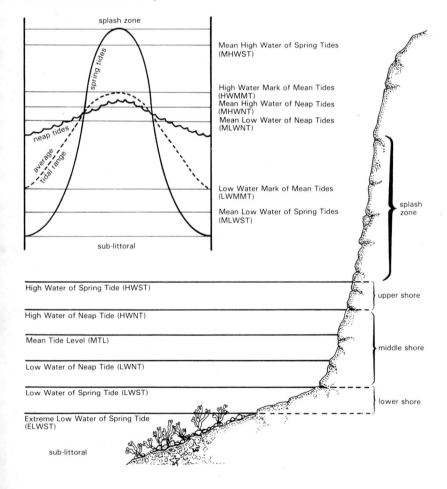

Estuary, ranges of over 15 yards (14 m) occur at Avonmouth. The tidal range is determined by the shape of the coastline as well as the submarine contours. At the time of the spring and autumn equinoxes (21 March and 21 September) when the sun and moon are more closely aligned, very spectacular high-ranging spring tides occur. At these times of year, when the lowest part of the shore becomes exposed, many interesting animals can be found which normally remain submerged in the sub-littoral.

The twice-daily ebb and flow of the tide means that at least one low tide occurs during daylight hours and in the summer months there may be even two low waters. The actual time of spring tides is fairly constant for a given locality: for example, low-water springs at Devonport occur around midday between 1100 and 1400 hours GMT, which is ideal both for observing and photographing seashore life. On the other hand, at Shoreham in Sussex, low-water springs occur in the early morning and in the late afternoon or early evening, which is not ideal for photography.

When the tide rises from low to high water it is known as a *flood* tide and when it falls it is known as the *ebb* tide. The rate at which a tide floods or ebbs is not constant. It usually rises more quickly during the first part of the tidal cycle than the second. On tidal flats, such as at Weston-super-Mare or in Morecambe Bay, the tide comes in so quickly you have to walk briskly or even run to avoid being overtaken by it.

Throughout this book, reference will be made to the tidal levels on the shore, since the distribution of many shore animals is determined by the amount of exposure to the air they will tolerate. Generally, the number of species increases as you walk down the shore from high water to low water. *All the abbreviated tidal levels are defined in the illustration opposite.* Another important level is 'mean sea level' (MSL) which is the average sea level from which all heights on land are measured. Since this varies slightly from one locality to another, the standard mean sea level used by the Ordnance Survey is the MSL at Newlyn in Cornwall.

Habitats

The type of shoreline around the coastline of the British Isles is clearly distinguished on the 1:25000 series of Ordnance Survey maps. Rocky shores are shown as black rocks, sandy beaches as fine orange stippling, while muddy shores are grey and shingle areas appear as orange circles. This provides a quick way of checking the type of beach before a visit is made. In addition, these maps mark in 'Low Water Mark of Mean Tides' (LWMMT) and 'High Water Mark of Mean Tides' (HWMMT), which clearly shows up those parts of the coastline which have big ranging tides.

Some books refer to the zones by the name of the dominant organism, e.g., the barnacle zone or the mussel zone, but, since there can be local variations from shore to shore, this is not too precise. Animals which live at MLWST are exposed to the air for only 4 per cent of a tidal cycle; those at MLWNT for 20 per cent; and those at MHWNT for 80 per cent.

Neither the seaweeds nor the animals which live on rocky shores are scattered haphazardly over a shore. Instead they occur in distinct zones, with the species most tolerant of exposure to air living at the top of the shore and those less tolerant at the bottom. This means that it is very often possible to describe the distribution of a species on a shore in relation to the tidal level. However, the length of time the species is exposed to the air is not the only factor which affects the zonation of seashore animals. Exposure to wave action and the aspect of the shore in relation to sun or shadow are also important.

Rocky shores represent the interaction of the sea with the land. They may appear hard and permanent but they are constantly being eroded away by pounding waves and also by weathering caused by frost, rain and wind. On exposed rocky shores, the constant wave action prevents brown seaweeds (wracks) from colonising rocks, and their place is taken by barnacles instead. Brown wracks are a feature of relatively sheltered rocky shores, which have a greater variety of species (and are a safer place for a marine biologist to work) than an exposed rocky headland.

Merging in with the cliff-top flowers are the maritime lichens. The most conspicuous ones are orange or grey encrusting growths or pale green tufts attached to rocks above the splash zone. Walking down a rocky shore past the lichens, various zones of brown wracks can be seen. When stranded by the tide, these seaweeds provide a moist blanket under which soft-bodied animals can crawl away from a hot sun. The wracks also provide a source of food for various molluscs.

Rock crevices, especially low down the shore, can be rich sites for sea anemones and sponges. Where the full force of the oncoming waves is broken on the outside walls of a cave, the interior walls can be encrusted with a colourful array of invertebrate animals. Hard-shelled barnacles and mussels survive exposure by closing their shells; while limpets and dog whelks stop moving around and pull their shells closer to the rock surface.

But most of the life seen exposed between the tides on rocky shores is merely surviving between meals. Rarely will seashore animals be seen feeding when exposed to the air, sun and wind. Filter-feeding animals, such as barnacles, can feed only when they are submerged. Hard-shelled grazing herbivores such as limpets can feed when exposed, but they will move around to feed only on overcast days or on shady north-facing rocks, where they are in no danger of drying out (desiccation). When covered by the sea, mobile animals are able to move around in search of food or a mate. Rock pools are places where some of these activities can be glimpsed during low tide.

Beaches which are built up from shingle, sand or fragmented shells (shell gravel) are known as deposition beaches. Sand, gravel, shingle and boulders arise from the weathering of rocks. The variation in particle size determines how effective a beach is at retaining water after the tide has receded. On shingle beaches, where water quickly drains away through the large spaces, and the shingle is constantly being churned up by the waves, life is sparse and confined to microscopic organisms living in the surface film around the shingle. Beaches made of fine sand hold water well and do not dry out when exposed.

Sandy beach fauna is dominated by bivalve molluscs and polychaete worms. Since sandy beaches have no convenient crevices, seaweeds or rocks where animals can take shelter, the only way they can survive being washed away or getting dried out is to burrow down into the sand before being exposed by the ebbing tide. Hence the barren appearance of an uncovered sandy beach. A closer look will reveal casts made by lugworms, holes marking burrow entrances and emergent ends of worm tubes—all clues to the life below the sand. While there is nowhere near such a variety of species in sandy beaches as occur on sheltered rocky shores, some species are extremely numerous.

When seaweeds die offshore or on adjacent rocky areas, their remains get carried up on to sandy beaches. These provide an essential source of organic debris for detritus (debris) feeders such as the tellins. Other sand dwellers are suspension feeders, drawing in fine particles—chiefly plankton—with sea water. Both methods of feeding take place when the beach is submerged.

On open beaches, waves tend to strike the shore at an angle, so that pebbles are moved sideways along the beach by being carried up at an angle and down in the backwash. Groynes or breakwaters built out at right angles to the shore check the sideways movement of pebbles and shingle which piles up on one side of the groynes.

When a shore is exposed at night, many animals which shelter during the daytime low tide will emerge to feed without fear of drying out or being eaten by bird predators. An excursion on to a rocky shore at night will reveal crabs out in the open walking over bare rock, limpets crawling over rocks and fish feeding in the open water of rock pools.

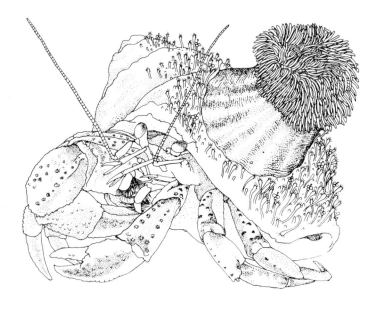

Sharing a hermit crab's shell home——sea anemone and hydroids.

Classification and Identification

Classification

On the seashore, examples can be found from all the major groups or phyla of the animal kingdom, including several which are exclusively marine such as the echinoderms. Within the animal kingdom, the major subdivisions are the *phyla*. Each *phylum* is further subdivided into *classes*, which contain the *orders*. Within the *orders* are the *families*, which contain the *genera*. Each *genus* is finally subdivided into *species*. It was Carolus Linnaeus, the 18th-century Swedish botanist, who created order from the chaos of biological nomenclature. He introduced the binomial ('two-name') method of naming individual species of plants and animals.

Take the spiny spider crab, *Maja squinado*, as an example. It is classified as follows:

Kingdom :	Animal	**Family :**	Maiidae
Phylum :	Arthropoda	**Genus** :	*Maja*
Class :	Malacostraca	**Species :**	*squinado*
Order :	Decapoda		

The colloquial name, spiny spider crab, is not the only common name of this crab in Britain; it is also known as the 'thornback'. Both these names will be meaningless in other countries, each of which have their own common names. For example, in Germany *M. squinado* is known as *grosse seespinne*, in France as *araignée* and in Greece as *kavouromàna*. By using Latin as the basis for scientific names, they can be readily accepted and understood internationally. Scientific names are printed in italics and only the generic name has an initial capital letter. The binomial *Maja squinado* is instantly recognisable in any language.

Biologists regard a species as a population of organisms which interbreed freely. Within a species there is genetic variation, so that it constantly adapts itself to the environment. In this way favourable genetic factors will be passed on from one generation to another, while genes which are unfavourable towards successful breeding, will gradually be 'lost'.

The marine phyla

As a preliminary guide to the marine phyla from which examples have been selected for the 50 detailed descriptions later in this book, a brief outline of the characteristics is given below.

Phylum Porifera: sponges: These primitive multicellular animals are fixed to rocks or seaweeds and so cannot move around. Sponges have no nervous system. There is a single cavity in their body with a large siphon through which water passes out of the sponge. Water currents are drawn in through small pores by minute whips called flagella beating inside the sponge cavity. The body of the sponge is supported internally by spicules made of either calcium carbonate or silica, or by horny fibres.

Phylum Cnidaria: In older books this phylum will be referred to as Coelenterata. These animals are basically constructed from two layers of cells which are folded into complex shapes; as a result they have soft bodies. Many of them superficially resemble flowers. There is often a jellyfish stage in the life history. There are three classes of cnidarians: the Hydrozoa (sea firs) which have flower-like polyps on stalks; the Anthozoa (sea anemones) which have well-developed polyps and no jellyfish stage; and the Scyphozoa (jellyfish) where the jellyfish stage predominates the life history. Corals and sea whips also belong to this phylum but, apart from rare cup corals, do not occur on British shores.

Phylum Annelida: segmented worms: This phylum is also divided into three classes: the Oligochaeta (earthworms); the Polychaeta (bristle worms); and the Hirudinea (leeches). There are marine leeches as well as freshwater and terrestrial ones, but none are illustrated in this book. Several examples of both errant (free-living) and sedentary (burrowing or tube-dwelling) polychaetes are described in this book. The name of this phylum is derived from the word *annellus*, meaning little ring, from the animals' numerous body segments.

Phylum Arthropoda: This highly successful group contains the largest number of species of any phylum. They are characterised by having jointed legs, and a hard outer skeleton. There are many classes of arthropods, including the Insecta; the Arachnida (spiders and mites); and the Crustacea (sea slater, barnacles, shrimps, prawns, crabs and lobsters). The crustaceans, which are chiefly marine, have a body divided into a head, a thorax and an abdomen. They can grow only by shedding their old skeleton.

Phylum Mollusca: This second largest phylum in the animal kingdom contains five classes: the Polyplacophora (chitons or coat-of-mail shells); Gastropoda (snails and slugs); Scaphopoda (tusk shells); Bivalvia (bivalves); and Cephalopoda (octopuses and squid). Many molluscs possess a hard shell which protects their soft body, although the shell has become lost or internalised in some species.

Phylum Echinodermata: This exclusively marine phylum is divided into five classses: the Crinoidea (feather stars); the Asteroidea (star-fishes); the Ophiuroidea (brittle stars); the Echinoidea (sea urchins); and the Holothuroidea (sea cucumbers). Echinoderms have a basic body pattern that is radially symmetrical, which is least obvious among the sea cucumbers. The name of this phylum means spiny-skinned, but by no means all echinoderms are spiny.

Phylum Chordata: This phylum is subdivided into two subphyla: the Urochordata and the Vertebrata. Among the vertebrates are the fishes, birds and mammals, which all possess a backbone surrounding the nerve cord. Although the urochordates have no trace of a backbone in the adult, in their larval stage they have a hollow dorsal nerve cord as well as gill slits. Compared with vertebrates, urochordates represent a very small number of species. Their larval stages resemble a tadpole in appearance. They are further subdivided into two classes: the Thaliacea (common name: salps), the adults of which are floating gelatinous barrels; and the Ascidiacea (sea squirts) which live attached to rocks as adults.

Identification

This book is not intended to be a field guide for the identification of large numbers of species likely to be found on the British coasts. There are a number of books which do just this.

For beginners
Heather Angel, *Seashore Life on Rocky Shores* (1975), *Seashore Life on Sandy Beaches* (1975), *Life in Our Estuaries* (1977), *Seaweeds of the Seashore* (1977), *Seashells of the Seashore, Books 1 and 2* (1978): all published by Jarrold.

Field identification guides
J. H. Barrett and C. M. Yonge, *Pocket Guide to the Seashore* (Collins, 1958); A. C. Campbell, *The Hamlyn Guide to the Seashore and Shallow Seas of Britain and Europe* (Hamlyn, 1976); de W. Haas and F. Knorr, *The Young Specialist Looks at Marine Life* (Burke, 1966).

General books on seashore life
Heather Angel, *The World of an Estuary* (Faber, 1974); J. R. Lewis, *The Ecology of Rocky Shores* (English Universities Press, 1964); D. Nichols, *The Oxford Book of Invertebrates* (Oxford University Press, 1971); T. Soper, *The Shell Book of Beachcombing* (David & Charles, 1972); T. Soper, *Beside the Sea* (BBC Publications, 1979); C. M. Yonge, *The Seashore* (Collins, rev. ed. 1968).

Reference books on specialised groups of marine life
C. I. Dickinson, *British Seaweeds* (Eyre & Spottiswoode, 1965); N. F. McMillan, *British Shells* (Warne, 1968); N. Tebble, *British Bivalve Seashells* (British Museum [Natural History], 1966); A. Wheeler, *The Fishes of the British Isles and North-West Europe* (Macmillan, 1969); C. M. Yonge and T. E. Thompson, *Living Marine Molluscs* (Collins, 1976).

Marine Boundaries

While the sea surrounding land masses provides a distinct geographical boundary to terrestrial flora and fauna, the oceans also have boundaries which demarcate assemblages of marine plants and animals.

To swim over a coral reef in tropical waters, or to view an underwater film made in these regions, is to appreciate the bewildering variety of life which lives in tropical seas. Polar seas, by contrast, although containing large numbers of animals, have a limited range of species. This trend—from a low diversity in the types of animals living in high polar latitudes to a high diversity in low tropical latitudes—is thought to reflect the change from the harsh seasonal extremes of the climate near the poles to the relatively constant climatic conditions on the equator. The change in the diversity of the animals does not occur gradually but in a series of well-marked steps. As a result there are bands or zones where collections of animals tend to remain very much the same. The divisions between these zones are known as zoogeographical boundaries and correspond to the northern or southern limits of many species. On a world scale, these zones are: tropical; subtropical; warm-water temperate; cold-water temperate; and polar.

Although Britain lies within the cold-water temperate zone, our shores are washed by currents originating from both warmer and colder zones. Therefore, the marine fauna of Britain is derived from three zoogeographical zones: the cold-water temperate (boreal); the polar (arctic); and the warm-water temperate (lusitanian).

In the North Atlantic, the southern boundary of the arctic fauna corresponds to the 'polar front', the southern limit of winter sea ice. Because of the influence of the warm North Atlantic Drift current, the polar front on the eastern side of the Atlantic is displaced to the north of Iceland and up to the north Cape of Norway. The position of the front has varied: in 1685 Iceland was ice-locked throughout the year, the Thames froze over in the winter and many people died as a result of the deterioration of the climate. During the last Ice Age the polar front coincided with the northern tip of Spain and there is evidence that icebergs regularly occurred off southern Portugal. These changes would have been accompanied by a movement of many arctic species of marine animals into western European waters. Many of the present boreal species would have been killed by the low water temperatures in mass mortalities similar to those that occurred in many shore-living animals such as the lugworm (*Arenicola marina*) and razor shells (*Ensis* spp) during the extremely cold winter of 1962/63. The zoogeographic boundaries which appear well defined on a map will fluctuate as they respond to quite subtle variations in climate.

The boreal zone has its southern limit around the English Channel, so anyone familiar with British seaweeds or shore animals will

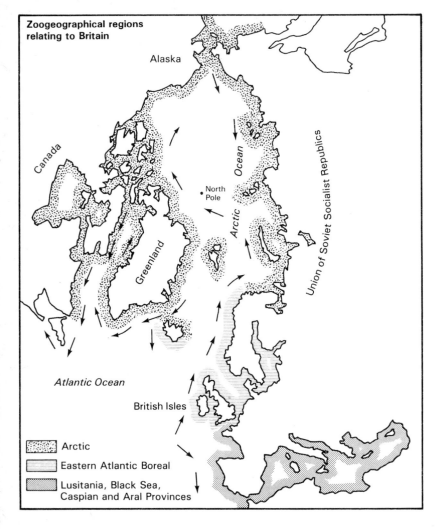

Zoogeographical regions relating to Britain

be able to recognise nearly all the seaweeds and animals encountered off northern France, Germany or western Norway. Generally, species which occur all round Britain originate from the boreal zone. Because of this, the Channel Islands are particularly interesting to marine biologists because many of the lusitanian—or warm temperate—species, that extend south to the Mediterranean and even some way down the north-west African coast, are just able to survive this far north.

The northern limit of lusitanian species is determined by temperature. The ocean currents carry warm water up the west coast of Britain, so that a few lusitanian species that are more tolerant of low temperatures can extend their distribution range up round Cornwall, Ireland and Wales. Examples of lusitanian species found around Britain are the sea urchin (*Paracentrotus lividus*; west Ireland), the spiny starfish (*Marthasterias glacialis*; south-west Britain) and the ormer (*Haliotis tuberculata*; Channel Islands).

The acorn barnacle (*Balanus balanoides*) is an example of a boreal species which occurs all round Britain. In the south-west, it breeds in the middle of our winter, whereas *Chthamalus stellatus* is a lusitanian barnacle which occurs only on the west coast of Britain and breeds in the summer. During the 1950s the northward spread of the barnacle *Chthamalus stellatus* was the result in the improvement of winter sea temperatures. The curled octopus (*Eledone cirrhosa*) is a boreal species which declines in abundance from northern Britain to the south. In contrast, the common octopus (*Octopus vulgaris*) is lusitanian and only in exceptional years when the deep water of the English Channel is warmed does it occur off Britain, often in plague proportions.

Lusitanian species with planktonic larvae may temporarily establish themselves on British shores, but be unable to breed here. Others may be killed as soon as the winter results in the drop of the water temperature. These changes are not of mere academic interest: during the 1930s the thriving herring fishing industry off Cornwall suddenly crashed. It was noticed that the plankton community, normally dominated by a boreal copepod *Calanus finmarchicus* and a particular arrow worm, had been replaced by another community. The herring larvae depended on a good supply of the copepods for their growth and survival and therefore died when the favoured plankton disappeared.

Life Histories

The two main aims of the living animal or plant are to survive and to produce offspring. Reproduction demands a considerable amount of energy, and so animals with different life-styles have evolved different life-history strategies.

Types of Reproduction

The simplest method of reproduction is just to divide into two animals (simple fission); this occurs in the amoeba. The asexual budding of small individuals from the parent occurs in some hydroids and sea anemones. This method of reproduction has the disadvantage that all the offspring are genetically identical. A species with genetic variation is better able to survive fluctuations in environmental conditions. This is also thought to be the basic mechanism whereby the evolution of new species occurs.

Hydroids have the advantage of asexual and sexual reproduction in alternating generations. The asexual stage is the colony which grows by budding. Special individuals then form either ovaries or testes which produce eggs and sperm. After fertilisation, the eggs develop into free-swimming jellyfish or medusae which are a dispersal phase—the means whereby the species colonises new habitats.

In the majority of marine invertebrates the larval stage consists of tiny drifting or floating individuals (i.e., it is *planktonic*) and this is an important agent for dispersing the species. Some of the longer-lived larvae get carried vast distances. Both polychaete worm and bivalve mollusc larvae have been tracked all the way from the east coast of America to off the African coast.

There is a great variety of types of sexual reproduction. In some species each individual is a true hermaphrodite, in other words, containing both fully functional ovaries and testes. This is beneficial in that, whenever two individuals meet, each one can fertilise the other's eggs. For animals which are sessile (fixed in one position) as adults, there is a clear advantage in being hermaphrodite, since, say, a barnacle can fertilise another barnacle only when it has settled adjacent to it. However, a chemical substance produced by adult barnacles attracts the late planktonic larval stages to settle nearby, so it is unlikely that a barnacle would settle on its own.

The slipper limpet is one of several species which changes sex.

When it first matures, it functions as a male. The newly-settling larvae are attracted to the shells of adult slipper limpets, so piles of animals develop. The testes of the older males regress and develop into ovaries so the slipper limpet then functions as a female.

Many marine species are dioecious and therefore have separate males and females. The sexes may be identical in appearance or they may differ in their coloration or their size, for example, the masked crab (*Corystes cassivelaunus*). Dioecious species often have mating

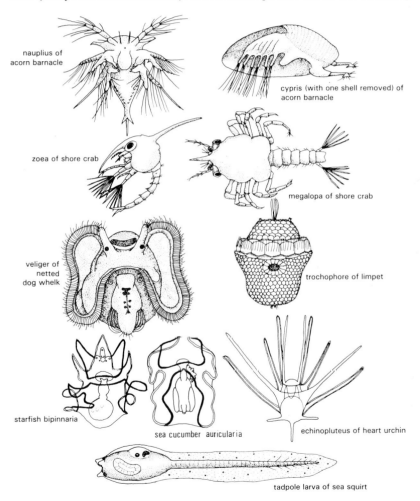

nauplius of acorn barnacle

cypris (with one shell removed) of acorn barnacle

zoea of shore crab

megalopa of shore crab

veliger of netted dog whelk

trochophore of limpet

starfish bipinnaria

sea cucumber auricularia

echinopluteus of heart urchin

tadpole larva of sea squirt

A selection of larvae of marine invertebrates

rituals. These courtship displays serve various functions. They help to ensure that mating does not occur between pairs of closely related species; they also help to maintain the vigour of the population by ensuring that only the most competitive male fertilises the female.

Some species breed once only and then die. Having grown to maturity the adults put all their energy into breeding and literally exhaust themselves. Female squids and octopuses produce one enormous clutch of eggs and subsequently die. Similarly, eels spend so much energy migrating back to the deeps of the Sargasso Sea that they cannot afford to try to return after the exhausting effort of spawning, so everything is sacrificed to the one big reproductive effort.

Types of Eggs

There are also variations in the numbers and sizes of eggs produced by different species. The mussel, for example, produces hundreds of thousands of tiny eggs lacking yolk, which hatch into tiny planktonic ciliated (having tiny hair-like structures) larvae. Since each individual larva has such an infinitesimal chance of surviving, vast numbers have to be produced, to allow for wastage. The larvae feed in the plankton—usually on the microscopic plant cells, *phytoplankton*, which float in the sunlit surface layers of the sea—so as to grow and eventually metamorphose into the adult form. There is more phytoplankton in the spring, so that breeding is usually timed to coincide with this 'bloom'. Animals with this type of reproductive strategy tend to be 'weed' species which, like their terrestrial colleagues, inhabit variable habitats and often have to disperse themselves as far as possible to find new sites in which to settle. Marine animals which do not have planktonic larvae need not breed to coincide with the spring bloom.

The dog whelk produces a few yolky eggs which develop inside capsules, feeding on infertile eggs. Young dog whelks emerge without passing through a planktonic larval stage. Since the vulnerable dispersal stage is cut out of the life history, a bigger investment can be made in the size of each egg and its food supply. Dogfish lay even larger but fewer eggs, each with a copious yolk supply on which the young dogfish embryo feeds until it hatches several months later. The infant mortality of young dogfish is very low, compared with any animal which produces planktonic larvae.

Invading Species

Man has repeatedly made deliberate introductions of marine species for commercial exploitation in British waters. But, indirectly, he has also been responsible for many others; the increase in speed of vessels has resulted in several accidental introductions to British waters.

When ships are tied up in ports, their hulls soon become encrusted with sessile marine organisms which provide cover and food for free-moving organisms. These all reduce the streamlining of the vessel and hence its effective speed. Although much research is being done on anti-fouling paints, it is known that several accidental introductions have been made to British waters via fouled ships.

The Australasian littoral barnacle (*Elminius modestus*) invaded our waters during the Second World War. It was first noticed in 1945 in the Thames Estuary and in Chichester Harbour, but it probably arrived at the beginning of the war. By 1947 it was widespread from Norfolk to Dorset, as the larvae drifted in the plankton around the coast. Isolated populations also sprang up at ports such as Plymouth, the Helford River in Cornwall and the Bristol Channel, as ships moved around the country.

The successful spread of *Elminius* can be attributed to many factors. It will tolerate lower salinities and muddier waters than our native *Balanus* or *Chthamalus* barnacles. It grows very rapidly, becoming mature in eight weeks and it also breeds frequently throughout the summer, whereas *Balanus* breeds once a year. The main limitation to the spread of *Elminius* is that it will not survive on exposed coasts, but in sheltered estuaries and creeks, it competes for space with young oyster spat.

The most recent accidental introduction to our waters has been the brown seaweed known as japweed (*Sargassum muticum*). The first record of attached (i.e., not free-floating) plants was made on 17 February 1973 at Bembridge in the Isle of Wight. This seaweed was introduced some years earlier into British Columbia in western Canada by importation with the Japanese oyster (*Crassostrea gigas*) from Japan. It therefore seems likely that japweed reached Britain in a similar way—from Japan or British Columbia.

Japweed fronds grow up to nine feet (3 m) in length with side branches bearing numerous small bladders, keeping the seaweed buoyant. Pieces of japweed as small as two inches (5 cm) long, can

↑ Direction of marginal
dispersal
↑ Probable route of dispersal
⁞ by shipping

The dispersal of the Australasian littoral barnacle, *Elminius modestus*
(information from J.R. Lewis, *The Ecology of Rocky Shores,*
English Universities Press, 1964).

float away to grow and produce sex organs, which increases the
effectiveness of dispersal. Japweed thrives in shallow-water lagoon
areas, including marinas, growing rapidly in the summer months by
as much as 4/5 inch (2 cm) per day. It easily fouls outboard motors,
and its attachment to boats accelerates its transportation around the
coast. The rapid growth of this alien seaweed soon swamps native
species such as serrated wrack (*Fucus serratus*), one of the wracks on
which flat winkles feed. Even more seriously, japweed competes
with and displaces eelgrass (*Zostera* spp) which is the sole food of
brent geese which overwinter in the Solent.

Three kinds of oysters have been deliberately introduced to Britain. One, the American oyster (*Crassostrea virginica*), has a deep
lower valve. While it will increase in size in our waters, it has not
established itself. Secondly, the Portuguese oyster (*Crassostrea
angulata*) also grows well in our waters, but breeds only in excep-
tionally hot summers. Finally, the most recent introduction to Britain is the Pacific or Japanese oyster (*Crassostrea gigas*) which is
now replacing the Portuguese oyster in our fisheries.

With the introduction of oysters from America, man unwittingly
introduced two pests of American oyster beds: the slipper limpet

(*Crepidula fornicata*) and the oyster drill or whelk tingle (*Urosalpinx cinerea*) which have established themselves along the Essex and Kent coasts. The slipper limpet has spread further round the coast, notably in the south. The oyster drill, which was first recorded in 1920, has not spread so extensively as the slipper limpet which arrived about 1890. The slipper limpet competes for space and food with the oyster. The oyster drill preys on the oyster by boring through the shell with its radula.

Oyster fishermen have their own method for attempting to control the oyster drill and the native sting winkle (*Ocenebra erinacea*) which also bores oysters: they cut the sting winkles' egg capsules away from oyster shells and from rocks. In an attempt to reduce the population of slipper limpets, they dredged oyster beds, separated the slipper limpets from the oysters and ground them up in a mincing machine. While this killed the adults, it also cross-fertilised the eggs which were returned to the sea with the ground-up remains!

To prevent the spread of shellfish pests and diseases, the Ministry of Agriculture, Fisheries and Food (MAFF) have imposed strict controls on the importation and the movement of shell fish around the coast.

The hard-shell clam or quahog (*Venus mercenaria*) is a thick-shelled bivalve mollusc which is a delicacy in North America. It has been intentionally introduced by man to several locations in Britain, including Humberside where a colony flourished for some years, but then died out. Several unsuccessful attempts were made to establish colonies of this clam in the Cheshire Dee and Mersey estuaries. However, once again, Southampton Water has been the site of an accidental introduction of an alien species, for it is here that the quahogs are flourishing. There were no deliberate introductions made by man, merely the disposal of kitchen waste overboard from transatlantic liners on which the quahogs are eaten.

Power stations which are sited on the coast utilise sea water to cool the condensed steam used to drive the turbines. Nuclear power stations tend to be sited on estuaries where there is a constant supply of cooling water. By the time this is discharged back into the estuary the temperature has increased by 50°F (10°C). Both shellfish and fish grow more rapidly in warm water and, for several years now, experiments have been carried out to determine which British and introduced species of commercial value grow best in warm-water effluents discharged from power stations.

Fluctuating Populations

The numbers of individuals of abundant marine species in particular show marked fluctuations not only from one area to another, but also from one year to the next in the same locality. Leaving aside accidental disasters induced by man's activities, these fluctuations are due to environmental changes, especially abnormal weather conditions, and to diseases.

The main factor which determines the distribution of marine organisms around our coasts is the water temperature. Individual animals are able to withstand and survive a much greater temperature range than the range needed for spawning to take place. This means that individuals within a species at different latitudes will breed at different times of year. It also means that the minimum (for arctic species) and maximum (for lusitanian species) sea-water temperature is the factor which limits whether an animal will breed or not in a given region. Our native oyster spawns all round our coasts when the sea water reaches 59°F (15°C), so therefore it begins to spawn in the south where the sea warms up first. On the other hand, since the imported Portuguese oyster requires 68°F (20°C) to initiate spawning, it is rarely able to spawn in our waters.

The development of eggs or larvae by marine organisms is related to the sea-water temperatures and the availability of food. So that, while the temperature of the sea will trigger off spawning, it can and does happen that this may not always coincide with a rich food supply. Filter-feeding animals consume large numbers of planktonic larvae quite indiscriminately; for example, a single adult mussel can eat 100000 larvae per day.

Sometimes spawning coincides with a great supply of food and this in turn has its effects. If huge numbers of acorn-barnacle larvae are produced to coincide with plenty of food, very heavy settlements of larvae result (see page 76). The small larvae can crowd together on the rock surface, but as the barnacles grow there is no room for the central barnacles to spread out sideways, so instead they grow upwards with a small basal attachment area and high-walled side plates. Quite pronounced barnacle 'mounds' result and are much shorter-lived than barnacles which develop from a less dense settlement because the 'mounds' do not adhere to the rock so well and tend to get eroded away in rough weather. This results in a temporary decline in the barnacle population in a localised area, which gradually builds up to a number of individuals which are more appropriate for the amount of rock surface available for settlement.

Aquatic organisms, in general, are very susceptible to sudden or prolonged temperature changes. In the 1904/5 winter, the seawater temperature was so cold that the Lancashire coastline was covered with ice-floes. Hundreds of tons of cockles died and were washed up on the shore.

Repeated references have been made throughout this book to the severe 1962/63 winter. During this winter, in Torbay, many intertidal animals were killed by freezing. For example, over 90 per cent of a population of snakelocks sea anemones (*Anemonia sulcata*) were killed in rock pools in Armchair Cove. It took four years for their numbers to build up to quarter of their original population before that severe winter. Prawns were also badly hit in this area. Leslie Jackman, Schools Museum Officer for the Devon County Education Committee at the time of the *Torrey Canyon* disaster, reports he had collected an average of 20 prawns per net haul from Princess Pier before that severe winter but, during the spring and summer of 1964, not one prawn was collected.

Burrowing animals in general will burrow deeper in an attempt to alleviate severe cold, but they may be killed from lack of oxygen if the surface layers become frozen. Fishes and crabs which can migrate will move offshore into deeper waters during severe winters. Shrimps and crabs move down estuaries into the sea in winter. In very cold weather, edible winkles become inactive and roll down the shore. Shore animals which are attached to rocks cannot take evasive action by migrating.

Abnormally high temperatures are just as lethal to marine organisms. During the summer, the day and night shore temperatures show the greatest variation. Organisms which live at the top of the shore are better adapted to temperature extremes than those living at the bottom. On British shores, the surface temperature of rocks on a hot summer's day may exceed 104°F (40°C); in rock pools on the same shore it will be 50°F (10°C) less.

Much work has been done on the effect of thermal stress on marine organisms and it was found that a long exposure to a low temperature may result in the same percentage of deaths as a brief exposure to a high temperature. Animals are better able to tolerate thermal stress if they can gradually acclimatise themselves to temperature increases or decreases. For example, if aquatic life (marine or freshwater) is collected on a cold winter's day, it should not be transported in a heated car, nor should it be placed in a centrally heated house. Instead, the container must gradually be allowed to warm up to the temperature inside an aquarium, before the animals are transferred to it.

The lethal temperature for a given species is regarded as the temperature at which more than half of the animals fail to survive when returned to their original temperature. So far as intertidal animals are concerned, there is a correlation between what temperatures they can tolerate and the zone they live in on the shore. High-level species have higher temperature tolerances and longer resistance times than low-level species, so that the thick topshell (*Monodonta lineata*), which lives from HWNT to MTL, is much better adapted to temperature fluctuations than the painted topshell (*Calliostoma zizyphinum*) which lives low down the shore. Marine animals are better able to tolerate temperature changes in air than in water, since there is some time-lag before the inside body tissues attain the outside air temperature.

Severe mortalities of seashore life which occur from extreme temperatures are unlikely to result in a species being totally destroyed in an area, since planktonic larval recruitment can usually take place from adjacent bays. Although recolonisation can be quite rapid, recovery may take several years. It may take a decade for organisms with a life-span of several years to return to a population with a balanced age structure. If larval recruitment does not take place from adjacent areas, another species may move in to fill the niche. The biggest impact on marine populations occurs when climatic extremes are repeated annually, so that the initial recovery suffers a severe setback.

Diseases of marine animals can have a much more devastating effect on population levels than climate, since they can totally wipe out a species in a given area. Early in the 1930s a mysterious disease wiped out nearly all our eelgrass (*Zostera* spp) beds, which resulted in widespread ecological implications. Muddy areas, previously stabilised by the eelgrass, eroded away, and the numbers of brent geese, which overwinter in our south-eastern estuaries, dropped as their sole food source disappeared.

Without interference by man, populations of marine animals will continue to fluctuate around a norm. But when natural high mortalities coincide with man-made disasters, the effects are likely to be much further reaching.

Marine Pollution

Pollution of our coastline by oil spillages receives more press coverage than any other kind of marine pollution, but there are many other types: an increase in sea-water temperature by constant warm-water discharges, the disposal of industrial and domestic waste, the accumulation of pesticides and heavy metals washed out of mine workings can also be serious threats to marine life.

Oil pollution has been with us for half a century. In the early days, spillages resulted from the deliberate dumping of waste oil from oil-carrying ships. The amount of oil spilled then was much less than in recent years, and also the remedy for counteracting the beached oil was to cart it away instead of using detergent. More recently, when huge tankers were built to transport crude oil from the country of origin to oil refineries in our country, not only did the amount of dumped waste oil increase, but also damage to these tankers resulted in accidental spillages of the crude-oil cargo. In 1964, the leading oil companies decided to adopt the procedure that the tankers would retain their waste residues on board instead of dumping them at sea. This meant the annual worldwide dumping of one million tons of crude oil was reduced to 600 000 tons per year.

The map on page 33 shows the major oil spillages around our coast since 1967 when the *Torrey Canyon* disaster hit our south-west coasts. An error of navigation resulted in the *Torrey Canyon* wrecking on the Seven Stones Reef off Land's End on 18 March 1967. Before the ship was destroyed, 60 000 tons of oil were released and, before the end of March, over six million gallons of detergent was issued from Falmouth for treating the beaches. These are the bare facts. But, with hindsight, we now know that it was the detergent which did more damage to our marine life than the oil itself. The *Torrey Canyon* disaster spurred a great deal of research into the effects of both oil and detergent on marine life, and by July 1967 a special supplement was published as part of the *Journal of the Devon Trust for Nature Conservation*, entitled 'Conservation and the *Torrey Canyon*', from which much of the data below originated.

Three lines of attack were made to prevent oil reaching our beaches. Firstly, the salvage of the *Torrey Canyon* failed; secondly, destruction of the oil by burning the crude-oil cargo was partially successful, with about one-fifth being destroyed; and thirdly, the dispersal of the oil by detergents proved disastrous to animals and seaweeds on the seashore and in the sub-littoral. Detergents do not destroy oil, they merely disperse it. This does help in the gradual natural breakdown of oil by bacteria which feed on it and which are fairly resistant to detergents. As they need a lot of oxygen for the breakdown process, they work most efficiently on small patches of oil. But, when detergents thin down the oil, this spreads it further so that it penetrates crevices and clings to fish gills as well as the gills of filter-feeding molluscs.

A week after the *Torrey Canyon* went aground, the oil began coming ashore. This coincided with one of the highest spring tides of the year, which meant the oil was carried high up the shore. As the tide receded, huge blankets of oil, resembling molten chocolate, were stranded on most Cornish beaches. One of the worst hit was the beach at the southern end of Whitesand Bay where oil was over one-foot (30 cm) thick.

Not unnaturally, the chief concern of the local authorities was to clean up the tourist resorts as quickly as possible. The Nature Conservancy (as it was then called) and the Cornwall Naturalists' Trust compiled a list of the 19 'Sites of Special Scientific Interest' (SSSIs) which were affected by the oil, together with their relative wildlife values. These organisations stressed that detergents were toxic and should be used only on the most popular holiday beaches. The Nature Conservancy also issued a statement relating to detergent emulsifiers. In this, they stressed several side-effects which could arise as a result of detergents being used: the destruction of littoral organisms; the formation of a layer of oil below the sand which would inhibit recolonisation of these beaches; and the damage to dunes by trampling and haulage of equipment. Estuaries would be particularly vulnerable since the water oscillates back and forth and is not completely replenished by each tide. In the end, detergents were not used in the Isles of Scilly or in the Hayle Estuary, but they were widely used on the tourist beaches.

The timing of this disaster could not have been worse for the sea birds such as puffins, guillemots, razorbills, cormorants and shags which were assembling in rafts offshore ready to move northwards to their breeding grounds. Also, the high tides meant that the oil was carried much higher up the shore than usual so that, when detergent was used at this high level, it was washed back down the shore by the ebbing tide. Leaving aside the toxicity of detergents, the oil itself will kill marine invertebrates by smothering them so they cannot

Major oil spills around the British coast since 1967

1 January 1967: German freighter, Isle of Wight. Widespread pollution.
2 January 1967: Damaged Greek tanker, Milford Haven. Considerable pollution.
3 March 1967: *Torrey Canyon*, Seven Stones Reef, off Cornish Coast. 60 000 tons of oil; 100 miles of coast affected. Minimum kill: 10 000 birds, especially guillemots and razorbills (probably 2 – 3 times or possibly 10 times this figure). Puffin, great northern diver, cormorant and kittiwake badly affected.
4 July 1967: Field tank, Barking Power Station. 200 tons in River Thames.
5 February 1968: Tank *Duchess*, Tay Estuary. Some of 10 000-ton cargo.
6 December 1968: Storage tank, Bantry Bay. Approximately 10 barrels (considered an underestimation).
7 April 1969: German coaster, *Hannes Knuppel*, and British tanker, *Hamilton Trader*, near bar light vessel in Liverpool Bay. 600 – 700 tons. Slick 1.5 x 3 miles. North Welsh coast affected, especially auks from Great and Little Orme Heads. Lancashire and Cumbria birds on St Bees Head affected.
8 April 1970: *Efthycosta II* and *Esso Ipswich*, Bristol Channel.
9 October 1970: *Pacific Glory* and *Allegro*, five miles from St Catherine's Point, Isle of Wight.
10 January 1971: *Texaco Caribbean* and *Paracas*, eight miles south of Dover.
11 March 1971: *Panther*, East Goodwins.

12 April 1971: *Hullgate* and *Ida Hoyer*, four miles from Beachy Head.
13 October 1971: *Current Trader*, Esso Marine Terminal, Fawley.
14 June 1973: *Conoco Britannia*, Humber Estuary. 208 tons.
15 May 1975: *Anangel Friendship*, St Bride's Bay, West Wales.
16 June 1975: *Hemitrochus*, Lyme Bay.
17 October 1975: *Natacina*, Lyme Bay.
18 November 1975: *Olympic Alliance* and HMS *Achilles*, Dover Strait.
19 May 1978: *Amoco Cadiz*, Portsall, Brittany. 220 000 tons and own fuel oil. Brittany extensively polluted; worst spillage ever.
20 May 1978: *Eleni V* and *Roseline*, six miles off Norfolk coast. 3000 – 4000 tons at time of collision; more later.
21 October 1978: *Litiopa*, Anglesea single-buoy mooring, Amlwch, North Wales. 200 tons. Conway estuary and North Wales coast affected.
22 October 1978: *Christos Bitas*, four-and-a-half miles off Smalls Lighthouse, South Wales. 300 tons. Skomer Island most polluted; also west Wales coast, North Devon and Gower coast.
23 December 1978: *Esso Bernicia*, Sullom Voe, Shetland. 1100 tons, then 600 tons later. 30 miles of coast polluted.
24 April 1979: *Baronventure*, Firth of Forth.
25 June 1979: *Tarpanbek* and *Sir Geraint*, off Selsey Bill.

breathe. Since the poisonous compounds of the oil soon evaporate they are not a great threat, but a thick layer of oil lying on the water surface will cut out light reaching the seaweeds below, which require light for the build-up of sugars during photosynthesis.

But the majority of the shore animal mortalities can be directly attributed to the use of detergents. Even on shores where only a single treatment of detergent was used to counteract one oil spillage, there were distinct strandlines of freshly killed limpets, mussels and dog whelks. When detergent was used repeatedly, huge beds of mussels with gaping shells could be seen. Limpets were so sensitive to the detergent that they were contaminated when washed by sea water from areas several hundred yards away where spraying took place. Limpets were then no longer able to grip on to rocks and so could be easily removed. In some areas no live limpets remained, and, several months later, previously bare rocks were covered with green algae which grew in response to the removal of grazing pressure by the limpets. Most of the shore in the west of the Lizard Peninsula was completely lifeless.

Only on shores where there was some delay in the use of detergents could comparisons be made of the abundance of shore life before and after spraying. At Porthgwarra, spraying did not take place until the end of the first week of April. Beforehand, apart from seaweeds which were covered with oil and limpets not gripping rocks tightly, the shore life appeared normal. One day after spraying, pools were littered with dead fish. Many limpets had dropped off the rocks and dead sea anemones and shore crabs were found.

Divers made repeated dives off Cornwall to assess the effects of pollution on the sub-littoral fauna. On 11 April, just below LWST, they found dead crabs, squat lobsters and rocklings. In deeper water, crabs were hobbling about on only a few of their legs. It is now known that concentrations of detergent as low as ten parts per million will induce legs to be shed from crabs and will also kill off oysters and cockles. On sandy bottoms, divers found dying burrowing heart urchins and razor shells projecting above the sand surface.

Sewage and Industrial Waste

The biggest volume of waste which is dumped at sea is domestic sewage. When untreated sewage is discharged, it is not only unpleasant for people walking on a beach or swimming in the sea; it can create a public health hazard by the contamination of shellfish by harmful bacteria or viruses. In high concentrations, sewage results in a lowering of oxygen levels by the sewage-feeding bacteria. Organic wastes discharged into the sea from brewing, distilling, woodpulping and some chemical industries are also broken down by bacterial action. In lower concentrations, these products have the effect of enriching the local flora and fauna; but if they are not quickly dispersed and diluted they will also result in oxygen depletion of sea water.

Some industrial waste contains heavy metals such as lead, mercury, zinc, cadmium and copper which are not broken down by bacterial action. Certain marine organisms, such as mussels, are able to concentrate these metals and, as a result, become toxic to humans and to other organisms. A notorious example of this kind of pollution occurred at Minimata in Japan, where people died as a result of eating shellfish contaminated with mercury. Other waste products which pollute the sea are pesticides and herbicides used in agriculture and forestry which reach the sea by water running off the land or in wind-blown dusts. Like heavy metals, they are not broken down by bacteria. They may also enter the sea in low concentrations but, if animals that are low down in the food chain accumulate DDT or dieldrin, eating them can result in the death of their predators.

Power Stations and Shipping

The Central Electricity Generating Board's Marine Biological laboratory, sited at the oil-powered Fawley Station in Southampton Water, was opened in 1969, principally to investigate the effects of warm-water effluents from power stations on marine organisms. Cooling water discharges can be as much as 54°F (12°C) higher than the surrounding water and so can be lethal to some plants and animals which normally live adjacent to the outfall. Warm water discharged into estuaries speeds up the heart beat, the respiration rate and the general metabolism of marine organisms, which in turn affects the whole ecology in the immediate vicinity of discharge outlets.

The discharge of radioactive wastes from nuclear power stations is both controlled and monitored. There is no present evidence that radioactive discharges have so far caused any damage to sensitive marine species. Coastal shipping which carries hazardous cargo is a potential threat to seashore life, but now special precautions are taken for cargoes which pose the greatest threat to damaging the coastal environment.

Marine Conservation

Legal Protection

Some measure of protection is given to our coasts by the laws relating to the use for pleasure of the foreshore (the area between high- and low-tide marks of ordinary tides in England and Wales and between low- and high-water marks of ordinary spring tides in Scotland). Much of our coastline is owned by local authorities, by private individuals or by the National Trust. Most of the foreshore, however, where the tides ebb and flow, belongs to the Crown and is administered by local councils. Usually, there is no restriction for using beaches for recreation, but areas may be restricted for swimmers on safety grounds (where there are strong currents) or where disturbance will result in desertion of nesting sea birds. It is an offence to remove pebbles, shells, sand or rocks from a public beach, but it is unlikely a council would bring about a prosecution except when lorry loads of the beach were disappearing. Under the Criminal Law Act, 1977, the maximum penalty for this offence is a £50 fine.

So far as the coastal zone as a whole goes, the existing law is very complex and covers aspects such as access, sea fisheries regulations, navigation, coastal protection and coastal defences, as well as pollution. The Control of Pollution Act, 1974, which covers land-based pollution, makes it an offence to permit polluted matter to enter waters within the three-mile limit. The Dumping at Sea Act, 1974, prohibits dumping, and the Prevention of Oil Pollution Act, 1971, prohibits the discharge of oil, both within the three-mile limit.

Nature Reserves

In Britain, at the present time, the setting up of inland nature reserves, including some estuarine and dune habitats, is the prime conservation concern. Of the 166 National Nature Reserves (NNRs) declared by the Nature Conservancy Council (NCC) by April 1980, only a few include portions which are on the coast. The background to the NCC, with a summary of the scale of marine conservation in Britain, is outlined in the NCC publication *Nature Conservation in the Marine Environment* on which many of the following statements and comments are based.

In 1973, the NCC was established by an Act of Parliament as

the official body concerned with nature conservation in Great Britain. In addition to establishing, maintaining and managing nature reserves, the NCC advises the Government about nature conservation. Under the 1973 Act, the NCC has the power to establish nature reserves only down to the limit of mean low-water mark of ordinary tides in England and Wales or of spring tides in Scotland.

Although many countries have declared underwater marine parks, we have no official marine reserves. The NCC appreciate that there is no biological justification for restricting nature reserves down to the bottom of the intertidal region and they have asked the Government to make provisions for marine nature reserves in the Wildlife and Countryside Bill. Three voluntary marine reserves exist, but until legislation is passed by the Government they will not be generally publicised.

To fully assess Britain's conservation requirements, a great deal of information is still needed. In 1965 a comprehensive review of conservation sites throughout Great Britain was begun in an attempt to see if the existing NNRs adequately represented the range of ecological variation over the breadth of the country. The results were published in 1977 as a two-volume work, *A Nature Conservation Review*, edited by D. A. Ratcliffe. This work excludes intertidal rocky shores and sub-littoral areas, but sandy and muddy shores are covered since they include salt marshes and estuaries which are such important sites for waders and wildfowl.

Code of Conduct

It is right that schoolchildren and university students, among others, should visit the coast, as part of their ecology studies, to learn how marine organisms live and interact with each other. This book is one of many which will encourage people in general to make shore excursions to see where the animals described here live and how they feed. Learning need not go hand in hand with collecting. If no cautioning is given, the activities of large parties of students working on a few shores near coastal field centres can result in some depletion of seashore animals and seaweeds by repeated carelessness and over-collecting. Sea anglers, bait diggers and skin divers can also cause localised damage by over-collection.

The original *Coastal Code*, published in 1974, has now been superseded by the NCC code, *The Seashore and You*, which provides guidelines for anyone working on the shore. It stresses that, if future generations are to enjoy the richness of our shores, all of us who use the shore and shallow seas must take heed of the code, which is divided into three main categories: disturbance, destruction and carelessness.

Coastal Preservation

The pressure on the coastal NNRs which have already been declared is linked with their location in relation to high population areas. Sand dunes, in particular, can suffer severe damage from trampling and, on the Gower Coast, areas have had to be fenced off to allow the dunes to be stabilised again by marram grass.

The pressure of tourism in coastal resorts seriously affects the intertidal species on 'honeypot' beaches, those areas which attract great numbers of people. In particular, beaches in the south and south-west of Britain are under greatest threat. But in the south-west there are also stretches of coastline controlled by the Ministry of Defence where public access is limited or even prohibited. These areas act as valuable reservoirs for replenishing battered beaches.

'Enterprise Neptune' was launched by the National Trust in 1965 to safeguard many coastal areas of outstanding beauty. The aim was to focus public attention on the problem of coastal development as well as to acquire and to preserve fine coastland areas. Between 1965 and 1973, £2 million were raised and 151 miles of coastline were purchased. In 1974, Stage II was launched to raise money to purchase an additional 100 miles of coastline and, by the end of April 1980, an additional 62 miles of coastline had been bought. But the National Trust calculate there are still 580 miles of coastline at risk.

The Pembrokeshire Coast National Park, which was designated in 1952, hugs the coastline of what is now known as Dyfed. The smallest of our national parks, it is also the only coastal park. Here can be seen extensive sandy beaches and spectacular rocky cliffs as well as several offshore islands which are important breeding sites for sea birds.

Although there is no direct evidence that marine species are as endangered as many terrestrial species, this is no reason for complacency. It is known that we do not have enough information about the state of most of our marine species. During the last 20 years, many of our threatened terrestrial habitats have been gradually bought or leased by the NCC so they can be conserved by the Nation. Now is the time to consider carefully marine sites in both the intertidal and sub-littoral.

The Pioneers

One of the first scientific studies of British marine invertebrate animals was written by John Ellis (1710 – 76) and published in 1755. As was the practice in these times, the title of his paper was very wordy: *An Essay towards a Natural History of the Corallines, and other Marine Products of the like kind, commonly found on the Coasts of Great Britain and Ireland.*

Thomas Pennant (who corresponded with Gilbert White of Selborne) wrote the first general account of life on our shores to be published. It appeared in 1777 in the fourth volume of *British Zoology* with illustrations of crustaceans, molluscs, starfish, sea urchins and worms. John Van Voorst, although not himself a naturalist or scientist, did a great deal to promote the interest in natural history—including marine life—by publishing a series of books over almost 50 years during the last century.

For a long time the hard-walled acorn barnacles were classified with the molluscs. It was not until an army surgeon, John Vaughan Thompson (1779-1847), studied the larval stages of the barnacles that he realised they were crustaceans. He also unravelled the mystery of the origin of stalked goose barnacles which attach themselves to buoys and driftwood. For centuries, these curious barnacles were believed to give rise to barnacle geese. Before Thompson's discoveries, branches washed ashore bearing goose barnacles were thought to bear fruit which developed into feathered and winged birds which then dropped off into the water.

It was Philip Henry Gosse (1810-88) who was the prime motivator of the great upsurge in interest in marine zoology during the Victorian era. Originally interested in birds, when his health failed Gosse was forced to move to Devon to recuperate. Here he began to write popular books on marine zoology and to lead shore excursions at Ilfracombe. Books of his such as *Naturalist's Rambles on the Devonshire Coast, A Year on the Shore* and *The Aquarium* made Gosse a household name.

Although Gosse did not invent the marine aquarium, he, more than anyone else, was responsible for popularising the home aquarium. He even devised a formula for the production of artificial sea water, if the collection of natural sea water proved too costly or took too much time. This enthusiasm for aquaria led to the

Drawing based on a thirteenth-century manuscript of the barnacle goose myth which supposed that the birds were spawned from goose barnacles which grew on trees.

founding of the first public aquarium at the Zoological Society of London in 1853, and Gosse was responsible for stocking it.

It was not uncommon for a strong crowbar to be included among the implements for fragmenting the shore to take home. Gosse's own account of his discovery of the beautiful scarlet and gold star-coral in a rock pool near Ilfracombe in 1852 illustrates that, in this era, the emphasis was very much on collecting and not on conservation:

> A very distinct species of Madrepore, and one of great beauty, I discovered to-day. It was spring-tide, and the water receded lower than I have seen it since I have been here... At length I fairly stripped, though it was blowing very cold, and jumped in. I had examined a good many things ... when my eye rested on what I at once saw to be a Madrepore, but of an unusual colour, a most refulgent orange. It was soon detached by means of the hammer, as were several more, which were associated with it. Not suspecting, however, that it was anything more than a variation in colour of a very variable species, I left a good many remaining, for which I was afterwards sorry.

As well as popularising the sea shore to the Victorians, Gosse made a major contribution to the scientific world with his *Actinologica Britannica* in 1860. This remained the standard work on British sea anemones and corals until Stephenson had his two-volume *British Sea Anemones* published by the Ray Society in 1927 and 1934.

Societies and Their Work

There is no national society which promotes the study of marine life at a popular level, but there are several societies concerned with the study of one aspect of marine life, and organisations involved in the conservation and teaching of this branch of natural history in Britain.

General Organisations and Societies

The Field Studies Council and the Scottish Field Studies Association run field courses chiefly for adults, sometimes for all the family, on a variety of topics from their centres. Some of the courses run by centres sited near the coast include 'Exploring Rocky Shores', 'Exploring the Pembrokeshire Coast National Park', 'Seaweeds' and 'Marine Biology for Divers'.

For further details about these and other courses, write to:
Field Studies Council, The Education Officer, Preston Montford, Montford Bridge, Shrewsbury SY4 1HW.
Scottish Field Studies Association, The Warden, Kindrogan Field Centre, Enochdhu, Blairgowrie, Perthshire PH10 7PG.

The British Naturalists Association
Hon. Secretary: Mrs W. A . Pauline, 2A London Road, Thatcham, Berkshire RG13 4LT.
This association is open to all naturalists throughout the British Isles and overseas, who wish to encourage and support schemes for the promotion and maintenance of national parks, nature reserves, conservation areas and to organise field surveys.

Society for the Promotion of Nature Conservation (SPNC)
The Green, Nettleham, Lincoln LN2 2NR.
Co-ordinates the 42 County Naturalists' Trusts, which themselves manage various reserves and organise lectures and field trips. The names and addresses of County Trusts in coastal counties, can be obtained from the SPNC.

Specialist Societies

Conchological Society of Great Britain and Ireland
Hon. Secretary: Mrs E. B. Rands, 51 Wychwood Avenue, Luton, Bedfordshire LU2 7HT.
Founded in 1876, this is one of the oldest existing societies devoted

to the study of the Mollusca, including their shells. Publications include the *Journal of Conchology, Conchologists' Newsletter, Papers for Students* and *Atlas of British Mollusca.*

Lectures, field meetings and census schemes are among the Society's activities. Membership is open to anyone interested in conchology and molluscs, and there is a junior membership section.

Malacological Society
Hon. Secretary: Dr Alan Bebbington, Department of Science, Bristol Polytechnic, Redland Road, Bristol BS6.
This society arranges meetings and lectures relating to living and fossil molluscs.

Porcupine Society
Hon. Editor of Porcupine Newsletter: Mr F. R. Woodward, Art Gallery and Museum, Kelvingrove, Glasgow G3 8AG.
Concerned with promoting interest in the ecology and distribution of marine fauna and flora in the north-east Atlantic, this society is named from the survey vessel *Porcupine* which worked on scientific expeditions in 1869 and 1870 in the north-east Atlantic and Mediterranean. The chief aims of the society are to promote interest in aspects of marine biology involved in the distribution and recording of marine organisms, to arrange meetings and publish a newsletter.

Professional Associations

These associations are concerned with promoting, via their scientific journals, knowledge gained through scientific research.
Estuarine and Brackish Water Biological Association
Marine Biological Association
Scottish Marine Biological Association

Shore Excursions and Photography

For anyone visiting the seashore, the aim should be to collect only the most common animals for observation in a temporary marine aquarium on the shore so they can be replaced where they were found. Once molluscs have died and their shells become beached, there is no harm in collecting them. But check first that they are not the home of a hermit crab.

The first place to search for shells, and for flotsam and jetsam in general, is the strandline, which is accessible during all states of the tide. Autumn and winter gales will often result in unusual objects getting beached, but they are also responsible for mounds of seaweeds piling up, which soon begin to rot.

Before setting out on a shore excursion beyond the strandline, it is important to make sure you are wearing suitable footwear. In the colder months, gum boots will prevent the cold sea water reaching your feet, but they are not much good at giving a firm grip on slippery seaweed-covered rocks. Tough, jagged barnacles will also soon ruin gum boots, but because of the temperature there is really no other alternative to them. In warmer weather, a pair of old plimsolls, which let the water in and out, are ideal.

The bits and pieces for collecting and examining shore life are best carried in an open bucket, so there is no danger of corrosive sea water getting near metallic parts. For small samples, old yoghurt pots make useful temporary containers and small plastic bags are ideal for shell collecting, while large plastic bags prevent wet trousers when kneeling on a wet sandy beach. For digging life out of sandy beaches, a fork will be much easier to use than a spade. Small shells are difficult to separate from the sand but, if a handful of sand is put into a plastic kitchen sieve and taken down to the sea, the sand can be washed out, leaving the shells in the sieve.

On rocky shores, a lightweight hand aquarium net is handy for catching prawns and small fish in shallow pools. The serious prawn collector uses a much more robust long-handled net with a rigid wooden or metal frame, for working beneath seaweeds in rocky gulleys. If a prawn is transferred to a transparent plastic lunch box topped up with sea water, the way in which it moves and swims through the water can be seen much more clearly than by peering into a pool with plenty of seaweed cover. Also, if flat-topped winkles and small hermit crabs in their shell homes are put in this mini-aquarium, they will emerge and crawl around.

Wind will cause ripples to form on larger pools lower down the shore, so that nothing can be seen easily. On a warm day, a skin-diver's mask can be worn and, if the glass front is placed just below the water surface, the details and colours of the pool interior will come to life. Alternatively, a glass-bottomed box held on the water will eliminate ripples from the viewing area and keep your face dry!

The underside of boulders, especially in gulleys where sea water continues to flow after the tide has fallen, are good sites for sponges, sea squirts, sea slugs, small crabs and worms. After examining a boulder, care should be taken to replace it carefully, so that the delicate organisms which have sought a wet, shady site are not left to dry out and die on top of an upturned boulder.

A torch is useful for illuminating dark crevices on rocky shores and essential for examining cave walls. Caves are, after all, like an enlarged crevice. Both offer a sheltered, damp and shady environment for seashore life. Before entering a cave, be sure to find out the time of low water, so there will be no danger of getting cut off.

For close examination of small shore organisms, a hand lens will be invaluable and reveal much which cannot be seen with the naked eye.

Recording and Photography

If species records are to be of value in the future, it is essential that the basic data is recorded at the time of the observation. This is where a field notebook is invaluable. It can be of any type that you find most convenient. In it, the date and the locality (with the six-figure Ordnance Survey grid reference) should be noted. Also, the type of shore (sand, mud or rock) together with the tidal level (HWST, MTL or LWST). It is also helpful to note the abundance of the species (very abundant, frequent, common or rare). No apparently rare species should ever be collected, and it is preferable not to collect any live specimens at all. If an interesting animal is found, sketch or photograph it, record its dimensions and notify the local museum or County Naturalists' Trust.

Field Observations

The strength of our knowledge of British botany and ornithology is based on the painstaking field observations made by amateur naturalists over the last two centuries. By comparison, our knowledge of the detailed distribution, feeding methods, predators and time of breeding of many marine species is far from complete. Without such basic information, it is impossible to be sure of the impact of, say, an oil spillage on animal populations whose numbers naturally fluctuate in climatic extremes.

Much useful information can be provided by careful observation and note-taking by anyone who is interested in a particular species or a group of species of marine animals. In addition to recording the absence/presence of certain species, behavioural studies can also be undertaken by patiently observing life in rock pools. Here, the frequency of feeding and selection of food, the interaction between individuals of the same species, and the way in which two species interact are the kinds of behaviour which can be observed on the shore in a pool. On sandy beaches, predators may leave tracks in the sand. Other clues as to which predators feed on which molluscs can be found by examining empty damaged shells. Bivalve shells with a small neat hole bored through one valve have been attacked by the carnivorous necklace shell, while an empty pair

Clues to look for on a sandy beach

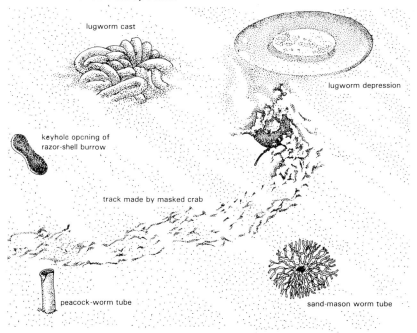

lugworm cast

lugworm depression

keyhole opening of razor-shell burrow

track made by masked crab

peacock-worm tube

sand-mason worm tube

of shells which have a larger rough hole centred on the shell margins will be the work of the oystercatcher.

Anyone who lives near to the coast, or who returns to the same beach at the same time each year, can record the relative abundance of egg capsules or spawn. The date when the first eggs were seen should also be noted.

Making a Shell Collection

Collecting empty shells, so they can be examined after a visit is made to the coast, is a good way of comparing the variation in shape and colour. *Collecting British Marine Molluscs* is a guide published by the Conchological Society (see 'Societies and Their Work'). It explains how to submit records for the Marine Census.

All museums with a natural history section will have some sort of shell collection, which is likely to include a lot of tropical shells. However, it is worth looking at any shell collection in a museum or a collector's home, to see the way in which the shells are stored and labelled. Large collections are housed in drawers in wooden cabinets. Initially each shell is labelled with the date and locality where it was collected, the habitat and the collector's name. The scientific name can always be added at a later date.

Shore Photography

Photography of life on the seashore and in pools should not be contemplated by anyone without the foresight to see that the camera must be at risk when exposed to an environment with corrosive sea water and abrasive sand. But, with care, accidents to the camera can be avoided.

Firstly, the camera should be wrapped in a tough plastic bag in a rucksack or a gadget bag. Since sea water will attack the protective coating on camera lenses, it is a wise precaution to use a skylight filter, as a protective barrier. A single sand grain inside a camera body can ruin a film by scratching the emulsion, so either load the camera before getting to the beach, or take shelter away from blowing sand before reloading in the open. Secondly, some means of preventing sea water from entering the base of the camera bag when it is put down on to damp seaweed or wet sand is essential. An old fertiliser sack or a large plastic bag is ideal for this purpose.

On a bright sunny day, a tripod may seem to be unnecessary, but it is useful for getting better close-ups by increasing the depth of field by using a slower shutter speed combined with a smaller aperture. For example, on a sunny day with Kodachrome 64, a typical hand-held exposure would be 1/125 second at f/8. By using a tripod, an exposure of 1/30 second at f/16 could be used for any static subjects such as dog whelks, limpets or sponges. The common limpets on page 87 were photographed on such an overcast day that an exposure of ½ second had to be used and so a tripod was essential. Even though many modern tripod legs are anodised, this is not adequate protection when the legs are repeatedly immersed in sea water and may be scratched by hard rocks. Plastic 'socks' made from tough plastic bags will prevent sea water coming into contact with metallic legs. 'Socks' will not be a protection from salt spray, so it is sensible to wipe all metallic parts and to lubricate moving parts with Vaseline or '3-in-1' oil, after working on the seashore.

Close-up Photography

Nearly all the animals photographed for this book, and indeed, most seashore life, are relatively small so that it is essential to get in fairly close if some detail is to be shown. The cheapest way of taking close-ups with a standard lens is to use a close-up (or supplementary) lens in front of the camera lens. For cameras with fixed lenses, this is the only way in which close-ups can be taken. When using close-up lenses, no increase in exposure is necessary. Cameras which have detachable lenses can have extension tubes or rings inserted between the body and the lens, which will allow for magnifications up to life-size (1:1) or even greater, to appear on the film. But when extension tubes are used, the light has to travel further to reach the film and so some increase in exposure has to be made. The most useful lens for all close-up photography, on the shore or on land, is a macro lens with its own built-in extension which allows a continuous focusing range from infinity to half- or life-size.

Photographing Rock Pools

Taking photographs through water is not nearly so straightforward as photographing in air. Firstly, reflections of the sky—and of a photographer bending over a pool—can spoil the image of the interior of the pool itself. When using a single-lens reflex (SLR) camera, these reflections can be seen in the viewfinder if the lens is stopped down to the pre-selected aperture before the exposure is made. Sometimes the reflections can be eliminated from the field of view by walking round a rock pool and viewing it from another angle. Anyone who has worn Polaroid sun glasses will appreciate how effective they are at reducing surface reflections on water.

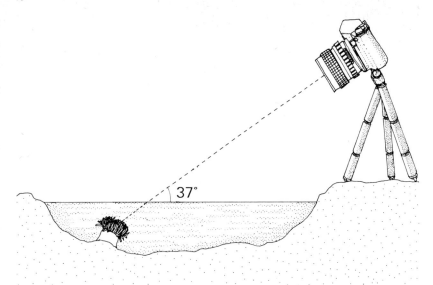

37°

Similarly, a polarising filter will eliminate surface reflections, providing it is used at an angle of approximately 37° to the water surface. The filter is screwed on to the front of the camera lens and rotated in its mount until the reflections disappear. Once again, a tripod is an asset here, because the camera can be kept in a fixed position. The main disadvantage of using a polarising filter is that it reduces the light reaching the film, so that an increase of one-and-a-half or two stops is required. This means that an exposure of 1/125 second at f/8 is reduced to 1/30 second at f/8, which presents problems if the subject is moving.

Small, shallow pools are easiest for beginning rock pool photography. On a sunny day, it should be possible to get sharply in focus the fringing seaweeds as well as the bottom of the pool.

Flashlight

A flash is essential for photography in caves or at night. It can also be used to prevent a blurred image of a moving animal on a dull day. When photographing through water, the flash should not be mounted on the camera itself, because it will be reflected off the water and appear in the photograph. If the camera has a hot-shoe attachment for a flash, a hot-shoe/cold-shoe attachment will have to be fitted so that the flash can be used remote from the camera on a flash extension lead.

A Selection of Species

The 50 individual species which are illustrated and described in detail on the following pages have been selected as examples of a range of animal types which can be found relatively easily on British shores. A few species, such as the common octopus, may rarely be seen on the shore, but it is included as it is often featured in public marine aquaria and its general biology is of interest.

The species have been grouped under eight habitats. Five of these relate to rocky shores (in pools, on seaweeds, on rocks, under boulders and in rocks) and one each to sandy beaches, estuaries and eelgrass beds. For quick reference, the habitat type is printed at the top left of each text page. In addition, a stylised representation of the animal group to which the species belongs is given on the top right of each text page (see pp. 16-18 for an explanation of each of these).

It must be stressed, however, that the distribution maps are provisional. Unlike the distribution of British birds and flowers which have been well documented for decades, marine mapping is in its infancy. The Marine Mapping Scheme, which got under way with the Marine Mollusc Survey in 1962, is not yet complete for the majority of groups. At the time of writing, provisional maps have been compiled for the marine molluscs only. Even then, since only 36 of the 40 Marine Sea Areas border the coastline of the British Isles and Ireland, the length of coastline each covers is relatively large compared to the 10-kilometre square terrestrial grid used for compiling the distribution maps of terrestrial species. Since the presence of an individual live specimen in a Marine Sea Area is recorded as a blue strip around the coastline for this area, it is therefore essential that the maps are not read too precisely. Instead, they should be taken as an indication of the distribution (e.g, southern, western or all round Britain) and that the presence of a species will, in any case, be limited to its particular habitat within the Sea Area.

The major sources for the maps appear on p. 4. There was also reference to local marine fauna lists, the author's personal observations, records in scientific papers and other general accounts. Even so, these maps cannot be regarded as complete, as the data is not yet available nationwide.

To use the maps

PRESENT distribution

Prawn

Palaemon serratus

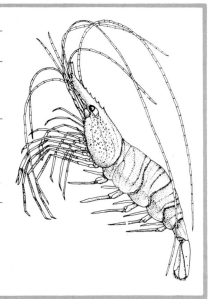

Size: body 1-3in (2.5-7.5cm).

Tidal level: LTL in seaweed-filled pools and gulleys in late summer.

Recognition: translucent body with purple, blue or yellow lines and dots. Pointed rostrum between eyes has 6-8 teeth on top and 4-5 teeth below.

Breeding: female ovaries ripen in early summer. After moulting, when still soft, she pairs and sperm spread over her underside to fertilise her 2500 eggs. Cement produced to bind eggs to hairs. Young prawns hatch out into larvae.

Feeding: weed fragments and animal debris picked up by nippers on first 2 pairs of legs and passed to other feeding limbs. Conspicuous eyes on movable stalks select food.

In late summer, prawns can be abundant in seaweed-filled gulleys low down on the shore, but they are difficult to spot because they are so transparent and they tend to hide under the seaweeds. When disturbed, a prawn darts backwards with a jet propulsive movement caused by opening the tail fan and rapidly flexing the abdomen beneath itself. It also moves forward by using the last 3 pairs of walking legs and by swimming with the 5 pairs of paddle-like swimmerets on the abdomen. The very long outer antennae are usually trailed backwards along the body. Prawns tend to be more active by night than by day. During the summer, they lose their outer skin by moulting every fortnight. The numbers of prawns fluctuate widely from one year to another. As the temperature drops in late autumn, they migrate offshore for the winter. Larger edible prawns are caught off Norway.

Shanny

Blennius pholis

Size: 2-4in (5-10cm).

Tidal level: MTL and below in pools and under stones.

Recognition: variable colour; olive or dark green, blotched black. Good disruptive coloration. Continuous dorsal fin. Small tentacle on each cheek bone. No scales so feels slimy.

Breeding: spawns from April to August; a few hundred yellow ovoid eggs with flattened underside laid on roof or side of rock crevice. Female then abandons eggs which are brooded by male. He changes colour to black with conspicuous white lips.

Feeding: broad flattened teeth used for biting barnacles off rocks. Also eats filamentous green algae, crustaceans and small fish.

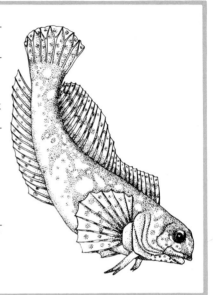

This fish abounds on both rocky shores and in sandy pools around breakwaters on which seaweeds grow. It also lives below LWST down to a depth of 30 ft (10 m). The dark blotchy patches help to break up its body outline in the same way as buildings and planes were disruptively painted for camouflage during wartime. The young fish larvae which hatch from the eggs live in the sea away from the shore for a few months, but they return to the shore by winter. They have dark heads and conspicuously marked pectoral fins, and they feed mainly on the feeding limbs (cirri) of acorn barnacles which they bite off with their sharp teeth. The shanny can withstand long periods out of water and, like the shore crab, can often be found sheltering beneath a boulder long after it has been stranded by the receding tide. It can crawl using the large paired pectoral fins.

Hermit Crab

Pagurus bernhardus

Size: body 1-4 in (2.5-10 cm).

Tidal level: lower shores in pools, larger hermits on sandy flats.

Recognition: reddish-yellow crab lives in empty marine snail shell. Withdraws inside shell home when danger threatens and closes opening with larger right pincer. Soft abdomen coiled to fit internal shell spiral.

Breeding: separate sexes pair. Eggs carried by female on underside of abdomen until hatch into planktonic zoeae larvae, which moult several times before becoming glaucothoë larvae; look like tiny hermits.

Feeding: stirs up muddy deposits which settle out from seawater and filters fine particles which are eaten. Sometimes scavenges.

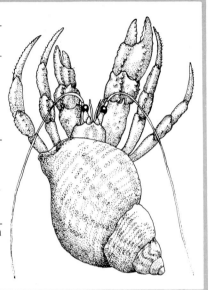

Hermit crabs are common on rocky shores in rock pools and under boulders. Small hermits live in winkle shells and move into a larger shell each time they moult. Large hermits use common whelk shells and live in the sub-littoral, sometimes getting washed up on to the lower shore. Hermits move by emerging from their shells and walking on their 2 larger pairs of legs, using their antennae to feel their way. If two hermits encounter one another, they signal their intent with their pincers: held tightly against the body shows submission, while moved outwards and upwards signifies a threat posture. Other animals may share the hermit crab home—a yellow sponge, a hydroid and a sea anemone may live on the shell and a polychaete worm may live inside. Since hermit crabs carry their own protection with them, they can be active during the day.

Common Octopus

Octopus vulgaris

Size: 2-3 ft (60-100 cm).

Tidal level: ELWST in pools or hidden in crevices on south coast.

Recognition: muscular bag-like body with 8 arms, each with a double row of suckers. Body colour varies to blend in with surroundings, but often brownish.

Breeding: separate sexes. After courtship, male transfers sperm packets to female using modified third right arm. 30000-50000 eggs laid in summer in clusters hanging from rock. Female broods and aerates eggs until small octopuses hatch after 10 weeks.

Feeding: active predator, feeding on crabs and fish which are caught by suckered arms and chewed by horny beak in centre of arms.

This octopus is a southern species which is most widespread in the English Channel. After mild winters, numbers can build up to form a plague, which causes extensive damage to crabs and lobsters in pots, as well as oysters in beds. The plague in 1900 meant 69000 less lobsters and 281000 less crabs were taken in south-coast pots. Normally living offshore among rocks and stones, the common octopus can sometimes be seen in pools low down the shore during low water of spring tides. It lives in a stony lair which it builds for camouflage and protection . Usually it moves over the bottom on its 8 arms but, when an octopus is alarmed, it swims by jet propulsion by forcing water out through the muscular funnel. Also when alarmed, it can squirt out a black inky smoke screen, which serves to distract predators. The curled octopus (*Eledone cirrhosa*) is much more widespread around Britain.

Snakelocks Sea Anemone

Anemonia sulcata

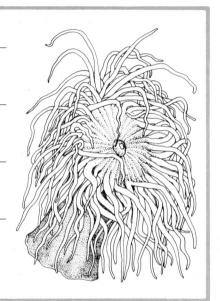

Size: column 1½ in (4 cm) tall; tentacles 2 in (5 cm) long.

Tidal level: MTL and below in sunny shallow pools, on rocks, in eelgrass (*Zostera*) and oarweed (*Laminaria*) beds.

Recognition: 180-200 tentacles, dull khaki or pale green with violet tips which are sticky to touch and do not contract.

Breeding: habitually reproduces asexually by dividing lengthwise into 2 or 3 anemones. Fission takes only 1-3 hours and tears body.

Feeding: preys on invertebrates and fish which are first paralysed by nematocysts in the tentacles and then pushed into mouth.

This sea anemone is easily spotted, since it seeks out the sunniest parts of pools where it can spread out its tentacles towards the light. Within the tentacles live microscopic algal cells which need light to photosynthesise food products. The intimate association of one species living in another is known as symbiosis. Here the algae are protected inside the sea anemone, which in return benefits by the algal cells removing waste carbon dioxide and giving off oxygen. When snakelocks sea anemones live attached to seaweeds or eelgrass, which are moved by the water currents, the anemone tentacles resemble a Gorgon's head as they wave to and fro with the motion of the water. Living down to a depth of 75 ft (23 m), snakelocks sea anemones have a westerly distribution around the coastline. They do not survive well on the shore during severe winters.

Club-headed Hydroid

Clava multicornis

Size: polyps up to 1 in (2.5 cm) high.

Tidal level: MTL and below.

Recognition: pinkish-yellow colony of polyps growing from creeping network of 'roots' on brown seaweeds. Each polyp club-shaped with threadlike tentacles.

Breeding: colony produces reproductive buds (gonophores) which develop into tiny medusae. Remain permanently attached to colony. This sexual state produces eggs and sperm. Fertilised eggs hatch into planula larvae. After release, sink to bottom. Activated by light, so tend to move up shore until come into contact with brown seaweeds.

Feeding: feeding polyps capture prey with tentacles.

There are three distinct parts to the club-headed hydroid colony: the branching root system, the stem and the terminal polyps. When exposed, the colonial polyps of this marine relative of the freshwater *Hydra* contract down to look like a yellowish pink gelatinous blob. Only when it is submerged, as shown in the photograph, can the structure of the delicate polyps be clearly seen. Since these polyps are not enclosed in a skeletal cup, they are referred to as 'naked'. *Clava* is usually attached to egg wrack (*Ascophyllum nodosum*) but can sometimes be found on other brown wracks. The gonophores or sex buds look like miniature bunches of grapes below the 20 white tentacles. The planula larvae are released during daylight, and light plays an important part in their release, activity and orientation. *Clava* is most common on relatively sheltered rocky shores with a good seaweed cover.

Flat Winkle

Littorina littoralis

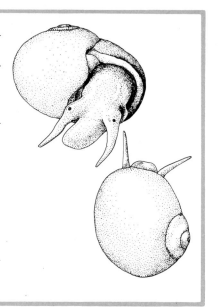

Size: ¾ in (1.5 cm).

Tidal level: mid-tide level of rocky shores on brown fucoid seaweeds.

Recognition: flat-topped shell varies in colour from yellow, orange, brown, green, black to banded. Shell aperture large and out-turned.

Breeding: spawns at night in early spring after pairing in the littoral surf zone where water contains plenty of oxygen. 90-150 eggs are laid in a flattened gelatinous mass on brown fucoid seaweeds. The jelly prevents the eggs from drying out during 2-3 weeks they take to hatch into miniature adults, which colonise the same or nearby brown seaweeds.

Feeding: on fucoid seaweeds, algal detritus, diatoms and lichens.

Flat winkles are common on brown seaweeds—especially bladder wrack and egg wrack—which blanket the mid-tide zone on sheltered rocky shores. Yellow-shelled winkles are conspicuous, while those with green shells mimic closely the air bladders on the bladder wrack itself. The winkles can still be seen crawling over the seaweeds after the ebbing tide has exposed them but, on warm sunny days, they soon crawl down in the damp fronds to resist desiccation during the several hours exposure before they are submerged once again. During development, the eggs pass through a veliger larva stage in the egg capsule. Scientists have recently split the intertidal winkles—including this species—into several species based on their reproductive biology, which makes it impossible to separate them on field characters alone. The distribution of flat winkles is limited to sheltered rocky shores.

Blue-rayed Limpet

Patina pellucida

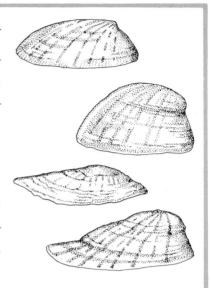

Size: ½ in (1 cm).

Tidal level: ELWST and sub-littoral in oarweed beds on rocky shores.

Recognition: smooth brown translucent shell, with blue dashed lines radiating from apex.

Breeding: separate sexes; male and female limpets move close together in winter and spring before gametes released and eggs fertilised outside female. Eggs hatch into free-swimming planktonic trochophore larvae, which develop into veliger larvae, each with a tiny shell and foot. Mature larvae settle as 2 mm long spat in May.

Feeding: rasps oarweed stipe, fronds and holdfast with radula. Also feeds on microscopic diatoms which settle on oarweed.

Blue-rayed limpets have two varieties, each with a distinct shell shape and colour: var. *pellucida* lives on oarweed fronds and has a smooth shell with 2-8 bright blue rays; while var. *laevis* lives in the holdfasts and has a rough shell with 2-46 pale blue rays. Some of the young limpets which settle on the fronds migrate down into the holdfasts during their first summer, to become the *laevis* form. This movement ensures the limpets are not lost when the oarweed fronds are destroyed by the autumn gales. In the autumn after settling, the limpets are ¼ in (5 mm) long and sexually mature. Most of them will die a year after they have settled. In some areas, blue-rayed limpets can be so plentiful that the oarweed stipes are pitted with feeding scars, like the ones in the photograph. Since blue-rayed limpets are almost restricted to laminarian forests they occur only where these forests develop.

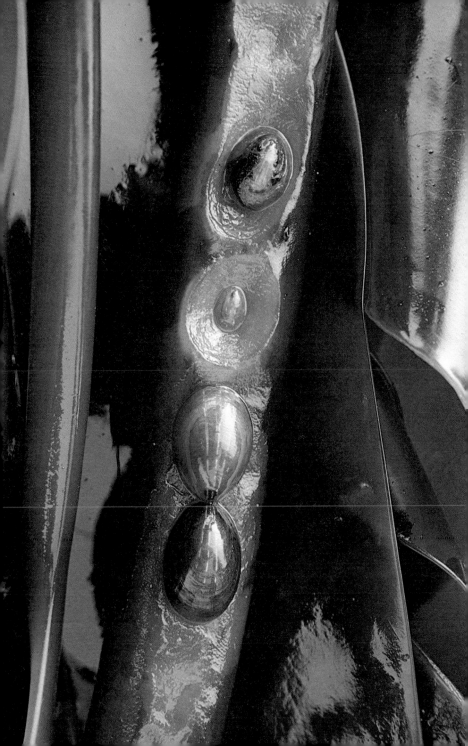

Star Sea Squirt

Botryllus schlosseri

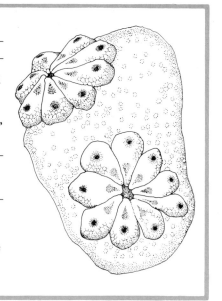

Size: gelatinous patches ¼ - 6 in (0.5 - 15 cm) across.

Tidal level: LTL and below.

Recognition: firm gelatinous encrusting growth on stones, rocks and seaweeds with 0.2-cm long individuals (zooids) arranged in star patterns. Colour, both of fleshy base and zooids, very variable, latter often yellow, blue or white.

Breeding: few large eggs produced, fertilised internally, and tailed tadpole larvae incubated inside.

Feeding: planktonic food is drawn in with the respiratory current, through the inhalent siphon of each individual, filtered and passed to gut opening. The waste food passes out through the shared central exhalent siphon.

The star sea squirt is a colony of individuals, none of which is capable of existing on its own The gelatinous growths live attached to seaweeds and rocks on the lower shore; sometimes they completely smother the seaweed so that only the basal holdfast attaching it to a rock is visible. In south Wales, star sea squirts can be found throughout the year, but the largest colonies occur during May, June and July. Usually living in shallow water, they can live down to a depth of several hundred metres. Star sea squirts feed on phytoplankton and organic detritus which is strained and trapped in a mucus secretion. They breed during June and July at Ardrossan in Scotland. The larval stage, which is the dispersal phase, does not feed. When it is released, the larva seeks out a suitable site for settling and forming a new colony.

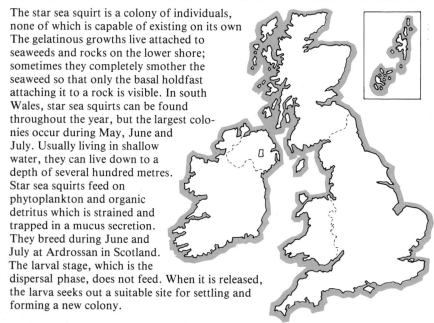

Purse Sponge

Grantia compressa

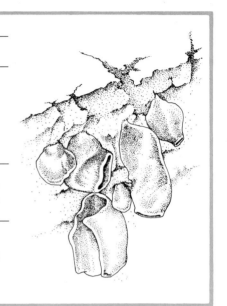

Size: 1-2 in (2.5-5 cm) long.

Tidal level: lower shore attached to rock, often among red seaweeds.

Recognition: white or straw-coloured flattened vases attached by stalk to rocks. Large opening at free end. Growth form and size relates to amount of exposure and wave action. Can reach 5-6 in (12.5-15 cm) in sheltered waters with plenty of food.

Breeding: asexually by small buds appearing on side of body which detach and develop into new sponges. Sex cells also formed.

Feeding: on small planktonic organisms and detritus which are drawn in through the large opening at the free end, by tiny cilia beating internally to create water currents.

The correct identification of many sponges can be done only by microscopic examination of the internal skeleton, which is made up of many needlelike spicules. However, this purse sponge is quite distinctive and can easily be recognised on the shore. It contains calcareous or limey spicules, while siliceous spicules are found in the glass sponges and soft spongin is present in the bath sponges. The diet of the purse sponge is chiefly protozoans, diatoms and bacteria which, once drawn inside the body of the sponge, are engulfed by individual collar cells which line it. This purse sponge is widely distributed around our shores, especially favouring shady rocky overhangs low down the shore where it will not get dried out during exposure. It will also grow attached to the submerged parts of pier supports and floating pontoons in marinas. In such sheltered positions, it reaches a much larger size than on open coasts.

Beadlet Sea Anemone

Actinia equina

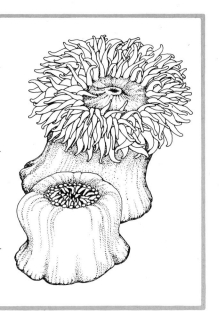

Size: column 3 in (7.5 cm) high, 2½ in (6 cm) across.

Tidal level: MTL to lower shore.

Recognition: wine red, green or brown gelatinous sac with 200 tentacles encircling the central mouth. When exposed to the air or disturbed, tentacles fold inside anemone which contracts down to a jelly-like blob.

Breeding: separate sexes, internal fertilisation. Eggs develop into planula larvae with cilia but no tentacles. Adults incubate young, which are released via mouth. Also reproduce by budding off young from basal disc margin.

Feeding: captures and paralyses prey with the nematocysts in the tentacles. Prey pushed into mouth.

This common colourful sea anemone is likely to be the first one seen by most people as they walk down a British rocky shore. Although the colour is variable, the red form is most widespread and all beadlets have a ring of 24 blue spots at the base of the tentacles. These spots can be seen most clearly when the tentacles have contracted inside the column. Beadlets attach themselves to rocks or pier supports by the basal disc, but they can detach and move around if necessary. They are active predators, feeding on prawns, worms and fish, and will tolerate exposure to air for long periods, which means a wide temperature tolerance. The colour photograph shows several attached to the wall of a cave. Beadlet anemones occur all around Britain, wherever there are stones, rocks or pieces of wood for attachment. They will even tolerate living in silty estuarine waters such as the Severn Estuary.

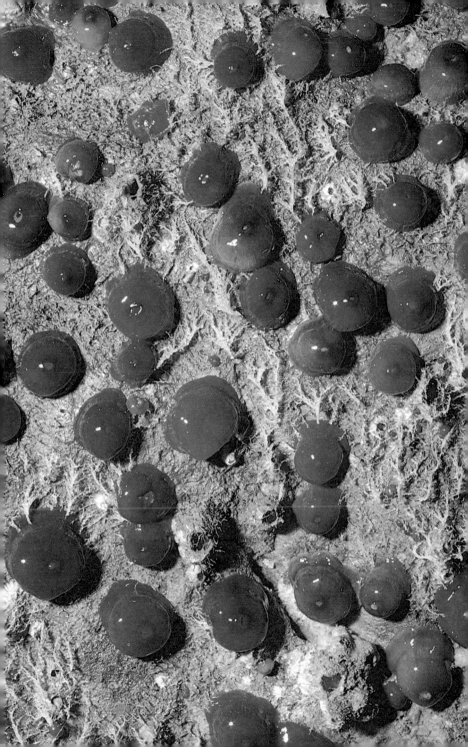

Dahlia Sea Anemone

Tealia felina

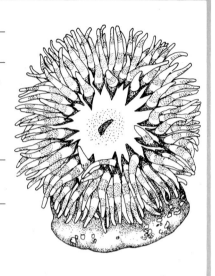

Size: 4 in (10 cm) across; up to 2 in (5 cm) high.

Tidal length: MTL down into sub-littoral.

Recognition: larger than beadlet sea anemone, with fewer (80-160), thicker tentacles, usually banded pink and white. Top of disc surrounding mouth has no tentacles. Column may have pieces of shell and gravel adhering to sticky warts.

Breeding: eggs are produced in May. Young anemones are found in *Laminaria* holdfasts.

Feeding: preys on variety of invertebrates and fish which come within reach of the tentacles. As tentacles bend over prey, nematocysts discharge and paralyse prey.

This is the largest and most spectacular of the sea anemones found on the shore between the tides. It lives attached to hard substrates low down on rocky shores, especially in cracks and fissures of rocks, in pools and beneath stones, wherever there are hideouts away from strong sunlight which it shuns. If a dahlia sea anemone is poked, it will squirt out sea water from the central mouth, withdraw its tentacles and contract down to a broad-based gelatinous blob. If the outside of the column is covered with shell fragments, then a contracted dahlia anemone is very well camouflaged and difficult to spot. The column of the dahlia anemone is variable in colour; it may be green, or crimson or pale grey or a mixture of colours. A pallid variety occurs in estuaries. The dahlia sea anemone is found all round our coasts on rocky shores and down to depths of 300 fathoms (1800 ft; 500 m).

Green Leafworm

Eulalia viridis

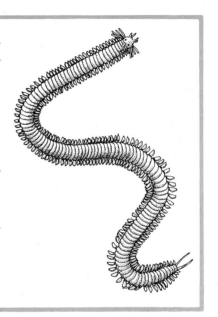

Size: 1½ - 4 in (4 - 10 cm) long.
Tidal level: MTL to lower shore.
Recognition: segmented bright green worm with 5 antennae at front. Small paddle-like lobes on both sides of each segment. Beneath seaweed on damp rocks. Freely crawls over bare and barnacle-encrusted rock when not sunny, but especially when tide is out at night.
Breeding: lays minute green eggs in gelatinous bags of translucent jelly attached to stones low down on shore in spring.
Feeding: food engulfed by unarmed proboscis which has no jaws. Feeds mainly on plant and animal debris which sticks to the proboscis and is wiped off inside the mouth.

Green leafworms are most evident when they are actively laying their translucent gelatinous pear-shaped egg sacs in March and April. These sacs can be seen attached by a narrow stalk hanging from seaweeds or rocks low down on the shore. Within each egg sac are hundreds of minute green eggs which hatch into trochophore larvae. Although the worms are abundant on rocky shores and are bright green in colour (which shimmers with a blue sheen in certain lights), they are not conspicuous for most of the year, as they tend to hide away beneath damp seaweed cover or in rock crevices when exposed by the ebbing tide. The errant 120-200 segmented worm actively swims in water and crawls over vertical rocks encrusted with barnacles, sponges, sea squirts and sea anemones. The green leafworm is more closely related to the highly active paddleworms, than to the ragworm.

Acorn Barnacle

Balanus balanoides

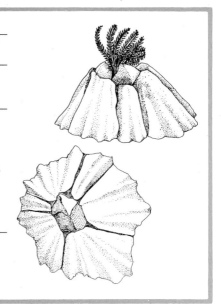

Size: up to ½ in (1.5 cm) in diameter.

Tidal level: beneath HWNT to LWST on rocks and shells.

Recognition: body surrounded by 6 hard white or dirty-white plates. Diamond-shaped area inside plates.

Breeding: hermaphrodite; internal cross fertilisation from neighbouring barnacle. After 4 months, nauplius larvae hatch, moult several times to become bivalved cypris larvae. Sink to bottom, are attracted to settled barnacles and cement themselves to adjacent rock by antennae. Solitary barnacles cannot reproduce.

Feeding: central plates open so 6 cirri can 'comb' water for food particles (larger than 0.03 mm), beating up to 140 times per minute.

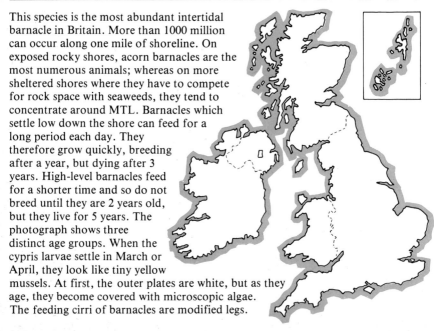

This species is the most abundant intertidal barnacle in Britain. More than 1000 million can occur along one mile of shoreline. On exposed rocky shores, acorn barnacles are the most numerous animals; whereas on more sheltered shores where they have to compete for rock space with seaweeds, they tend to concentrate around MTL. Barnacles which settle low down the shore can feed for a long period each day. They therefore grow quickly, breeding after a year, but dying after 3 years. High-level barnacles feed for a shorter time and so do not breed until they are 2 years old, but they live for 5 years. The photograph shows three distinct age groups. When the cypris larvae settle in March or April, they look like tiny yellow mussels. At first, the outer plates are white, but as they age, they become covered with microscopic algae. The feeding cirri of barnacles are modified legs.

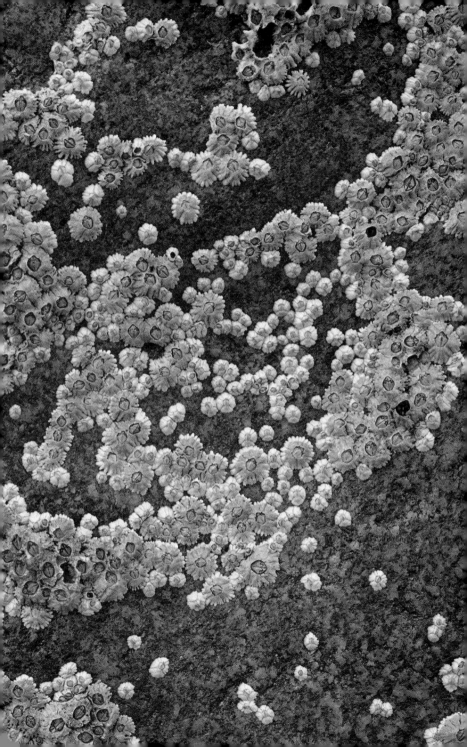

Sea Slater

Ligia oceanica

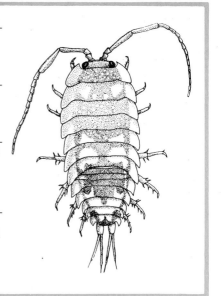

Size: up to 1 in (2.5 cm).

Tidal level: upper shore at HWM wherever hideouts, such as rock crevices, occur for shelter during the day.

Recognition: flattened greyish mottled body resembles large wood-louse with large pair of antennae. Pair of black eyes.

Breeding: sperm transferred from male to female using modified hind limbs. Eggs carried by female in brood pouch on her underside until they hatch into small slaters.

Feeding: emerges at night to feed on channelled wrack (*Pelvetia*) and animal debris. Very sensitive to light and will stop feeding on bright moonlit nights.

This largest species of British wood-louse lives in a very restricted zone on the upper limit of the seashore. It should be regarded as a terrestrial animal which has ventured into the marine environment to gain both shelter and food. Usually it cannot survive living more than a few yards away from the edge of the sea; but on exposed coasts where the sea spray is carried up cliffs, it can live in grass up to 165 yards (150 m) above sea level. Being a nocturnal feeder, it is not often seen by day, even though it is abundant in suitable localities around the coast. Crevices, caves, groynes and cracks in quays all provide daytime hideouts. Several sea slaters often pack into one small crevice. At night during a low tide, they move over the rock surface, as in this flashlight photograph. Sea slaters can darken or lighten their bodies to blend in with their surroundings by contracting or expanding pigment cells.

Dog Whelk

Nucella lapillus

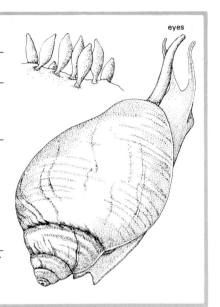

eyes

Size: height: 1½ in (4 cm); breadth: ¾ in (2 cm).

Tidal level: from HWNT downwards on rocky shores.

Recognition: thickened shell, colour often dirty white, sometimes yellow, black, pink or with brown bands. Groove in shell where siphon emerges.

Breeding: separate sexes. Congregate in rock crevices in winter and spring. After pairing female lays 6-31 yellow flask-shaped capsules on rock. Each capsule contains several hundred eggs, only few fertile, rest provide food for others. Four months later 10-12 tiny shelled dog whelks emerge.

Feeding: carnivore on barnacles (upper plates prized open) or mussels (shell bored with a neat hole by radula).

Young dog whelks have a thinner shell and a larger shell opening than mature whelks. When collected from the rock, the dog whelk withdraws into its shell and closes the opening with a brown horny operculum. Mussel shells which have neat round holes in them have been mechanically bored by dog whelks. Both mussels and barnacles are attached to rocks, and so cannot move from the predatory dog whelk. This marine snail is the main predator of intertidal barnacles. After the dog whelk has prized open the upper plates and eaten the barnacle flesh, all that remains is the outer wall enclosing the central hole. Very young dog whelks feed on small calcareous tube worms—*Spirorbis*—instead of barnacles. Dog whelks occur all round Britain, wherever there are rocks which are not too exposed. On rough shores, they can shelter from the waves in rock crevices.

Edible Winkle

Littorina littorea

Size: height: 1 in (2.5 cm); breadth: ¾ in (2 cm).

Tidal level: from HWNT to LWST on rocky, stony and muddy shore. Also in estuaries.

Recognition: pinky/grey or blackish sharply pointed shell with a distinct angle where the outer lip meets the body whorl. Young shells ridged.

Breeding: in spring, 1 mm capsules with 1-5 pink eggs, laid 1-2 hours after mating. Planktonic capsules resemble soldiers' steel helmets. After 6 days, eggs hatch into larvae each with a coiled shell. Young winkles settle on the shore in May and June.

Feeding: make browsing excursions using sun as a light compass. Feed on detritus and algal growths on rocks.

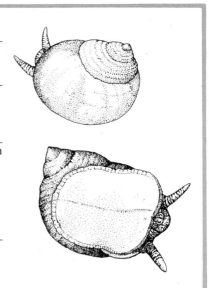

This largest British winkle is common between tide marks all around Britain. The size of the shell alone is diagnostic, but this is also the only winkle which has dark cross bands on its tentacles. The thick shell protects the winkles from wave action for, unlike limpets, winkles do not cling on to rocks in rough seas. Instead, they survive by dropping off the rock and withdrawing inside their shell. The shell opening is then sealed off with a horny operculum so that the animal is completely protected as it is buffeted by the waves and currents. In this way, large numbers can collect in gulleys. Even though this winkle is eaten by gulls and oystercatchers and is also collected by man for food, it is still abundant on rocky shores. It also lives in estuaries, where it tolerates polluted water. Winkle-gathering goes back to the days of Queen Anne and is known as 'triggering'.

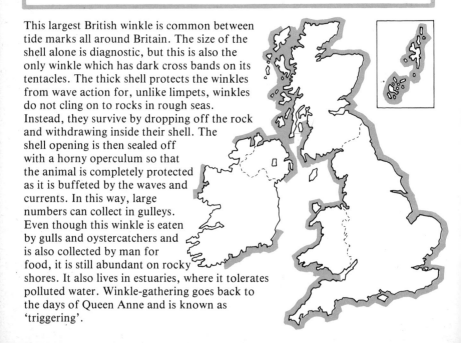

Thick Topshell

Monodonta lineata

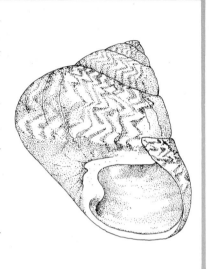

Size: shell 1 in (2.5 cm) tall.

Tidal level: HWNT to middle shore. Will tolerate some exposure.

Recognition: grey or greenish thick conical shell with overlying zigzag dark purple streaks, mother-of-pearl lining. Aperture with obvious tooth on inner side. Umbilicus not easily seen in adult. Shell top eroded to show pearly layer in older shells.

Breeding: separate sexes but do not pair. Male and female topshells move in close so eggs fertilised after they leave female. Hatch into planktonic trochophore larvae and then into veliger larvae.

Feeding: weak chitinous jaws can only rasp at small algal particles and vegetable detritus.

This topshell is the largest one found on British shores, where it prefers sheltered shores with big boulders and lots of gulleys without much loose sand. It is most often found on bare rock without seaweeds and in gulleys and shallow pools. It may be confined to a very narrow zone extending only a few feet on either side of mean high water of neap tides. The thick topshell is a southern species locally common on rocky shores in the south-west. Its most northerly limit in the British Isles is the north coast of Ireland. Low temperatures have a marked effect on thick topshells, which grow more slowly when the temperature drops. They show a distinct seasonal migration by moving down the beach in winter and up in the summer.

They do not survive harsh winters, such as the one in 1962/63, unless they can hide in deep crevices.

Common Limpet

Patella vulgata

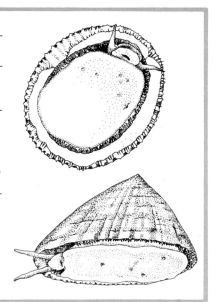

Size: 2 in (5 cm) long shell.

Tidal level: HWNT to ELWST on rocky shores and in pools.

Recognition: conical shell with broad base, grey-green inside. No white pigment on tentacles.

Breeding: October to December. Separate sexes, but do not mate. Eggs released from female and fertilised externally. 24 hours later hatch into free-living trochophore larvae then into veliger larvae, before settling.

Feeding: intertidal herbivore, feeds when covered by sea and waves not strong. In damp weather and at night, exposed limpets will feed in air. Algae are rasped by tiny teeth on file-like radula which gets worn, so radula moves forward with new teeth.

The conical limpet shell is well adapted for survival in stormy seas. It offers the minimum resistance to waves and any slight pressure makes it cling all the harder. Even when the tide goes out, a limpet can still breathe with its gills by using the sea water trapped inside its shell clamped to the rock. On hard rock, the limpet grinds its shell margin to fit the rock profile; whereas on soft rock it wears a circular scar in the rock itself by shell rotations. This perfect fit of the shell with the rock means that each limpet has its own 'home' to which it returns after its feeding forays. Constant browsing by limpets prevents the establishment of larger intertidal seaweeds, such as sea lettuce (*Ulva*). One of the most striking visual effects of the 1967 *Torrey Canyon* disaster was the colour change of intertidal rocks in the south-west from brown to bright green: limpets killed by detergent no longer browsed on the *Ulva* sporlings.

Mussel

Mytilus edulis

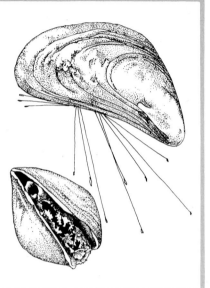

Size: 2-4in (5-10cm).

Tidal level: MTL and below. Often with barnacles on open rocky coasts. Form extensive beds on rocks in muddy estuaries.

Recognition: dark blue/black shell, pointed at one end.

Breeding: spawns early in year. Eggs and sperm shed into sea stimulate other mussels to spawn, so increasing chance of external fertilisation. Eggs hatch into planktonic veliger larvae. Young settling mussels known as spat. Attach to rock by byssal threads.

Feeding: on plankton when submerged and shells open. Water drawn in through frilly siphon and food strained by orange gills. Waste goes out via plain-edged siphon with water stream.

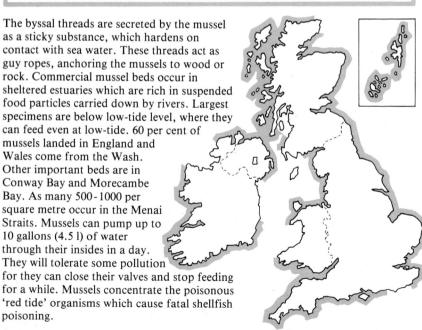

The byssal threads are secreted by the mussel as a sticky substance, which hardens on contact with sea water. These threads act as guy ropes, anchoring the mussels to wood or rock. Commercial mussel beds occur in sheltered estuaries which are rich in suspended food particles carried down by rivers. Largest specimens are below low-tide level, where they can feed even at low-tide. 60 per cent of mussels landed in England and Wales come from the Wash. Other important beds are in Conway Bay and Morecambe Bay. As many 500-1000 per square metre occur in the Menai Straits. Mussels can pump up to 10 gallons (4.5 l) of water through their insides in a day. They will tolerate some pollution for they can close their valves and stop feeding for a while. Mussels concentrate the poisonous 'red tide' organisms which cause fatal shellfish poisoning.

Common Starfish

Asterias rubens

Size: diameter, usually 4-5 in
(10-12.5 cm), may be up to 20 in (50cm).

Tidal level: lower shore and below
especially on mussel beds.

Recognition: usually 5 arms, may be 4
or 6, tapering towards tips. Top rough
with row of spines in midline.
Yellow/brown or red/brown.
Underside of each arm has many
suckered tube feet.

Breeding: in spring. Separate sexes
with 2 gonads in each arm. Eggs and
sperm shed into water which stimulate
shedding of sex cells from opposite sex.
Fertilisation external. Eggs hatch into
bipinnaria larvae, present in plankton
May-September.

Feeding: mainly on bivalve molluscs,
especially mussels.

Starfish all have an internal system of
waterfilled canals which end in suckered tube
feet, which are moved by water being pumped
in and out of them. A starfish crawls around
by pushing the tube feet on the leading arm
forward and then gripping the rock with the
suckers. As the tube feet are contracted, so
the body of the starfish edges forward.
Starfish can grip tightly to vertical rock
faces, and to live mussel shells on which
they feed. The body is humped
over the bivalve, so that the shells
are gripped by the tube feet and
gradually pulled apart by the
starfish exerting a continuous
force. A starfish has no teeth; so
it digests its food externally by
pushing its stomach between
the mussel shells and secreting
enzymes so that the liquid food
can then be sucked up. Sometimes small molluscs are
swallowed whole and the empty shells discarded.
The numbers of common starfish vary annually.

Shore Crab

Carcinus maenas

Size: shell 1-4in (2.5-10cm) across.

Tidal level: MTL into sub-littoral on all shores including estuaries.

Recognition: colour variable, often dark green. 3 blunt teeth between eyes and 5 sharp teeth on shell on each side of eye.

Breeding: mates after female moulted, while her shell is still soft. He carries her beneath him for several days beforehand. Pair for several hours. Female spawns January to May; carries eggs beneath her abdominal flap until hatch into planktonic zoeae larvae after 16-18 weeks in winter and 12-14 weeks in summer.

Feeding: pincers seize and kill food, which can be worms or molluscs. Also scavenge on dead animals.

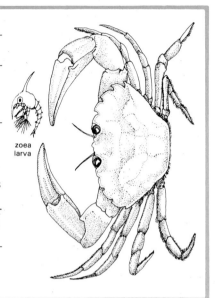

zoea larva

Of all the crabs living on the shore, this one is most likely to be found, hiding beneath stones or seaweed cover when exposed. Like all crabs, the hard outer skeleton must be shed if the animal is to grow. Before the old shell is cast, a new one is laid down beneath it and the crab blows itself up to a much larger size. Since the new shell is soft, and takes several days to harden, 'soft' crabs are very vulnerable to attack from predators. Man also uses them as bait for sea fish. Shore crabs can be sexed by the shape of the abdominal flap tucked beneath their shell; females have a broad 7-jointed flap and males a narrow 5-jointed one. Shore crabs sense their surroundings using their stalked eyes, their antennae and smell. They are preyed on by eels and other fish as well as various birds including gulls, shags and cormorants. The safest way to hold a crab is by the back of the carapace.

Edible Crab

Cancer pagurus

Size: shell 2-10in (5-25cm) across.

Tidal level: MTL down into sub-littoral.

Recognition: pinky-brown shell with piecrust margin. Huge pair of pincers with black tips.

Breeding: female moults in September followed by pairing but eggs not laid until December of following year. Fertilised as laid. Orange eggs carried under female's abdominal flap. Pass through zoea and megalopa larval stages. Edible crab larvae appear in plankton from April to August.

Feeding: heavy pincers crush molluscs and other crustaceans and flesh then picked out. May excavate pits up to 8in (20cm) deep to get at burrowing bivalve molluscs.

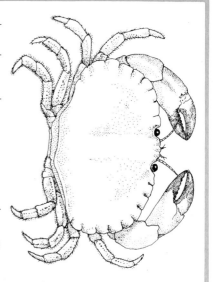

Very small edible crabs will live inside the branching holdfasts of the large brown oarweeds. When disturbed, they lie on their backs with their legs tightly interlocked. Large crabs tend to live offshore, but some live in rock crevices or beneath boulders on the lower shore. They move offshore in winter to spawn, and back into warm shallower waters in spring for the eggs to hatch in summer. Edible crabs are caught commercially in baited pots along the east coast and in the south-west, and in creels off Scotland. Nearly three-quarters of the 1792-lb (813-kg) catch in 1975 was landed in the south and south-west of England. The flesh inside the big pincers and the legs provide the edible white flesh. Tagging experiments have shown that crabs—especially females—migrate west and south-west down the English Channel for as much as 10 miles (16 km) or more.

Spiny Squat Lobster

Galathea strigosa

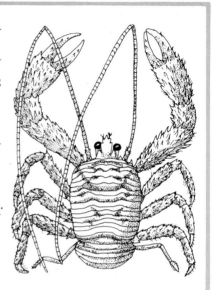

Size: up to 5 in (12.5 cm) long.

Tidal level: under stones and rocks from LWST into sub-littoral.

Recognition: body red with blue lines. Abdomen tucked beneath thorax. Long first pair of legs end in pincers. These and next 3 pairs of legs spiny. Sharply pointed rostrum between eyes has 3 spines on each side.

Breeding: 2 broods, eggs fertilised as laid and then cemented on to abdominal appendages where carried by female until hatch into planktonic zoeae larvae in May and in late summer.

Feeding: on fine particles mixed with sand and detritus collected by hairy mouth parts sweeping over bottom or by pincers grasping plant and animal remains.

This is the largest species of squat lobster to be found on the shore and it is also the most spiny, notably the pincers. The handsome colouring belies the ferocious behaviour it adopts when it is attacked. The flat claws are quite capable of giving a very painful nip if it is carelessly handled. Although this squat lobster is widely distributed around our coasts, it is not common. *Galathea squamifera* is a smaller species which can also be found beneath stones. It has a greenish-brown body with red flecks. The zoeae larvae of both species occur commonly in British plankton hauls. All squat lobsters have a very reduced hind pair of legs, which are usually carried tucked beneath the body, so that they appear to have only 3 pairs of walking legs. The abdominal flap is used by the females for carrying their egg masses, which are pale at first and darken to a bright red as the eggs develop.

Sea Lemon

Archidoris pseudoargus

Size: 2-4in (5-10cm) long.

Tidal level: LTL and below, often where encrusting sponges present.

Recognition: broad slug-like with yellow foot. Upper side rough, yellow with green, pink or brown blotches. Pair of yellow head tentacles. Anus surrounded by a circle of 8-9 plumed retractile gills. No shell.

Breeding: hermaphrodite; pair (as shown opposite) to fertilise each other. Frilly white spawn ribbons laid (1in [2.5cm] wide) on underside of boulders on lower shore in the spring. Eggs hatch into planktonic veliger larvae.

Feeding: on sponges, especially breadcrumb sponge *Halichondria panicea* which encrusts rocks.

spawn ribbon

The gills of this sea slug are used as secondary respiratory structures and, because they are naked, they give rise to the name of the whole group of sea slugs—the nudibranchs. Inside the body of the sea lemon are needles of calcium carbonate which help to support the body and can make up to half the dry body weight. One of the largest of the intertidal sea slugs, it moves up on to the lower shore to spawn in the spring. It lays a coiled gelatinous spawn ribbon up to 32 in (81 cm) long and containing some 300000 eggs. The first part of the egg ribbon is smeared with mucus which glues it to the rock; then, as the sea lemon moves away, the egg ribbon is gradually pulled out. It can take up to an hour to lay ½ in (1.27 cm) of ribbon. After spawning, the adults die. Sea lemons were once used as a fish bait in Shetland. The bright orange variety, var. *flammea*, prefers to feed on red sponges.

Cowrie

Trivia monacha

Size: shell ½ in (1.5 cm) long.

Tidal level: LW and below on rocks and beneath boulders.

Recogniton: white/pale pink shell with 20-25 ribs and 3 purple spots above and a slit below.

Breeding: late spring and summer. Vase-shaped egg capsules (4.5 mm) laid in holes made in sea squirt test. End of vase projects from sea squirt. Each capsule has 1000-2000 unshelled eggs which float in fluid retained by neck plug. Each egg hatches into veliger larva (echinospira) with a large light shell which keeps it afloat.

Feeding: when submerged, on compound sea squirts. Bites off pieces of test with jaws so can get at sea squirt zooids which are swallowed whole.

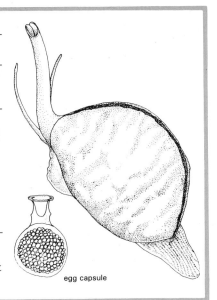

egg capsule

The underside of rocky overhangs and boulders, which are encrusted with compound sea squirts, are the most likely haunt of our beautiful, but small, relatives of tropical cowries. When exposed to the air, the animal withdraws into its ribbed shell. The narrow slit on the underside reduces the chance of the soft body drying up inside during the short time the lower shore is exposed to the air. When a cowrie is submerged, as illustrated in the photograph, the paired tentacles and orange siphon emerge and reach forwards, while the spotted mantle skin-folds extend up on each side of the shell. When the mantle is completely extended, very little of the shell itself is visible. This cowrie has a south-western and northern distribution around Britain. *Trivia arctica* is a similar cowrie which occurs on British shores, but it is slightly smaller and has an unspotted shell.

Sea Gherkin

Cucumaria saxicola

Size: body 2-4in (5-10cm) long.

Tidal level: lower shores among rocks, under stones and in crevices.

Recogniton: cucumber-shaped body with 2 rows of suckers below and 3 above. 10 dark branched tentacles surround the mouth.

Breeding: eggs and sperm released into sea. Fertilised eggs develop into planktonic auricularia larvae followed by several larval stages before the cilia disappear and the young sea gherkin attaches itself to bottom with tube feet.

Feeding: sea gherkin clings to rock by 2 rows of short tube feet. Food particles, such as detritus, adhere to sticky mouth tentacles which are wiped clean inside mouth.

This is one of several kinds of sea cucumbers which live between the tides. They all belong to the marine group of echinoderms, which show a distinct 5-rayed symmetry. This is not so apparent in the sea cucumbers as in the starfish, but the sea gherkin does have its tube feet arranged in 5 rows. The pinkish worm cucumber *Leptosynapta inhaerens* has lost all the tube feet as an adaptation to its burrowing life in sandy beaches. Although the white body of the sea gherkin shows up very clearly against dark rocks, when exposed it is often difficult to spot, hidden away in rock crevices or in holes made by rock-boring molluscs, since the tentacles are contracted. Once they are covered by the sea, they extend and emerge from the crevices to feed. The thin, but flexible outer skin is strengthened with internal calcareous plates. The sea gherkin is not found in Scotland.

Sea Squirt

Ciona intestinalis

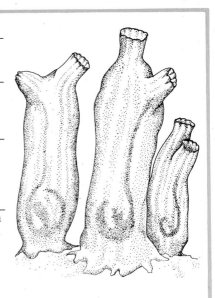

Size: body 3-5 in (7.5-12.5 cm) long.

Tidal level: lower shore into sub-littoral. Attached by base to rocks, piles, buoys and boat hulls.

Recogniton: transparent gelatinous retractible sac with two siphons edged in yellow with red spots at free end. 5 longitudinal internal muscles bands.

Breeding: hermaphrodite; eggs and sperm shed into sea for external fertilisation. Develop into tailed tadpole larvae only a day after fertilisation.

Feeding: filter-feeds on plant plankton and detritus which is drawn in through larger terminal siphon by cilia beating inside. Plankton trapped in mucus is ingested.

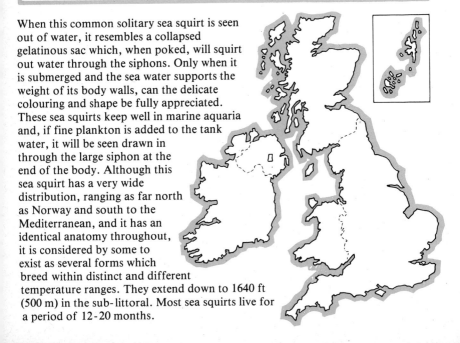

When this common solitary sea squirt is seen out of water, it resembles a collapsed gelatinous sac which, when poked, will squirt out water through the siphons. Only when it is submerged and the sea water supports the weight of its body walls, can the delicate colouring and shape be fully appreciated. These sea squirts keep well in marine aquaria and, if fine plankton is added to the tank water, it will be seen drawn in through the large siphon at the end of the body. Although this sea squirt has a very wide distribution, ranging as far north as Norway and south to the Mediterranean, and it has an identical anatomy throughout, it is considered by some to exist as several forms which breed within distinct and different temperature ranges. They extend down to 1640 ft (500 m) in the sub-littoral. Most sea squirts live for a period of 12-20 months.

Green Sea Urchin

Psammechinus miliaris

Size: up to 2 in (5 cm) in diameter.

Tidal level: lower shore.

Recognition: green globular limy skeleton or test covered with short green spines tipped with purple. May cover itself with bits of seaweed.

Breeding: eggs and sperm shed into sea for external fertilisation in spring and early summer. Hatch into echinopluteus larvae which occur in summer plankton. When adult skeleton forms, larvae are 1 mm in size and sink down to the bottom.

Feeding: on barnacles and cockles. Uses its 5 teeth-like plates which project through mouth on centre of underside to erode hinge ligament of bivalves so it can eat out the inside.

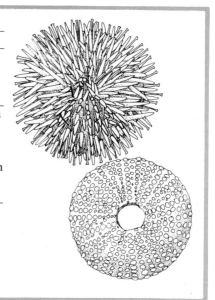

Live urchins often cover themselves with pieces of seaweed or eelgrass held in place by the upper tube feet. The strong spines can bore holes in soft rocks, in which the urchins will shelter. When the urchin dies, the spines fall from the test to reveal the rounded part of the ball-and-socket joints which allow the spines to move in any direction. The teeth shown in the photograph are the only visible part of a complex structure called 'Aristotle's lantern' which has 5 internal large calcareous plates called pyramids, operated by internal muscles. As the urchin feeds, the 5 teeth can be opened or closed. As well as barnacles, of which it may eat as many as 21 per day, the green sea urchin will also eat algae and eelgrass. During the severe 1929 winter, this urchin was wiped out on the Whitstable oyster beds where it had been abundant.

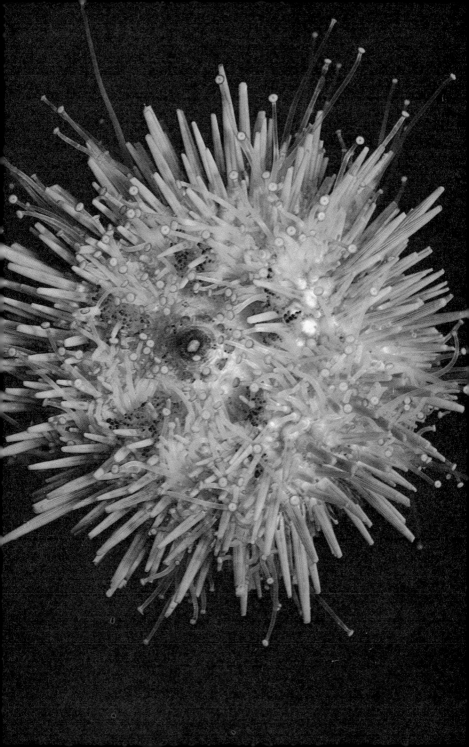

Piddock

Pholas dactylus

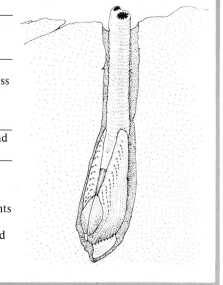

Size: shell up to 3 in (7.5 cm) long.

Tidal level: LTL in shale, chalk, sandstone and wood; shells often remain in burrow after animal dies.

Recognition: bivalve mollusc with white shells covered with ribs and cross ridges. Lives in neat circular hole in rock or wood which it makes by boring action.

Breeding: eggs fertilised externally and develop into ciliated larvae.

Feeding: filter-feeder; paired siphons project above burrow into sea water. Internal ciliated gills create water current which draws microscopic plants in through inhalent siphon. Food particles are sieved out by the gills and the waste passes out through exhalent siphon.

The piddock bores using a mechanical action with its 2 shells. Each shell has 5 rows of fine teeth near the front edge which rasp away the hole. Although beached shells appear thin and brittle, they are hard enough to penetrate the soft rocks or wood in which the piddock lives. Unlike most bivalves, there is no shell ligament connecting the two shells together and the hinge teeth are reduced to a rounded ball on each valve which act like a double ball joint. As the piddock bores, it uses its foot as a sucker to grip the rock near the head end of the bore, so the shells are alternately rotated left and right in a see-saw motion against the ball joint, making an even, rounded bore hole as the shell teeth grind away. The bore hole measures 1 in (2.5 cm) across and 6 in (15 cm) deep. The piddock produces a strong green-blue light from 5 regions which produce a luminous slime. The purpose of this light is not known.

Lugworm

Arenicola marina

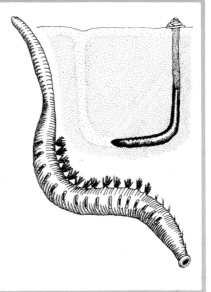

Size: 4-8in (10-20cm) long.

Tidal level: from MTL in muddy sand.

Recognition: worms reddish, yellow/black or greenish. Middle portion with 13 pairs of red feathery gills. Tail thinner; no gills or bristles.

Breeding: in mid-October. Worms remain in burrows and liberate sex cells simultaneously so maximum chance of fertilisation in sea. Eggs hatch into trochophore larvae which remain on bottom, metamorphosing into worms.

Feeding: on muddy sand in its burrow. Rough pharynx pushed out so particles stick to it and then swallowed. Head end of burrow shows as a funnel-like depression on beach above. Moves up tail end of burrow to defecate and add to its cast. Feeds 5-8 hours a day.

Worm casts on a sandy beach are a sure sign that lugworms are living down below. Black casts show their burrow extends to anaerobic sand. In beaches with plenty of organic food, lugworms can reach densities of 32800 per hectare. A shallow depression in the sand, adjacent to the cast, marks the position of the head end of the lugworm burrow. When the tide flows up the shore, it infills the depression with more sand and food particles. Lugworms can remain in the same position in their mucus-lined burrows for weeks at a time, and they never chose to leave their burrows. The oxygen level in the burrow drops right down when the tide goes out and the burrow is left partially filled with stagnant sea water; but the lugworm's rich blood supply stores up plenty of oxygen for use during this period. Many fish enjoy eating lugworms and so they are very popular bait.

Sand Mason Worm

Lanice conchilega

Size: tube 12in (30cm) long, encrusted with sand grains. Worm 8-10in (20-25cm) long.
Tidal level: lower shore.
Recogniton: tufted upper end of tube projects up from beach and can be seen at low tide. Pink worm has long pink tentacles and a pair of red tufted gills.
Breeding: eggs fertilised in sea. Hatch into planktonic trochophore larvae, which metamorphose into small worms.
Feeding: tentacle feeder. When tide is in, worm moves up tube, extends tentacles to wipe off detritus particles which get entangled in tufted end of tube. Tentacles also extend over beach surface to feed.

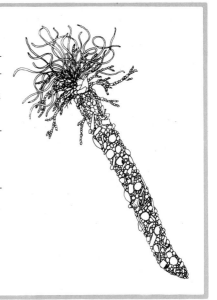

The photograph shows a concentrated patch of tufted ends of sand-mason worm tubes resembling a forest in miniature. Each worm selects sand and gravel for its tube building, and uses bi-lobed lips around the mouth to sort out the smaller particles for the tufted end. Most of the tube which lies buried in the sand is built from coarse sand and shell fragments which are mixed with mucus secreted by pairs of gland shields on the underside of the body. The grains are added to the tube by the lips which also make repairs to a damaged tube. Tufts of bristles on the first 17 body segments allow the worm to grip the inside of its tube and make a hasty retreat. The tentacles which emerge from the tube are highly mobile. On the underside of each are microscopic hairs called cilia, which help to move small food particles to the mouth. Larger ones are held by the tentacles and reeled into the mouth.

Peacock Worm

Sabella pavonina

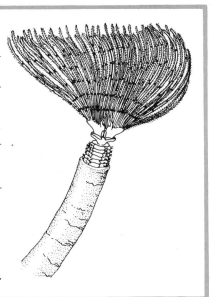

Size: tube 18in (45cm) long, ¼ in (6mm) diameter. Worm 4-10in (10-25cm) long.	

Tidal level: lower shore on muddy/sandy beaches.

Recognition: smooth brown tube projects 3-4in (7.5-10cm) above beach. Front of worm ends in fan of striped feathered tentacles.

Breeding: external fertilisation of eggs in sea, which develop into planktonic trochophore larvae.

Feeding: filter-feeder. When covered by sea, tentacle fan emerges from open end of tube. Hairs beat towards fan centre creating current carrying particles which are sorted. Large ones rejected, smallest swallowed while intermediate are used for tube building.

When exposed to the air, the tentacular fan of the peacock worm may remain projecting a few millimetres above the smooth tube, but any vibrations on the beach surface will cause the worm to withdraw out of sight down its tube. Like the sand mason worm, forests of peacock worm tubes may occur on some beaches. The smooth walled tubes are made from fine silt which is mixed with a mucus secretion. A sudden and high temperature rise will result in the death of peacock worms, which are one of many intertidal fan worms which filter-feed on fine particles suspended in sea water. As the tide submerges the peacock worm tubes, a brightly coloured tentacular fan can be seen to emerge from each, providing no disturbance is made to the water or to the beach surface. The feeding worms are also highly sensitive to a falling shadow which makes them withdraw immediately.

Honeycomb Worm

Sabellaria alveolata

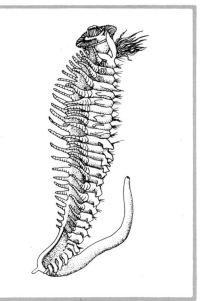

Size: colonial sand grain reefs up to 2 ft (60 cm) across. Worm up to 2 in (5 cm) long.

Tidal level: LWST and below.

Recognition: interlocking structure of individual worm tubes, each opening on reef surface, give it a honeycombed appearance when exposed at low tide.

Breeding: spawn in July and eggs hatch into planktonic trochophore larvae. Settle out of plankton 2-4 months after fertilisation, attracted to settle by substance from existing worm tubes.

Feeding: when covered by sea, worms emerge from tube so tentacles can collect microscopic food particles and sand grains for repairing tube.

The yellowish reefs made by this marine worm are conspicuous against the rocks on which they are built. Each worm constructs its own tube by gluing single sand grains or shell fragments on top of one another by the lobed lip around the mouth. As new worms settle out from the plankton, the outer edges of the colony advance over the bare rock. If limpets are living beside an active colony, they may have to move away to find a home, whereas acorn barnacles which cannot move get overgrown by an enlarging colony. Honeycomb worms will live for 4-5 years and, if no new worms settle, the reef will slowly break down. Strong wave action during stormy weather will speed up the destruction of the reef.

Even if a reef is completely destroyed, planktonic larvae from worms in neighbouring bays can begin a new colony because long-dead colonies are still attractive to settling larvae.

Shrimp

Crangon crangon

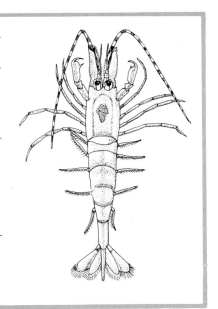

Size: body 1-3 in (2.5-7.5 cm) long.

Tidal level: lower shore in sandy pools and estuaries.

Recognition: grey or dark brown body with darker spots. No rostrum. First pair of legs short and stout with movable spine which curves over to meet sharp point; not pincer-like.

Breeding: after moulting, female lies on her side to pair. Carries the eggs attached to base of swimming limbs and last 2 pairs of walking legs. Eggs hatch into zoeae larvae then develop into mysis larvae. Common in spring inshore plankton.

Feeding: variable through year; diet includes green plants, organic remains, small crustaceans, molluscs, worms, eggs and even young fish.

The shorter antennae, the lack of a pointed rostrum, a more flattened body and mottled body markings are all characters which help to distinguish a live shrimp from a prawn. When boiled, shrimps turn brown, whereas prawns turn pink. Shrimps live buried in sand by day and emerge at night to feed. They burrow using the legs and swimmerets to scoop out underlying sand so that they gradually sink down. Finally, the antennae are used to sweep sand over the top so that the shrimps are completely buried. As shrimps can adapt to the low salinity of estuarine water, they are often abundant in estuaries in the summer. Shrimps can be caught by raking the top few inches of sand so they are disturbed and emerge on the surface, where they can be picked up by hand or with a net. Morecambe Bay, the Bristol Channel and the Essex and Kent coasts are all sites of local shrimping fisheries.

Masked Crab

Corystes cassivelaunus

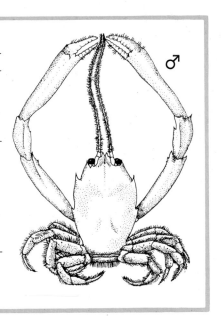

Size: male shell 1 in (2.5 cm) across, 1½ in (4 cm) wide; female smaller.

Tidal level: LTL in sandy beaches.

Recognition: straw-coloured crab with human face-like markings on upper surface. Shell longer than broad. Male has pincers twice body length; female pincers smaller.

Breeding: male attracted to female by hormones. He carries her around for several days. Female shell is hard when they pair. Eggs cemented to her abdominal appendages. Planktonic larvae pass through 5 early stages, all abundant in inshore plankton, March – June.

Feeding: forages at night. Active predator on any animal it can catch with its pincers.

This crab is well adapted for life in sand. As the tapering legs begin to dig, the crab adopts an upright position, so that within seconds it disappears until only the tips of its long pair of antennae remain above the sand. On the inside edge of each antenna is a double row of hairs which interlock to form a breathing tube. While it is buried, the crab breathes by drawing a fresh supply of sea water down the tube, passing through a sand filter before reaching the internal gills. Like the shrimp, the masked crab hides in the sand by day to avoid being eaten by fish predators. At night, it emerges to forage on the sand surface. It then reverses the direction of its breathing current by drawing water in through the side of the carapace and pushing it out via the breathing tube. Old crabs which have not recently moulted have acorn barnacles attached to their shells. The sexes are easily distinguished by their pincer size.

Necklace Shell

Natica alderi

Size: shell ¾ in (2 cm) in diameter.

Tidal level: lower shore and below in sandy beaches.

Recognition: rounded polished yellow/brown shell with spiral rows of dark red spots and large umbilicus. Large aperture sealed with yellow operculum.

Breeding: in June after pairing, spawn beneath sand. Egg cases mixed with sand in a gelatinous stiffened egg 'collar'. Same colour as sandy beach on which it lies freely. Eggs hatch directly into small snails.

Feeding: preys on bivalves, especially banded wedge shell (*Donax vittatus*), as shown opposite, and tellins. Bivalve held with muscular foot and circular hole bored through one shell by chemical action, when insides eaten.

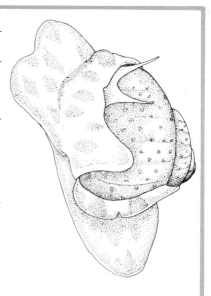

Empty shells of this predatory mollusc are more often found washed up on sandy beaches than the live animal, which moves beneath the sand using its bi-lobed muscular foot like a miniature plough. The foot is so large it covers both the head and front of the shell. When a necklace shell finds a living bivalve, it covers it with slime, feeling with its foot over the two shells to see if they are damaged and, if so, no boring is necessary. But if the bivalve shells are intact, it bores a neat circular hole with tapering sides and inserts its proboscis so the toothed radula can pull pieces of flesh into the mouth, where they are cut off with powerful jaws. Empty bored shells are easy to find on beaches with a high population of necklace shells. The necklace shell has a pair of widely spaced tentacles with an eye at the base of each one. It occurs all round Britain wherever there is a suitable sandy bottom.

Thin Tellin

Tellina tenuis

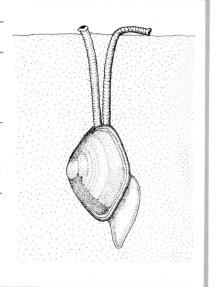

Size: up to ¾ in (2 cm) long.

Tidal level: MTL down into sub-littoral.

Recognition: very flattened glossy white, or rose-pink shells. Tough persistent ligament holds valves together after mollusc dies, so shells are like butterfly wings on sand.

Breeding: ripe eggs or sperm shed in May through exhalent siphon above sand surface where fertilised externally. Hatch into free-swimming trochophore larvae; turn into veligers.

Feeding: deposit-feeder. Long inhalent siphon sucks up organic detritus and diatoms on sand surface like a mini-vacuum cleaner. Food replenished by tidal movements, but tellins can move around.

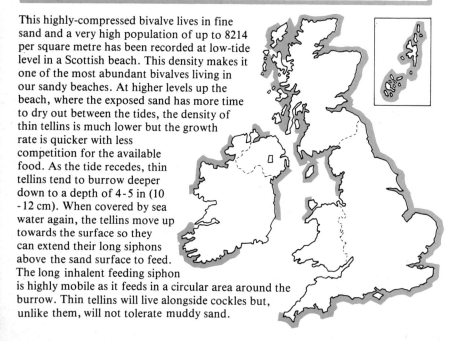

This highly-compressed bivalve lives in fine sand and a very high population of up to 8214 per square metre has been recorded at low-tide level in a Scottish beach. This density makes it one of the most abundant bivalves living in our sandy beaches. At higher levels up the beach, where the exposed sand has more time to dry out between the tides, the density of thin tellins is much lower but the growth rate is quicker with less competition for the available food. As the tide recedes, thin tellins tend to burrow deeper down to a depth of 4-5 in (10 -12 cm). When covered by sea water again, the tellins move up towards the surface so they can extend their long siphons above the sand surface to feed. The long inhalent feeding siphon is highly mobile as it feeds in a circular area around the burrow. Thin tellins will live alongside cockles but, unlike them, will not tolerate muddy sand.

Razor Shell

Ensis siliqua

Size: shell up to 8 in (20 cm).

Tidal level: LTL and below in clean sand, burrow often has a distinct keyhole opening on sand surface.

Recognition: straight-edged dirty yellow shells, blackened if living in anaerobic sand. Tough ligament keeps valves together after razor has died.

Breeding: in early spring. Fertilisation external. Eggs hatch into trochophore larvae which occur in plankton during April to May. Develop into bivalved veliger larvae.

Feeding: when submerged, on fine particles drawn in with water through inhalent siphon projecting above surface of sand when tide is in. Particles strained by internal gills. Waste leaves through other siphon.

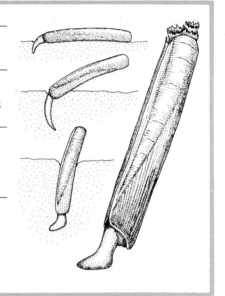

The razor shell is so named from its resemblance to an old-fashioned cut-throat razor. It burrows very rapidly into sand by using its cream-coloured muscular foot. If a live razor shell is laid on sand, the wedge-shaped foot emerges from one end and pushes into the sand. Blood is pumped into the foot so the end swells out and anchors the razor as it suddenly contracts and pulls down the shells. Once a razor starts to burrow, it repeats the pushing of the foot and contracting the body so quickly that it is impossible to hold the smooth shells and pull them out. Sea anglers use razors as bait and collect them by pouring salt down their holes. During the severe 1962/63 winter so many razor shells were killed off that graveyards of gaping shells could be seen strewn over the lower levels of sandy beaches in spring. Also known as 'razorfish' and 'spoutfish'.

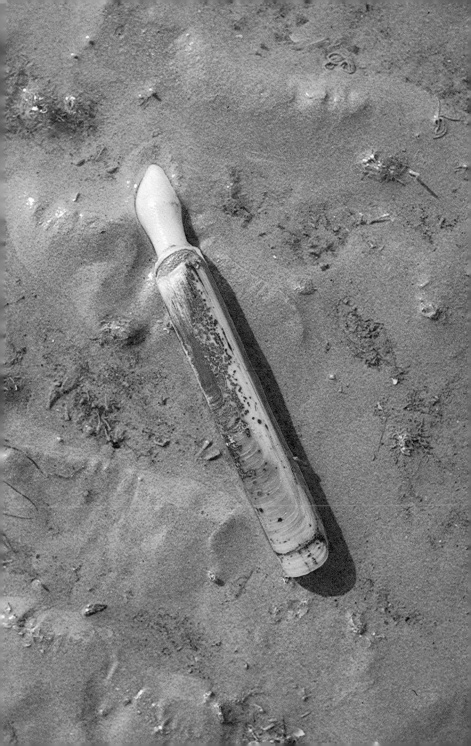

Common Cockle

Cerastoderma edule

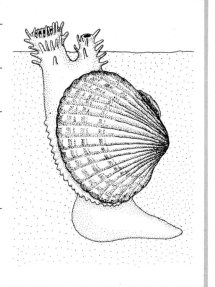

Size: 2½ in (6 cm) in diameter.

Tidal level: MTL and below on sandy and sandy/mud shores. Will tolerate low salinities in estuaries.

Recognition: dirty white or brownish bivalve mollusc with 22-28 radiating ribs on both shells.

Breeding: hermaphrodite, breed in summer when fertilisation occurs in sea water. Eggs hatch into trochophore larvae, developing into veligers. Young cockles, known as spat, settling from plankton. Huge spat falls occur once every 3-4 years.

Feeding: filter-feeds on plankton drawn in through one of 2 siphons which extend up above the sand when the tide is in. Waste leaves cockle via small exhalent siphon.

Cockles can occur in such dense concentrations that they form an almost continuous layer beneath the sand surface. As many as 10000 cockles have been recorded in one square metre. The largest cockles live low down the shore where they have more time to filter-feed. It is now known that cockles have a distinct cycle of feeding activity and inactivity associated with the tidal regime. When exposed, cockles cannot feed and so digestion takes place. As cockles burrow down to only 2 in (5 cm), they can be collected by raking. Commercial cockle beds occur in Morecambe Bay, the Wash, the Cheshire Dee and the Burry Inlet of Carmarthen Bay. High summer temperatures can cause mass mortalities in cockle beds, as happened in 1973 in Morecambe Bay and the Dee Estuary, when huge numbers of dead cockles produced a powerful stench.

Burrowing Starfish

Astropecten irregularis

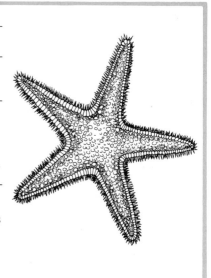

Size: diameter 3-5 in (7.5-12.5 cm).

Tidal level: LWST down into sub-littoral in sand.

Recognition: pink, flattened, usually with 5 arms. Side margins of arms fringed with spines.

Breeding: pair of gonads in each arm. Eggs and sperm shed into sea, which stimulates more sex cells to be shed. Fertilised eggs hatch into planktonic bipinnaria larvae which change into brachiolaria larvae.

Feeding: cilia on upper surface beat to move food particles falling on top of starfish to the mouth below. Also feeds on worms, sponges, crustaceans and molluscs. Any undigested remains are later rejected from the mouth.

Although usually pinkish in colour, it may have purple tips to the arms or be a brick-red colour. The edge plates which form a distinct border around all 5 arms are yellow or red. The upper edge plates bear large spines in 2 alternating rows, while the lower edge plates are densely spined. As an adaptation to life in sand, the tube feet end in points. This means the burrowing starfish cannot climb up vertical faces nor feed on large bivalves. Its diet includes small molluscs and crustaceans, which means it competes for food with bottom-living plaice. The burrowing starfish has a rhythmic activity pattern, being most active at dawn and lying passively beneath the sand at midday. This diurnal activity is controlled by light for, although the rhythm can be maintained for several days in complete darkness, it gradually breaks down. This starfish may carry a scale worm (*Acholae astericola*) in a groove beneath an arm.

Heart Urchin

Echinocardium cordatum

Size: body 2 in (5 cm) long by 1½ in (4 cm) broad.

Tidal level: LTL and below in sand.

Recognition: dirty white brittle test covered with golden-yellow soft spines. Large spatula-like digging spines on underside. 5 double rows of holes in test mark positions where suckered tube feet emerge.

Breeding: separate sexes. Reproduce in mid-summer of second year. Eggs fertilised in sea and hatch into planktonic echinopluteus larvae. Settle in sub-littoral zone and migrate up above LTL in first year.

Feeding: modified tube feet clustered around slit-like mouth collect detritus in burrow and on sand surface and pass into mouth.

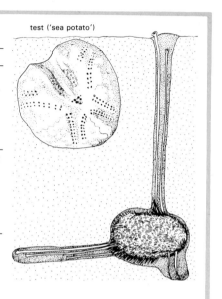

test ('sea potato')

Once a heart urchin dies, the spines soon fall away to leave the brittle test which is known as a sea potato. This is so light that it can be blown along the beach by wind. The heart urchin is well modified for its burrowing existence. The larger spines are more flexible and the test is slightly flattened. Using the flattened spines, it burrows into sand to a depth of 6-8 in (15-20 cm) but keeps a shaft open up to the surface. It lines the burrow and the shaft with mucus to prevent sand from falling on it. Extra long tube feet can extend up the shaft to pick up food on the sand surface. The slit-like mouth has no teeth or 'Aristotle's lantern'. Fishermen used to believe that when heart urchins buried deeper into the sand, this was a forewarning of storms. In suitable beaches, heart urchins are gregarious which increases the likelihood of the eggs being fertilised outside the body.

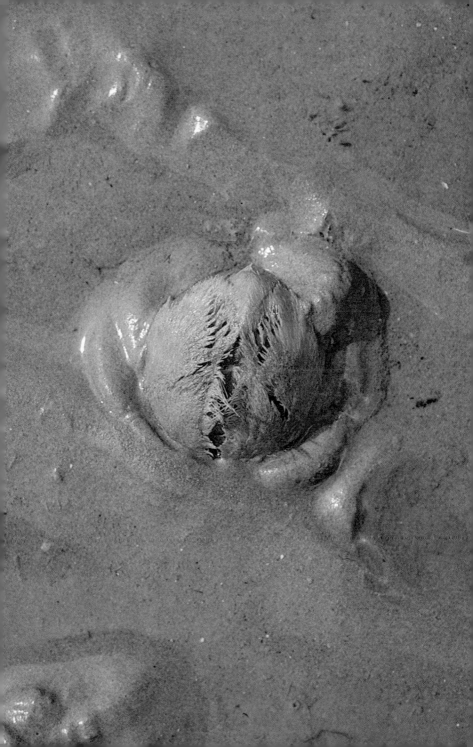

Slipper Limpet

Crepidula fornicata

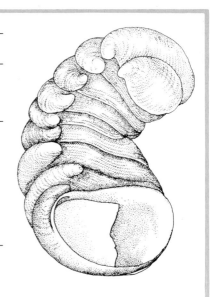

Size: shell up to 1½ in (4 cm) long.

Tidal level: LTL and offshore, often on oyster beds.

Recognition: oval pinkish/brown shell with some spiral coiling; has darker streaks. Horizontal shelf across half of underside.

Breeding: live in chains of up to 12 limpets, youngest at top are males, which pass through a hermaphrodite stage before changing sex as they grow larger. Male fertilises female below in chain. Several eggs laid, embedded in albumen in a capsule and brooded by female under foot. Hatch into free-swimming veliger larvae.

Feeding: filter-feeds on plankton. Competes with oysters for food and also smothers oysters with faeces.

This mollusc, which is more closely related to the winkles than to the true limpets, was accidentally introduced to this country with oysters from America at the end of the last century. It is now a pest of oyster beds, not by being a predator but by utilising the suspended food before it reaches the flattened oysters below them. Slipper limpets have long gill filaments which increase the surface area for collecting plankton which is trapped on the filaments in mucus. A male limpet will remain a male so long as it is attached to a female limpet but, once it is removed, it will develop into a female. Also, if large numbers of males are present, this will induce some to become fe- males. There is no alternation of sex changes; once a male has become a female, it remains as such. Slipper limpets have a strong southern and eastern distribution and can be abundant in sheltered estuaries on oyster beds.

Spiny Spider Crab

Maja squinado

Size: up to 7in (17.5cm) long.

Tidal level: LTL into sub-littoral on sand and among rocks.

Recognition: pinkish/brown crab with triangular spiny carapace. 2 points between the eyes. First pair of legs long with small pincers, 3 pairs walking legs long and thin.

Breeding: form large conical heaps (60-80 crabs) below LTL in summer. Young males and females moult in centre of heap, females then mate with mature males. Female carries eggs beneath abdominal flap. Hatch into planktonic larvae in late summer.

Feeding: on small animals and on seaweeds. Beak-like pincers adept at plucking food from crevices.

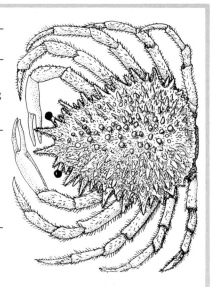

The spiny carapace of this crab gives rise to its other name of 'thornback'. Young crabs place seaweeds on the spines to help camouflage their shells. Larger crabs are better able to defend themselves and so have fewer seaweeds. The large breeding piles which form in summer may be several feet high. The larger mature male crabs cover the outer edges of the heaps and so protect the smaller crabs from predatory lobsters and octopuses. Pubescent crabs moult during the summer and are at their most vulnerable, so heaping of spider crabs serves both for protection and reproduction. In some years these crabs are so abundant during the summer that they completely fill up lobster pots so there is no room for the lobsters. On stony beaches, thornbacks bury themselves and in the past fishermen would locate the crabs by walking over the beach with their bare feet.

Ragworm

Nereis diversicolor

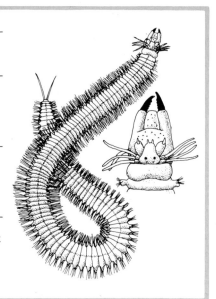

Size: body 3-4in (7.5-10cm) long.

Tidal level: MTL-LTL in sand and mud, especially in brackish water in estuaries.

Recognition: yellow/brown segmented worm with green sheen, and red blood vessel along back. Conspicuous head tentacles and paired paddle-like lobes on each segment.

Breeding: male and female worms spawn in burrows or on mud surface. Eggs hatch into trochophore larvae, which are not active swimmers and remain on the bottom.

Feeding: food grasped by powerful black chitinous jaws which are shot out on end of short muscular proboscis. Omnivorous, feeding both as predator and scavenger.

As well as crawling over mud, ragworms can also swim using their paddles. This worm is widespread in brackish estuarine water. The larvae will not tolerate such a wide salinity range as the adults. Ragworms are active hunters using their antennae and eyes to locate food, which is anything their jaws can grasp. They live in burrows in the mud where they are not exposed to the wide fluctuations of water flowing up and down the estuary. Spawning takes place when the water temperature rises above 41°F (5°C), and the body ruptures to release the eggs or sperm. As the larvae are not planktonic, they do not get carried from one estuary to another and so ragworms exist in estuaries as isolated populations. Sea anglers use ragworms as bait, especially for flounders. If carelessly handled, the black jaws can give a painful nip. Ragworms are eaten by long-billed wading birds.

Hydrobia Snail

Hydrobia ulvae

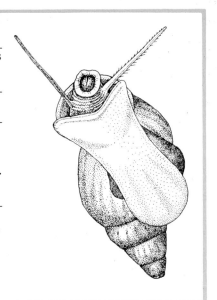

Size: height ¼ in (6mm); breadth ⅛ in (3mm).

Tidal level: very common between tides in estuaries and salt marshes, often with sea lettuce.

Recognition: small grain-sized brownish shell, with horny operculum.

Breeding: time depends on location. Eggs (usually 4) laid in capsule with albumen. Capsules often attached to adult shells if no firm substrate present. Eggs hatch into veliger larvae which spend only short time in plankton.

Feeding: on sea lettuce (*Ulva*), blue/green algae, bacteria and detritus. Will also feed on faeces of own and other species, digesting bacteria growing on them.

Densities of up to 42 000 per square metre have been recorded in the Clyde Estuary, making this tiny snail one of the most abundant animals of estuarine mud flats. The behaviour of the snails is closely linked with the tidal cycle. When exposed by the receding tide, *Hydrobia* crawls over the mud to browse. It then burrows into the mud and emerges before the tide ebbs up the flats, when it forms a mucous raft which keeps it afloat and also traps planktonic food. The ebbing tide then carries it back to its former level, when it breaks from the surface film, withdraws into its shell and sinks down to the mud. Hydrobia snails are an important food source for many wading birds. The snails concentrate as they settle on the ebb tide. Shelduck feed almost exclusively on *Hydrobia* and many birds starved to death in the 1962/63 winter when the intertidal zone froze.

Common Eel

Anguilla anguilla

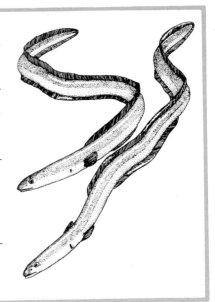

Size: young elvers or glass-eels 3-6 in (7.5-15 cm) long.
Tidal level: submerged in estuaries where they migrate through from the sea to freshwater.
Recognition: when first enter estuaries, body transparent so gills, head, gut and backbone can be seen; after few weeks dark pigment starts to develop and obscures insides.
Breeding: adult eels migrate to Sargasso Sea to breed, then die. Clear eggs (1 mm) develop into flattened leaf-like leptocephalus larvae which take 3 years to migrate to European coasts as elvers with a rounded eel-like body.
Feeding: elvers feed on small crustaceans and worms.

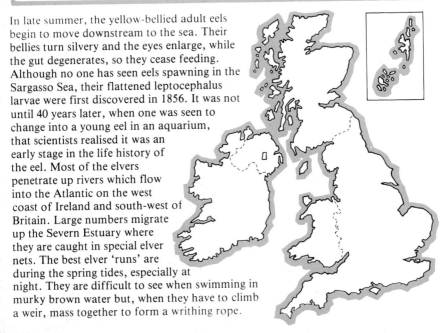

In late summer, the yellow-bellied adult eels begin to move downstream to the sea. Their bellies turn silvery and the eyes enlarge, while the gut degenerates, so they cease feeding. Although no one has seen eels spawning in the Sargasso Sea, their flattened leptocephalus larvae were first discovered in 1856. It was not until 40 years later, when one was seen to change into a young eel in an aquarium, that scientists realised it was an early stage in the life history of the eel. Most of the elvers penetrate up rivers which flow into the Atlantic on the west coast of Ireland and south-west of Britain. Large numbers migrate up the Severn Estuary where they are caught in special elver nets. The best elver 'runs' are during the spring tides, especially at night. They are difficult to see when swimming in murky brown water but, when they have to climb a weir, mass together to form a writhing rope.

Native Oyster

Ostrea edulis

Size: up to 4in (10cm) in length.

Tidal level: LW and below down to 15-45 fathoms (90-270ft; 27-82m) offshore. In creeks and estuaries in SE and SW lying on silty shells or gravel.

Recognition: bivalve mollusc with irregular rounded brownish shells. Upper valve rests inside lower valve.

Breeding: in summer when water temperature reaches 59°F (15°C), especially at full moon. Begins life as male and changes sex throughout life. Eggs fertilised internally, by sperm drawn in with water currents. Incubate eggs to larval stage. Larvae released into sea. Young oyster spat settle where other oysters are present.

Feeding: small particles filtered from sea water by the internal gills.

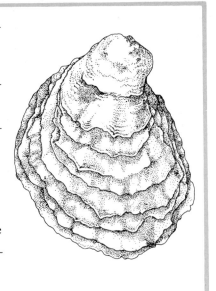

Today, oysters are an expensive luxury for a few but, some 150 years ago, they were a staple part of the diet of the poor. In the 1950s some 8 million oysters were landed annually, but by the late 1960s this figure had dropped to 3 million. Several east-coast estuaries, including the Blackwater, Crouch and Roach, used to support good oyster beds, but severe winters (especially 1962/63), predation by sting winkles and competition with slipper limpets have all contributed towards their decline. Now, one of the most prolific oyster-producing areas is on the south coast from Chichester Harbour to Poole Harbour. In the south-west, oysters are also cultivated in the Rivers Fal and Helford in Cornwall. Stocks are now boosted by bringing in oyster spat from other areas, and also by rearing larvae in hatcheries. Mature oysters are harvested using dredges from boats.

Netted Dog Whelk

Nassarius reticulatus

Size: shell up to 1½ in (4cm) long.

Tidal level: lower shore and below in sand.

Recognition: brown shell with spire of 10 whorls criss-crossed with spiral ridges and longitudinal ribs. Outer lip has teeth on inner margin.

Breeding: in spring and summer. Flattened yellowish egg capsules laid in neat rows on eelgrass or on hard objects. Each capsule contains 50-2000 eggs which hatch into veliger larvae with a long planktonic life.

Feeding: scavenges on dead or decaying flesh including lobsters and whelks in pots. Uses long siphon to detect food source. Food taken in by a long proboscis which can probe inside shells to get at flesh.

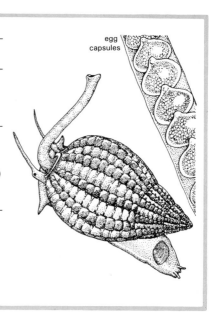

egg capsules

These whelks use their foot to bury themselves in muddy sand and shell gravel when the tide goes out. On the ebbing tide, the whelks either plough through the sand with their long grooved siphon projecting above the surface like a periscope or they emerge to glide over the surface of the sand. Both when the whelk is buried and crawling over the bottom, it waves the siphon backwards and forwards through the water to detect the presence of food in all directions. The scent of a dead crab or whelk is detected by the siphon and within seconds the netted dog whelks emerge from hiding and converge on the food. The mobile foot is used to push food towards the long proboscis which has a rasping radula at the end. As well as bait in crab pots netted dog whelks will also take advantage of freshly dead crabs which fishermen use as bait for catching the larger edible whelks in whelk pots.

Sea Hare

Aplysia punctata

Size: body up to 6in (15cm) long.

Tidal level: lower shore and below.

Recognition: fleshy red, brown or olive-green body, sometimes spotted. 2 pairs of tentacles on head. Small internal horny shell covered by mantle. When disturbed, sea hares eject purple slime which stains.

Breeding: hermaphrodite; form a mating chain, each sea hare acting as a male to one in front and as a female to one behind. Spawn inshore in spring and early summer, laying tangled threads of pinkish spawn. Young hatch from spawn and settle offshore. Adults die after spawning.

Feeding: on seaweeds which are grasped by the foot, so pieces bitten off with jaws are pushed into mouth.

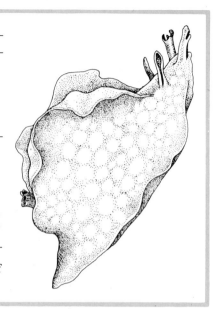

For most of the year, sea hares live offshore, but they move inshore to spawn in the spring. When exposed to the air on a beach, a sea hare appears an unattractive lump of purplish flesh but, when submerged, it moves underwater with a graceful motion. As the sea hare has the remnants of a shell, it is not a true sea slug, but forms a link between the shelled molluscs such as winkles and whelks and the sea slugs proper. The slender pink spawn ribbons which are laid among tufted seaweeds resemble an untidy mass of pink wool. Sea hares will eat a variety of seaweeds, which may be the most common species present. Young sea hares tend to eat red seaweeds, unlike older animals which eat green sea lettuce, brown wracks and also eelgrass. Different seaweeds have marked effects on their growth. This sea hare, which is one of several British species, is found in shallow water all round Britain.

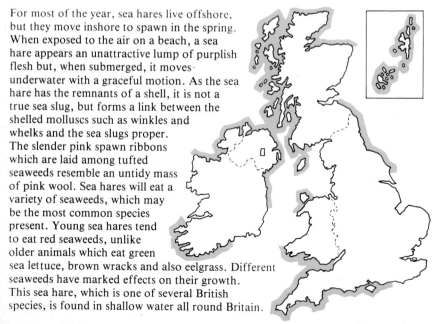

Conclusions and Future Prospects

Britain is on the edge of the distribution boundaries of many marine animals. Our waters are the southernmost limit of some arctic species and the northernmost limit of some lusitanian species. These animals are sensitive indicators of changes in environmental conditions, especially sea water temperatures. As well as climatic fluctuations, populations are affected by man's activities such as overfishing and pollution. To understand and monitor these changes, the common marine animals need to have their distributions carefully mapped and need a census of the sizes of their populations.

Even then, in-depth knowledge of a few species will not show the interrelationships of species within a community. A recent example of how man misinterpreted the decline of one species by natural predation is shown by the cockle/oystercatcher controversy in south Wales. The cockle is one of several shellfish on which oystercatchers feed. When the cockle fishery in the Burry Inlet on the Gower Peninsula declined in the early 1970s, the Nature Conservancy Council decided to cull the oystercatchers. During 1973 and 1974, 9238 birds were shot. This resulted in no increase in the cockle stocks, but merely slowed down the decline. There were obviously other factors contributing to the decrease in the cockles on these commercial grounds.

So, as well as detailed studies of individual species, we also require much more knowledge about animal communities and ecosystems as a whole. Indeed, this is one of the recommendations of the World Conservation Strategy (WCS) which was launched in March 1980. WCS was commissioned by the United Nations Environment Programme (UNEP) and prepared by the International Union for Conservation of Nature and Natural Resources (IUCN). Without knowing how animal populations wax and wane in response to climatic variation, it is impossible to decide whether sudden visible changes are natural or in response to man's activities. More detailed studies of ecosystems would enable us to predict with more certainty the effects of pollution or exploitation on the complete ecosystem.

As the energy crisis deepens, so the search for energy is going to impinge more and more on the shore life of our coasts. The threat of oil pollution is all too familiar after the disasters of the *Torrey Canyon* and the *Amoco Cadiz,* among others.

It took a disaster the size of the *Torrey Canyon* to provide the necessary impetus for research into the toxic effects of different detergents. As a result, the ones used today are much less toxic than those used in the 1960s. We now know that, if the oil is treated at sea, there is much less damage done to shore life than when oil is treated on the shore, and, if oil does reach the shore, spraying should be done just before the rising tide reaches the oil/detergent mix.

Above all, the top priority must be the prevention of massive oil pollution disasters since, as far as marine life is concerned, the cure for oil pollution is worse than the pollutant itself. If an oil spill does occur, it can be held back in enclosed areas, such as estuaries and sea-water lochs, by floating booms and the oil can then be sucked up from the surface.

It was 16 days after the Cornish mainland was polluted by *Torrey Canyon* oil that the first oil reached the French coast. This gave the French authorities time to observe our approach to the problem. They decided against using detergents and instead removed the oil (which in many places was much worse than in Cornwall) mechanically. During the first week they took 4200 tons (4267 tonnes) of oil from their beaches. The remnants of oil remaining were, as always, broken down naturally with time.

The current view held by the Nature Conservancy Council and the Ministry of Agriculture, Fisheries and Food is that, except where breeding sea-bird colonies or commercial fisheries are at risk, it is less damaging to leave natural processes to gradually overcome oil pollution.

The building of the giant oil terminal at Sullom Voe in the Shetlands has been preceded by one of the fullest ecological surveys of an area that has ever been conducted. Here, for once, there is at least some prior knowledge of what marine animals occur there, so that, when the inevitable disaster does happen an efficient ecological advisory service could ensure its effects would be minimised by knowing which areas had priority for protection.

It is impossible to learn from mistakes of this sort without both 'before' and 'after' information. Considerations on the siting of further terminals, storage facilities and manufacturing plants on the coast should take account of the wildlife in the immediate area. If a disaster befalls large numbers of birds overwintering in an estuary, or gathering on the sea surface for moving up to breeding grounds (as happened with the puffins, razorbills and guillemots after the *Torrey Canyon* spill), this is likely to evoke a bigger outcry from the public than if large numbers of uncommercial invertebrates suffer a similar fate, since they are unknown to most people. Nuclear power plants have vast requirements for cooling water, so they are often sited on the coasts or estuaries. Once again, environmental considerations may not have an adequate influence because inadequate information is available. Much more detailed studies of ecosystems are required so that we can predict with more confidence the effects that exploitation or pollution will have on an ecosystem as a whole and not just on commercially important species.

Obtaining such information is impossible without amateur help. There are not enough professional marine biologists in Britain and there are never likely to be enough. The distribution of British flowering plants was worked out with the help of a massive array of amateur botanists. Up and down the country, amateur ornithologists carry out regular censuses on the number of nesting birds in Britain. In the entomological field, amateurs operating a network of light traps all over Britain help to map the arrival of migrant insects. These records will spot, for example, the arrival of migrant aphid swarms from the Continent so that farmers can be tipped off to spray their crops in time to prevent a plague of aphids developing. When the botanist David Bellamy co-ordinated 'Operation Kelp' in the 1960s he showed how amateur divers can help in the amassing of huge quantities of data which scientists need to assess variations in natural populations. Kelps are large brown seaweeds which can easily be recognised by a diver. Samples were collected and weighed and the turbidity of the water noted. When all the results had been analysed, it was clear that polluted water, carrying particles in suspension, restricted the penetration of light through sea water which limited the plant growth. For records to be of value, however, it is essential that identifications are correct and observations meticulous.

Unlike on land, where exotic introductions have been made and cultivated for centuries from all corners of the globe, nearly all marine organisms in British waters are wild, which means that there are fewer problems with the invasion of exotic species crowding out of native species. Native species which are commercially exploited are in more danger of being affected by man than most others, with the exception of attractive-looking species which are on the limits of their distribution and which appeal to the amateur collector.

Various methods are available for restricting catches of commercial species that have depleting stocks. The size of the catches can be reduced by protecting some areas, by having close seasons or by controlling the mesh size of nets or trawls.

All the species selected for detailed description in this book are seashore animals. Since several are dependent on seaweeds for food or shelter, their way of life is dependent on these marine plants. Brown seaweeds (especially the oarweeds *Laminaria* spp) are exploited by man as a source of alginates, which are used both in the food and pharmaceutical trades; for example, sodium alginate is used as a stabiliser for ice cream. Seaweeds beached on the foreshore are gathered as a source of fertiliser. As the demand for alginates and fertilisers grows, it is possible that certain seaweeds may be cropped both underwater and intertidally in future. This would affect a very wide range of both plant and animal life in the shallow sub-littoral.

MAFF laboratories have bred fish larvae for stocking offshore waters, and also imported stocks of shellfish spat for fattening up in coastal waters. Marine farming on a scale comparable to agriculture on land is not too far-fetched if we require more food from the sea. The selection of commercially preferable genetic strains, the setting up of marine enclosures, the selection of shellfish monocultures, with associated destruction of 'weed' species, as well as the introduction of more alien species could not fail to affect the resident organisms in an adverse way.

The exploitation of sand and gravel for the building industry may appear harmless enough, but gravel collected offshore can ruin fishing grounds by making it too rough for fishing. It can also result in erosion taking place elsewhere, by sediments being moved by the sea to infill the holes created. This movement of sediments from one place to another may affect the deposition of sediments in the sub-littoral and the lower shore.

With repeated annual visits to a favourite sandy bay it may be difficult to notice any changes which are taking place, but sand particles are not stable. There can be very marked visual differences between a peaceful sandy bay in summer and one subjected to rough winter seas which can suddenly remove all the sand: by the summer, the sand has gradually accumulated and appears as it was in previous years. The hard sand reefs built by honeycomb worms appear indestructible, but fierce seas can break up extensive reefs, which may take years to be built up to the original size. So nothing is permanent on the shore: populations fluctuate and terrain changes, as the tide continues to ebb and flow over the shore.

Marine habitats can be lost to man-made coastal defences: breakwaters, quays, sea walls and marinas. During the building, destruction inevitably takes place and, although afterwards some colonisation may take place, the smooth steep vertical faces of coastal defences in no way simulate rock pools, horizontal platforms and crevices of the original rocky shore. Seaweeds, sea anemones and mussels will also colonise breakwaters, but these cannot be described as rich sites, although pier pilings can have an interesting associated fauna—including sponges, sea squirts and sea slugs—which can be viewed at low tide.

One of the renewable energy resources that we may try to exploit is that of tidal energy. It has been estimated that a barrage built across the Severn Estuary could generate nearly ten per cent of Britain's electricity. To try to predict what effects the building of such a barrage would have on the marine environment, the Institute of Marine Environmental Research (IMER) has been developing a tidal ecosystem model of the Severn Estuary. A mathematical model of this sort is a replica of the system, that seeks to describe how the ecosystem works in terms of complex mathematical equations, in much the same way that a sculptor describes what a person looks like by using stone. Using a powerful computer to run the model, many years' events can be condensed into a few minutes. By introducing the barrage into the model, it is hoped that its effects on the biology can be predicted. Beyond that, it is hoped that the model can be extended to take into account other estuaries. For example, it has been suggested that a barrage should be built across Morecambe Bay partly as a huge freshwater reservoir, and partly to provide a good roadway to north Lancashire and Cumbria.

Another renewable energy resource is wave energy. Lines of wave-rider generators may be set out offshore which may change the wave environment of our coasts. The biology of fouling organisms will need to be fully understood, otherwise they may seriously reduce the wave-riders.

Further in the future, we may see the application of biotechnology in the marine environment. Micro-organisms are at present used to brew beer, synthesise antibiotics and other industrial chemicals. In future, they may be used to extract minerals from seawater: the Japanese have already found a micro-organism that will concentrate uranium 4000 times from sea water. Another suggestion is that micro-organisms grown in massive culture vessels may be used as our future fuel; a 60 x 60 mile (97 x 97 km) area could grow all our energy requirements. The only place where that sort of area is available is our coastal seas.

At the present time, although the coastline and seashore are under increasing pressure so that we cannot afford to be complacent, compared with our terrestrial habitats (nearly all of which have had either vegetation felled, or burned, or ploughed for agriculture, forestry or building), parts of our seashore—especially in more remote areas—are comparatively untouched. Here one aspect of Britain's natural heritage can still be seen and appreciated today. But for how much longer?

Glossary

Albumen: protein solution in egg.

Algal: relating to algae, a large group of lower plants, which includes seaweeds.

Anaerobic: without oxygen.

Antennae: the long slender paired sensory head appendages on some arthropods and worms.

Aperture: an opening.

Aristotle's lantern: jaw apparatus of sea urchins.

Ascidian: sea squirt, member of Urochordata.

Asexual: reproduction like budding and simple division which does not involve cross-fertilisation between different sexes.

Basal disc: disc at base of sea anemones.

Bilobed: having two lobes.

Bivalve: mollusc with body enclosed by two shell valves.

Boreal: a cold-temperate water zoogeographical zone which lies between the arctic and subtropical zones.

Byssal threads: hair-like threads which anchor some bivalve molluscs to rocks.

Calcareous: made of calcium carbonate or chalk.

Capsule: a gastropod mollusc egg case containing several eggs.

Carapace: dorsal covering overlying thorax of most crustaceans; often extends around side of body.

Chitinous: made of chitin, a tough resilient material within outer arthropod skeletons.

Cilia: microscopic, actively moving threads used by animals either to propel themselves through water or to move substances internally.

Cirri: large, compound cilia providing same function as cilia, but more powerfully.

Collar cell: specialised cell lining the insides of sponges.

Detritus: particles of debris from decaying plants and animals.

Diatom: a microscopic one-celled alga, with sculptured, two-part siliceous shell.

Ebb tide: receding tide.

ELWST: extreme low water of spring tides.

Errant: free-living; used to describe a group of polychaete worms.

Filamentous: finely thread-like.

Filter-feeder: animal which feeds by filtering food particles from water.

Flagella: very long, fine threads which beat actively in a spiral manner.

Flood tide: inflowing tide.

Frond: leafy part of seaweed.

Fucoid: belonging to 'brown' groups of algae, the wracks.

Gamete: reproductive cell: sperm (male); egg (female).

Gastropods: group of molluscs including snails, sea slugs and sea hares.

Gelatinous: jelly-like.

Gonad: sexual organ which produces gametes.

Gonophore: sexual reproductive buds of hydroid coelenterates.

Hermaphrodite: individual producing both male and female gametes.

Holdfast: attachment of seaweed at their bases.

HWM: high water mark.

HWMNT: high water mark of neap tides.

HWMST: high water mark of spring tides.

Intertidal: occurring between high and low tide marks.

Invertebrates: animals having no backbone (vertebrae).

Larvae: immature forms of animals which are totally different from adults.

   auricularia: sea cucumber.

   bipinnaria: early starfish.

   brachiolaria: late starfish.

   cypris: late barnacle.

   echinopluteus: echinoderm.

   echinospira: cowrie.

   glaucothoë: late hermit crab.

   leptocephalus: migratory larva of eel.

   megalopa: late crab.

   nauplius: early crustacean.

   planula: late coelenterate.

   tadpole: sea squirt.

   trochophore: polychaete and mollusc.

   veliger: gastropod.

   zoea: early crab.

Littoral zone: intertidal zone between high and low water spring tides.

LTL: low tide level.

Lusitanian: the subtropical warm-water zoogeographic zone in the north Atlantic.

LW: low water.

LWMNT: low water mark of neap tides.

LTMST: low water mark of spring tides.

Medusae: 'jellyfish': free-swimming dispersal phase of coelenterates.

Metamorphosis: transformation from larval to adult form, which involves reorganisation of body tissue.

Moult: to shed outer covering.

MTL: mean tide level.

Neap tide: the smallest ranging tide (compare with spring tide).

Nematocyst: stinging cell in coelenterates.

North Atlantic Drift: the diffuse ocean current which flows north-eastwards across the north Atlantic towards northern Europe, considered by some to be an extension of the Gulf Stream.

Omnivorous: animal which eats both plant and animal matter.

Operculum: horny plate which closes opening of gastropod

mollusc shell when animal withdraws.

Pharynx: region of gut immediately behind mouth.

Photosynthesis: process occurring in green plants whereby organic compounds are synthesised from water and carbon dioxide using the sun's energy.

Phytoplankton: microscopic plants which drift in the sea.

Plankton: plants and animals which drift at all depths in the oceans, but which are most abundant near the surface.

Podia: water-filled appendages (tube feet) of echinoderms.

Polychaete: marine, segmented (annelid) worm; may be errant or sedentary.

Polyp: coelenterate or part of coelenterate colony which has a sea anemone-like body form.

Proboscis: extendible mouth structure.

Protozoan: microscopic, single-celled organism.

Radula: horny teeth-bearing 'tongue' of molluscs.

Rostrum: pointed projection on front of crustacean head.

Salinity: degree of 'saltiness'. Usually expressed as parts of salt per thousand parts of water.

Scavenger: animal feeding on carrion.

Semi-diurnal: occurring half daily, i.e., twice a day.

Sessile: living attached to substrate—rock, shell or seaweed.

Siliceous: containing silica.

Siphon: tube through which water is either sucked in or pumped out in molluscs and sea squirts.

Spat: mass of newly metamorphosed forms of molluscs.

Spicule: minute internal skeleton which supports body of some sponges.

Splash zone: region of shore above HWM subject to sea spray.

Spongin: horny substance which forms internal skeleton of some sponges.

Sporling: young plant developing from spore.

Spring tide: the biggest ranging tide (compare with neap tide).

Stipe: stalk of seaweed.

Strandline: line of debris left at HWM when tide recedes.

Sub-littoral zone: zone below low water of spring tides.

Surf zone: region of shore where waves break.

Swimmerets: the six pairs of appendages found on the abdominal segments of crustaceans.

Test: exoskeleton of echinoderms or outer sac of sea squirts.

Thorax: group of segments behind arthropod head, which bears limbs.

Tidal range: distance between high and low water marks.

Tube feet: see podia.

Umbilicus: opening or hollow at base of some gastropod shells, which have a hollow central pillar to the shell.

Wrack: a brown seaweed.

Zooid: individual member of a colonial animal.

Index

160

THE VINEYARDS OF CALANETTI

Saying 'I do' under the Tuscan sun...

Deep in the Tuscan countryside nestles the picturesque village of Monte Calanetti. Famed for its world-renowned vineyards, the village is also home to the crumbling but beautiful Palazzo di Comparino. It's been empty for months, but rumours of a new owner are spreading like wildfire...and that's *before* the village is chosen as the setting for the royal wedding of the year!

It's going to be a roller coaster of a year, but will wedding bells ring out in Monte Calanetti for anyone else?

Find out in this fabulously heart-warming, uplifting and thrillingly romantic new eight-book continuity from Mills & Boon® Romance!

A Bride for the Italian Boss
by Susan Meier

Return of the Italian Tycoon
by Jennifer Faye

Reunited by a Baby Secret
by Michelle Douglas
Available September 2015

Soldier, Hero...Husband?
by Cara Colter

His Lost-and-Found Bride
by Scarlet Wilson

The Best Man and the Wedding Planner
by Teresa Carpenter

His Princess of Convenience
by Rebecca Winters

Saved by the CEO
by Barbara Wallace

Dear Reader,

A lot of times the thought of going home can make a person smile broadly as a sense of eager anticipation has them racing out through the door...homeward bound. Then there are those other times—those not-so-great trips home. You know...the ones where an impending homecoming sends a nervous tremor through a person's stomach and makes their palms moist.

Well, Angelo Amatucci is about to have one of those not-so-great homecomings. When he's summoned back to Italy it isn't for a joyous reunion with his brother and sister. And it doesn't help matters that returning to the small Tuscan village will cause him to come face to face with a tangled web of emotions. But he doesn't let any of that deter him—not when his family needs him.

Kayla Hill is a loyal assistant with her eyes on a promising career. She's a small-town girl making her way in the big city. And now that she's latched her wagon on to Angelo, a brilliant star in the advertising industry, she's certain that success is at last within her grasp—if only she can keep her thoughts focused on work and not on her exceedingly handsome boss. But when Angelo leads her on a wondrous romantic journey through the rolling hills of the Tuscan countryside all bets are off.

I hope you enjoy this special story of love—not only the romantic kind, but the kind that holds a family together through thick and thin.

Happy reading

Jennifer

RETURN OF THE ITALIAN TYCOON

BY
JENNIFER FAYE

MILLS & BOON

First published in Great Britain 2015
by Mills & Boon, an imprint of Harlequin (UK) Limited,
Eton House, 18-24 Paradise Road, Richmond, Surrey, TW9 1SR

© 2015 Harlequin Books S.A.

Special thanks and acknowledgement are given to Jennifer Faye
for her contribution to *The Vineyards of Calanetti* series

ISBN: 978-0-263-25856-1

Harlequin (UK) Limited's policy is to use papers that are natural,
renewable and recyclable products and made from wood grown in
sustainable forests. The logging and manufacturing processes conform
to the legal environmental regulations of the country of origin.

Printed and bound in Great Britain
by CPI Antony Rowe, Chippenham, Wiltshire

Award-winning author **Jennifer Faye** pens fun, heart-warming romances. Jennifer has won the RT Reviewers' Choice Best Book Award, is a Top Pick author and has been nominated for numerous awards. Now living her dream, she resides with her patient husband, one amazing daughter—the other remarkable daughter is off chasing her own dreams—and two spoiled cats. She'd love to hear from you via her website: jenniferfaye.com

Books by Jennifer Faye

Mills & Boon® Romance

The DeFiore Brothers

The Playboy of Rome
Best Man for the Bridesmaid

Rancher to the Rescue
Snowbound with the Soldier
Safe in the Tycoon's Arms
The Return of the Rebel
A Princess by Christmas

To Michelle Styles, an amazing friend,
who taught me so much, including that
the important part of writing was what I decided to do
after the dreaded 'R'. Thank you!

CHAPTER ONE

"CAN I SMELL YOU?"

Kayla Hill's fingers struck the wrong keys on her computer. Surely she hadn't heard her boss correctly—her very serious, very handsome boss. "Excuse me. What did you say?"

Angelo Amatucci's tanned face creased with lines as though he were deep in thought. "Are you wearing perfume?"

"Uh...yes, I am."

"Good. That will be helpful. May I have a smell?"

Helpful? With what? She gave up on answering an email and turned her full attention to her boss, who moved to stand next to her. What in the world had prompted him to ask such a question? Was her perfume bothering him? She sure hoped not. She wore it all the time. If he didn't like it or was allergic to it, she thought he'd have mentioned it before now.

Kayla craned her neck, allowing her gaze to travel up over his fit body, all six-foot-plus of muscle, until she met his inquisitive eyes. "I'm sorry but I... I don't understand."

"I just finished speaking with Victoria Van Holsen, owner of Moonshadows Cosmetics. She has decided that her latest fragrance campaign, even though she painstakingly approved it each step of the way, just won't do."

"She doesn't want it?" Kayla failed to keep the astonishment out of her voice.

A muscle in his jaw twitched. "She insists we present her with a totally new proposal."

"But this is a Christmas campaign. Everything should be finalized, considering it's already March." Then, realizing that she was speaking to a man with far more experience, she pressed her lips together, silencing her rambling thoughts.

"Now that information about her competitor's upcoming holiday campaign has been leaked, she wants something more noteworthy—something that will go viral."

"I thought the campaign was unique. I really like it." Kayla truly meant it. She wasn't trying to butter up her boss—that was just an unexpected bonus.

"The fact of the matter is, Victoria Van Holsen is a household name and one of our most important clients. Our duty is to keep her happy."

It was the company's motto—the client's needs come first. No matter what. And if Kayla was ever going to rise up the chain from her temporary detour as the personal assistant to the CEO of Amatucci & Associates Advertising to her dream job as an ad executive on Madison Avenue, she could never forget that the clients were always right. It didn't matter how unreasonable or outrageous their requests might be at times, keeping them happy was of the utmost importance.

"How can I help?"

"Stand up."

His face was devoid of emotion, giving no hint of his thoughts.

She did as he asked. Her heart fluttered as he circled her. When he stopped behind her and leaned in close, an army of goose bumps rose on her skin. Her eyes drifted closed as a gentle sigh slipped across her lips. Angelo Amatucci truly did want an up close and personal whiff of her perfume.

He didn't so much as touch a single hair on her, but she could sense him near her neck. Her pulse raced. If this most unusual request had come from anyone else, she'd swear they were hitting on her. But as Mr. Amatucci stepped to the front of her, his indifferent expression hadn't changed. Her frantic heart rate dipped back to normal.

There had never been any attempt on his part to flirt with her. Though his actions at times could be quite unpredictable, they were always ingenuous. She deduced that his sudden curiosity about her perfume had something to do with the Van Holsen account. But what could he be thinking? Because there was no way she was wearing a Moonshadows fragrance. One ounce of the stuff would set her back an entire paycheck.

"It seems to have faded away." A frown tugged at his lips.

"Perhaps this will be better." She pulled up the sleeve of her blue suit jacket and the pink blouse beneath it before holding out her wrist to him. "Try this."

His hand was warm and his fingers gentle as he lifted her hand to his face. Her heart resumed its frantic tap dancing in her chest. *Tip-tap. Tip-tap.* She wished it wouldn't do that. He was, after all, her boss—the man who held her career aspirations in the palm of his very powerful hand. A man who was much too serious for her.

Still, she couldn't dismiss that his short dark wavy hair with a few silver strands at the temples framed a very handsome, chiseled face. His dark brown eyes closed as he inhaled the fragrance, and she noticed his dark lashes as they swept down, hiding his mesmerizing eyes. It was a wonder some woman hadn't snatched him up—not that Kayla had any thoughts in that direction.

She had narrowly escaped the bondage of marriage to a really nice guy, who even came with her Mom's and Dad's stamp of approval. Though the breakup had been hard, it had been the right decision for both of them. Steven had wanted a traditional wife who was content to cook, clean and raise a large family. Not that there was anything wrong with that vision. It just wasn't what she envisioned for her future. She wanted to get out of Nowhereville, USA, and find her future in New York City.

When Mr. Amatucci released her arm, she could still

feel warmth where his fingers had once been. Her pulse continued to race. She didn't know why she was having this reaction. She wasn't about to jeopardize her rising career for some ridiculous crush on her boss, especially when it was perfectly obvious that he didn't feel a thing for her.

His gaze met hers. "Is that the only perfume you wear?"

She nodded. "It's my favorite."

"Could I convince you to wear another fragrance?"

He was using her as a test market? Interesting. She could tell him what he wanted to hear, but how would that help him develop a new marketing strategy? She decided to take her chances and give him honest answers.

"Why would I change when I've been using this same perfume for years?"

He rubbed his neck as she'd seen him do numerous times in the past when he was contemplating new ideas for big accounts. And the Van Holsen account was a very big account. The fact that the client had the money to toss aside a fully formulated ad campaign and start over from scratch was proof of their deep pockets.

Mr. Amatucci's gaze was still on her, but she couldn't tell if he was lost in thought. "How long have you worn that fragrance?"

"Since I was a teenager." She remembered picking out the flower-shaped bottle from a department store counter. It was right before her first ever school dance. She'd worn it for every special occasion since, including her first date with Steven. And then there was her high school graduation followed by her college commencement. She'd worn it for all the big moments in her life. Even the day she'd packed her bags and moved to New York City in search of her dreams.

"Talk to me." Mr. Amatucci's voice cut through her memories. "What were you thinking about just now?"

She glanced hesitantly at him. In all of the weeks she'd worked as his PA, they'd never ventured into a conversation that was the slightest bit personal. Their talks had always centered around business. Now, he'd probably think she was silly or sentimental or both.

"I was thinking about all the times in my life when I wore this perfume."

"And?"

"And I wore it for every major event. My first date. My first kiss. My—" A sharp look from him silenced her.

"So your attachment to the fragrance goes beyond the scent itself. It is a sentimental attachment, right?"

She shrugged. "I guess so."

She'd never thought of it that way. In fact, she'd never given her perfume this much thought. If the bottle got low, she put it on her shopping list, but that's as far as her thoughts ever went.

"So if our client doesn't want to go with a sparkly, feel-fabulous-when-you-wear-this campaign, we can try a more glamorous sentimental approach. Thanks to you, we now have a new strategy."

She loved watching creativity in action. And she loved being a part of the creative process. "Glad I could help."

He started to walk away, then he paused and turned back. "You were just promoted to a copywriter position before you took this temporary assignment as my PA, right?"

She nodded. What better way to get noticed than to work directly for one of the biggest names in the advertising industry.

"Good. You aren't done with this project. I want you to dig into those memories and write out some ideas—"

"But don't you have a creative team for this account?" She wanted to kick herself for blurting out her thoughts.

Mr. Amatucci sent her a narrowed look. His cool, professional tone remained unchanged. "Are you saying you aren't interested in working on the project?"

Before she could find the words to express her enthusiasm, his phone rang and he turned away. She struggled to contain her excitement. This was her big opening and she fully intended to make the most of it.

This was going to work out perfectly.

A smile tugged at Kayla lips. She'd finally made it. Though people thought she'd made a big mistake by taking a step backward to assume a temporary position as Mr. Amatucci's PA, it was actually working out just as she'd envisioned.

She'd gone after what she wanted and she'd gotten it. Well, not exactly, but she was well on her way to making her dreams a reality. With a little more patience and a lot of hard work, she'd become an account executive on New York's famous Madison Avenue in the exclusive advertising agency of Amatucci & Associates.

Her fingers glided over the keyboard of her computer as she completed the email to the creative department about another of their Christmas campaigns. Sure it was only March, but in the marketing world, they were working months into the future. And with a late-season snowstorm swirling about outside, it seemed sort of fitting to be working on a holiday project.

She glanced off to the side of her computer monitor, noticing her boss holding the phone to his ear as he faced a wall of windows overlooking downtown Manhattan. Being on the twenty-third floor, they normally had a great view of the city, but not today. What she wouldn't give to be someplace sunny—far, far away from the snow. After months of frigid temperatures and icy sidewalks, she was most definitely ready for springtime.

"Have you started that list?" Mr. Amatucci's piercing brown gaze met hers.

Um—she'd been lost in her thoughts and hadn't even realized he'd wrapped up his phone call. Her gaze moved from his tanned face to her monitor. "Not yet. I need to finish one more email. It shouldn't take me long. I think your ideas for the account are spot-on. Just wait until the client lays her eyes on the mock-ups."

Then, realizing she was rambling, she pressed her lips firmly together. There was just something about being around him that filled her with nervous energy. And his long stretches of silence had her rushing to fill in the silent gaps.

Mr. Amatucci looked as though he was about to say something, but his phone rang again. All eyes moved to his desk. The ringtone was different. It must be his private line. In all the time she'd been working for him, it had never rung.

It rang again and yet all he did was stare at the phone.

"Do you want me to get it?" Kayla offered, not sure what the problem was or why Mr. Amatucci was hesitant. "I really don't mind."

"I've got it." He reached over and snatched up the receiver. "Nico, what's the matter?"

Well, that was certainly a strange greeting. Who picked up the phone expecting something to be wrong? Then, realizing that she was staring—not to mention eavesdropping—she turned her attention back to the notes she'd been rewording into an email. She glanced up to see Mr. Amatucci had turned his back to her. He once again faced the windows and spoke softly. Though the words were no longer distinguishable, the steely edge of his voice was still obvious.

She looked at the paper on her desk, her gaze darting over it to find where she'd left off. She didn't want to sit here with her hands idle. No, that definitely wouldn't look good for her.

She was sending along some of Mr. Amatucci's thoughts about the mock-up of an ad campaign for a new client—a very demanding client. The account was huge. It would go global—like most of the other accounts her boss personally handled. Each of his clients expected Mr. Amatucci's world to revolve around them and their accounts. He took their calls, no matter the time—day or night. Through it all, he maintained his cool. To say Angelo was a workaholic was being modest.

As a result, he ran the most sought-after advertising agency in the country—if not the world. Stepping off the elevator, clients and staff were immediately greeted by local artists' work and fresh flowers. The receptionist was bright and cheerful without being annoying. Appointments were kept timely. The quality of the work was exemplary. All of it culminated in Amatucci & Associates being so popular that they had to turn away business.

"*Cosa!* Nico, no!" Mr. Amatucci's hand waved about as he talked.

Her boss's agitated voice rose with each word uttered. Kayla's fingers paused as her attention zeroed in on the man who never raised his voice—until now. He was practically yelling. But she could only make out bits and pieces. His words were a mix of English and Italian with a thick accent.

"Nico, are you sure?"

Had someone died? And who was Nico? She hadn't heard Mr. Amatucci mention anyone with that name, but then again, this call was on his private line. It was highly doubtful that it had anything to do with business. And she knew exactly nothing about his personal life—sometimes she wondered if he even had one.

"Marianna can't be pregnant!" The shouts spiraled off into Italian.

Pregnant? Was he the father? The questions came hard and fast. There was a little voice in the back of her mind that told her she should excuse herself and give him some privacy, but she was riveted to her chair. No one would ever believe that this smooth, icy-cool man was capable of such heated volatility. She blinked, making sure she hadn't fallen asleep and was having some bizarre dream. But when her eyes opened, her boss was standing across the room with his hand slicing through the air as he spoke Italian.

The paramount question was: Who was Marianna?

Angelo Amatucci tightened his grip on the phone until his fingers hurt. This had to be some sort of nightmare and soon he'd wake up. Could it be he'd been working a bit too much lately? Perhaps he should listen to the hints from his business associates to take a break from the frantic pace. That would explain why just moments ago when he'd been examining Ms. Hill's perfume—a scent he found quite inviting—that he'd been tempted to smooth his thumb along the silky skin of her wrist—

"Angelo, are you listening to me?" Tones of blatant concern laced Nico's voice, demanding Angelo's full attention. "What are we going to do?"

Nico was his younger brother by four years, and though their opinions differed on almost everything, the one area where they presented a unified front was their little sister, Marianna—who wasn't so little anymore.

"There has to be another answer to this. You must have misunderstood. Marianna can't be pregnant. She's not even in a serious relationship."

"I know what I heard."

"Tell me again."

"I wanted her to taste the wine from the vineyard. I think it's the best we've ever produced. Just wait until you try some—"

"Nico, tell me about Marianna."

"Yes, well, she has looked awfully pale and out of sorts since she returned home after her year of traveling. I thought she'd done too much partying—"

"*Accidenti!* She wasn't supposed to waste the year partying." Unable to stand still a moment longer, Angelo started to pace again. When his gaze met the wide-eyed stare of Ms. Hill, she glanced down at her desk. He made a point of turning his back to her and lowering his voice. "She was sent to Australia to work on the vineyards there and get more experience in order to help you. If I'd have known she planned for it to be a year of partying, I'd have sent for her. I could have put her to work at the office."

Nico sighed. "Not everyone is like you, big brother. We aren't all driven to spend every last moment of our lives working."

"And you didn't do anything about her being sick?"

"What was I supposed to do? I asked if she needed anything. She said no, that it was some sort of flu bug. What else was I supposed to do?"

Angelo's hand waved around as he flew off in a string of Italian rants. Taking a calming breath, he stopped in front of the windows and stared blindly at the snow. "And it took her confessing she was pregnant for you to figure it out?"

"Like you would have figured it out sooner? What do either of us know about pregnant women…unless there's something you haven't told me?"

"Don't be ridiculous!" Angelo had no intention of getting married and having a family. Not now. Not ever.

"She didn't have any choice but to come clean when I offered her some wine. She knew she couldn't drink it. Hard to believe that you and I will be uncles this time next year."

"Don't tell me you're happy about this development?"

"I'm not. But what do you want me to do?"

"Find out the father's name for starters."

"I tried. She's being closemouthed. All she said was that she couldn't drink the wine because she's eight weeks pregnant. Then she started to cry and took off for her room."

"Didn't you follow? How could you have just let her get away without saying more?"

"How could I? I sure don't see you here trying to deal with an emotional pregnant woman."

How had things spun so totally out of control? Angelo's

entire body tensed. And more importantly, how did he fix them? How did he help his sister from so far away?

Angelo raked his fingers through his hair. "She has to tell you more. How are we supposed to help if we don't even know which man is the father. She isn't exactly the sort to stay in a relationship for long."

"Trust me. I've tried repeatedly to get his name from her. Maybe she'll tell you."

That wasn't a conversation Angelo wanted to have over the phone. It had to be in person. But he was in the middle of overseeing a number of important projects. Now was not the time for him to leave New York. But what choice did he have? This was his baby sister—the little girl he remembered so clearly running around with a smile on her face and her hair in braids.

But a lot of time had passed since he'd left Italy. Would she open up to him? The fact his leaving hadn't been his idea didn't seem to carry much weight with his siblings, who were left behind to deal with their dysfunctional parents. Though he dearly missed his siblings, he didn't miss the constant barrage of high-strung emotions of his parent's arguments and then their inevitable reunions—a constant circle of epic turmoil.

Maybe the trouble Marianna had got herself into was some sort of rebellion. With their parents now living in Milan, there was only Nico at home to cope with their sister. And to Nico's credit, he never complained about the enormous responsibility leveled solely on his shoulders.

Now that their parents had moved on, Angelo didn't have any legitimate excuse to stay away. But every time the subject of his visiting Monte Calanetti surfaced, he pleaded he had too much work to do. It was the truth—mostly. Perhaps he should have tried harder to make more time for his siblings.

Stricken with guilt, anger and a bunch of emotions that Angelo couldn't even name, he couldn't think straight. As the oldest brother, he was supposed to look out for his brother and sister. Instead, he'd focused all of his time and energy on creating a thriving, wildly successful company.

In the process, he'd failed their wayward and headstrong sister.

And now her future would forever be altered.

He owed it to Marianna to do what he could to fix things. But how could he do that when he was so far away?

CHAPTER TWO

THIS ISN'T GOOD. Not good at all.

Kayla pressed Save on the computer. She needed to give Mr. Amatucci some space. She reached for her wallet to go buy a—a—a cocoa. Yes, that would suit the weather outside perfectly.

She got to her feet when her boss slammed down the phone. He raked his fingers through his short hair and glanced at her. "Sorry about that. Where were we?"

The weariness in his voice tugged at her sympathies. "Um…well, I thought that I'd go get some um…cocoa—"

"The Van Holsen account. We were talking about how we need to put a rush on it."

"Um…sure." She sat back down.

Kayla wasn't sure how to act. She'd never before witnessed her boss seriously lose it. And who exactly was Marianna? Was it possible Mr. Amatucci really did have a life outside this office—one nobody knew about? The thought had her fighting back a frown. Why should it bother her to think that her boss might have fathered a baby with this woman? It wasn't as if they were anything more than employee and employer.

Mr. Amatucci stepped up to her desk. "I'll need to go over this with you tomorrow afternoon."

"Tomorrow?"

She knew that he asked for the impossible at times and this happened to be one of those times. He'd caught her totally off guard. It'd take time to think out innovative ideas for the new campaign platform. And she had an important meeting that night, but there was no way she was telling her boss about that.

Mr. Amatucci arched a brow at her. "Is that going to be a problem?"

"Uh…no. No problem." She would not let this opportunity pass her by. "I'll just finish up what I was working on, and I'll get started."

He paused as though considering her answer. "On second thought, it'd be best to go over your ideas first thing in the morning."

"The morning?"

His gaze narrowed in on her, and she wished that her thoughts would quit slipping across her tongue and out her mouth. It certainly wasn't helping this situation. She was here to impress him with her capabilities, not to annoy him when he was obviously already in a bad mood.

"Ms. Hill, you seem to be repeating what I say. Is there some sort of problem I should be aware of?"

She hated that he always called her Ms. Hill. Couldn't he be like everyone else in the office and call her Kayla? But then again, she was talking about Angelo Amatucci— he was unlike anyone she'd ever known.

He was the first man to set her stomach aquiver without so much as touching her. She'd been so aware of his mouth being just a breath away from her neck as he'd sniffed her perfume. The memory was still fresh in her mind. Was it so wrong that she hadn't wanted that moment to end?

Of course it was. She swallowed hard. He was her boss, not just some guy she'd met at a friend's place. There could never be anything serious between them—not that he'd ever even noticed her as a desirable woman.

"Ms. Hill?"

"No, there won't be a…uh…problem." Who was she kidding? This was going to be a big problem, but she'd work it out—somehow—some way.

Her gaze moved to the windows and the darkening sky. With it only nearing the lunch hour, it shouldn't be so dark, which could only mean that they were going to get pounded with more snow. The thought of getting stuck at the office turned her nervous stomach nauseous.

Snow. Snow. Go away.

He gazed at her. "I didn't mean to snap at you—"

"I understand. You've got a lot on your mind."

"Thank you."

His gaze continued to hold hers. The dark depths of his eyes held a mystery—the story of the real man behind the designer suits and the Rolex watches. She had to admit that she was quite curious about him—more than any employee had a right to about her very handsome, very single boss. And that odd phone call only made her all the more curious. Maybe he wasn't as single as she'd presumed. The jagged thought lodged in her throat.

Mr. Amatucci's steady gaze met hers. "You're sure you're up for this project?"

She pressed her lips together, no longer trusting her mouth, and nodded. She'd have to reschedule tonight's meeting for the fund-raiser.

"Good. If you need help, feel free to ask one of the other PAs to take over some of your other work. The Van Holsen account is now your priority."

He gathered his tablet computer and headed for the door. "I've got a meeting. I'll be back later."

"Don't worry. I've got this."

Without a backward glance, he strode out of the room, looking like the calm, cool, collected Angelo Amatucci that everyone respected and admired for his creative foresight. But how he was able to shut down his emotions so quickly was totally beyond her.

What was she going to do about her meeting tonight? It didn't help that she'd been the one to set it up. Somehow she'd been put in charge of the Inner City League after-school program fund-raiser. The program was in a serious financial bind. ICL was a great organization that kept at-risk kids off the streets after school while their parents were still at work.

Kayla had been volunteering for the past year. Helping others was how her parents had raised her. They had always been generous with their spare time and money—not that they had much of either. Kayla may have hightailed it out of Paradise, Pennsylvania, as soon as she could, but there was still a lot of Paradise in her. And she'd swear that she got more back from the kids and the other volunteers than she ever gave to any of them. For a girl who was used to living in a small town of friends, it was a comfort to have such a friendly group to keep her from feeling isolated in such a large city of strangers.

There was no way she could reschedule tonight's meeting. They were running out of time until the charity concert and there was still so much to plan. Somehow she had to make this all work out. She couldn't let down the kids nor could she let down her boss. The thought of Angelo Amatucci counting on her felt good.

Not only was he easy on the eyes, but she really enjoyed working with him, even if he was a bit stiff and withdrawn most of the time. But now that she'd witnessed him emotionally charged, she couldn't help but wonder what it'd be like to get up close and personal with him.

Angelo shook his head.

Marianna pregnant! Impossible.

Okay, so it wasn't impossible, but why had she been acting so irresponsible? It wasn't as if she was married or even considering it. She changed romantic interests faster than he changed ties—never getting too serious—until now. Nico didn't even know the father's name. What was up with that?

"What do you think, Mr. Amatucci?"

He glanced up at his youngest and most promising account executive. This was a meeting to discuss the campaign for a new sports car that was going to be revealed later that year. The car was quite nice and was sure to create a buzz of attention.

But for the life of him, Angelo couldn't keep his mind wrapped around business—no matter how important the account. His head was in Italy at the village of Monte Calanetti—where he should be dealing with his sister's life-changing event.

Angelo glanced down at the presentation on his digital tablet and then back at the account executive. "I think you still have work to do. This presentation is flat. It isn't innovative enough. There's nothing here to sway a twentysomething consumer to take out a sizable loan on top of their college debt in order to have this car. I want the 'must have' factor. The part that says if I have this car all of my friends will be envious. This isn't just a car—this is a status symbol. Do you understand?"

Mike glanced down and then back at Angelo. "But this is what the client asked for."

"And it's your job to push the envelope and give the client something more to consider—to want." Maybe he'd been too quick in his determination that Mike was going to be an asset to Amatucci & Associates—unlike Kayla, who was constantly proving she was an independent thinker. "Try again."

Mike's mouth started to open but out of the corner of Angelo's eye he could see the copywriter give a quick shake of his head. Mike glanced back at Angelo. He nodded his agreement.

"Good. I expect to see something new in forty-eight hours."

Again the man's mouth opened but nothing came out. His lips pressed together, and he nodded. Now if only Angelo could handle his little sister in the same no-nonsense manner. He liked when things were easy and uncomplicated.

But now, with time to cool down, he realized that his only course of action was to return home—to return to Italy. His gut knotted as he thought of the expectations that he'd failed to fulfill. Back in Monte Calanetti he wasn't viewed as someone successful—someone influential. Back home he was Giovanni's son—the son who'd fled his family and their way of life, unlike his younger brother who took great pride in their heritage.

With the meeting concluded, Angelo made his way back to his office. With the decision made to leave first thing in the morning, he had to figure out how to handle his current workload. His clients would never accept having their accounts turned over to anyone else. They paid top dollar for one-on-one attention, and they would accept nothing less.

In order for him to stay on top of everything while traveling abroad, he needed someone who was good in a crisis, levelheaded and an independent worker. Kayla's beautiful face immediately sprang to mind. Could she be the answer?

He hesitated. She did have a habit of being a bit too chatty at times. But this was an emergency. Allowances would have to be made.

More importantly, he was impressed with her work ethic and her attention to details. She was hungry and eager—two elements that would serve her well. And best of all, she had an easy way with people—something that might come in handy on this trip.

He stopped next to her desk. "Ms. Hill." She glanced up. Her green eyes widened. How had he missed their striking shade of jade until now? He cleared his throat, focusing back on the business at hand. "How's the Van Holsen account coming?"

Color pinked her cheeks. "Mr. Amatucci, I... I haven't gotten to it yet. The phone has been ringing and I've been sending out information for some other accounts."

She looked worried as though she'd done something wrong. For the first time, Angelo wondered if everyone who worked for him was intimidated by him. He didn't like the thought of Ms. Hill being uncomfortable around him. He knew he wasn't an easy man to get to know, but he didn't like the thought of striking fear in the hearts of his employees.

"Relax. That's fine. Besides you'll have plenty of time to brainstorm on the flight."

"Excuse me. The flight?"

Since when did he speak without thinking it through first? It had to be this mess with Marianna. It had him off-kilter. "Something urgent has come up. I need to travel to Italy. And I need a competent person to accompany me."

"Me?" Excitement lit up her whole face. Before today, he'd never noticed that behind those black-rimmed reading glasses were not only mesmerizing green eyes but also a beautiful face—not that he was interested in her, or anyone. Ms. Hill clasped her hands together. "I've never been to Italy. I'd love it."

"Good. That's what I was hoping you'd say." But suddenly he wasn't sure spending so much time alone with her was such a good idea, especially now that he'd noticed the unique color of her mesmerizing eyes and her intoxicating scent. He swallowed hard. But it was too late to back out now. "You need to understand this trip will be business only, not a holiday."

"Understood."

"If you go, you'll need to be committed to your work 24/7. We can't afford to miss any deadlines. Is that acceptable?"

She hesitated and, for a moment, he worried that she would back out.

But then Ms. Hill's head bobbed. "I can do it."

"Make sure you are ready to go first thing in the morning."

"As in tomorrow morning?"

He nodded. "And expect to be gone for at least a week—

maybe two." Her mouth gaped and her eyes widened. It was obvious that he'd caught her off guard. But she wasn't the only one to be surprised today—by so many things.

When he'd approved her transfer to be his temporary PA, he'd made it perfectly clear that he demanded 100 percent focus and commitment from his employees. It was that extra push and attention to detail that put Amatucci & Associates head and shoulders above the competition.

If you wanted to be the best, you had to give it your all. And that is what he expected from all of his employees, even if it meant dropping family, hobbies and extracurricular activities in order to focus on the job. What he was asking of Kayla was no different than he'd ask of anyone.

When she didn't jump to accept his offer, he had no patience to wait for an answer. "That won't be a problem, will it?"

From the little he knew about his assistant, she didn't have a family. At least not in the city. And he hadn't seen or heard any hints of a man in her life. Maybe she was more like him than he'd originally thought.

Or was there something else bothering her? Was it the incident with the perfume? Perhaps that hadn't been one of his better moves. He was used to following his instincts when it came to his creative process, but there was something about his assistant that had him leaning a little closer to her slender neck and, for the briefest second, he'd forgotten the reason. His mind had spiraled in a totally inappropriate direction. That wouldn't happen again. He'd see to it.

After all, she wasn't his type. Her nondescript business suits, the way she pulled back her hair and the way she hid her luminous green eyes behind a pair of black-rimmed glasses gave off a very prim, old-fashioned persona. So why was he letting one unexplainable moment bother him?

"I could make arrangements to go, but I have so much work to do on the Van Holsen account—"

"If that's your only objection, then don't worry. The account can wait one day. In fact, take the rest of the day off. I expect to see you at the airport at 6:00 a.m.. Unless you'd like me to pick you up on the way."

"Uh, no." She shook her head vehemently. "I'll find my own way there."

He felt a bit obligated. He was, after all, asking her to drop everything on a moment's notice to help him out. He needed to make a concerted effort to be a little friendlier. "Are you sure? It's really no problem to swing by your place."

"You don't even know where I live."

"True. But since you're going out of your way to help me, I wouldn't mind going out of my way for you."

"Thank you. I appreciate it." She smiled, easing the stress lines from around her mouth.

Angelo found his attention straying to her kissable lips coated with a shimmery light pink gloss. Okay, so not every aspect of her was prim and proper. A fantasy of her pulling off her glasses and letting down her hair played in his mind. Realizing the direction of his wayward thoughts, he halted them.

With effort, his gaze rose over the light splattering of freckles on her pert nose to her intense green eyes. How had he failed to notice her beauty up until today? Had he been that absorbed in his work that he'd failed to see what was standing right in front of him?

He cleared his throat. "I'll pick you up at say five-thirty?"

"Mr. Amatucci—"

"If we're going to travel together, we should at least be on a first name basis. Please, call me Angelo." Now where in the world had that come from? He made a point of keeping his distance from his employees. But then again, he was taking her home with him, where she would meet his family, and that broke all of his professional rules. He reconciled himself with the fact that Kayla's time working for him was limited—soon his regular PA would be back. So maybe he could afford to bend the rules a bit.

"And please call me Kayla." She smiled again, and this time it reached her eyes, making them sparkle like fine jewels.

"We're going to my home in Italy. It's a small village in the Tuscany countryside—Monte Calanetti."

"I'm afraid I've never heard of it, but then again, I've never had the opportunity to travel abroad. Is it big? The village that is?"

He shook his head. "The last time I saw it— granted it has been quite a while—but it was as if time had passed it by. It is rather small and quaint. It is entirely a different world from New York City. Now, are you still interested in going?"

She hesitated and he worried that he'd have to come up with an alternate plan. As of right now, he didn't have one. He needed someone who was familiar with his accounts and wouldn't need a bunch of hand-holding. Kayla was his only viable option. He wasn't one to beg, but at this particular moment he was giving it serious consideration.

Her dimpled chin tilted up. "Yes, I am. It sounds like it'll be a great adventure."

"I don't know about that. The reason I'm going there isn't exactly pleasant, but then again, that isn't for you to worry about. You need to go home and pack."

"Okay. But what should I plan on wearing for the trip? Business attire?"

"Definitely something more casual. There won't be any business meetings, so use your best judgment." He had no doubt her casual attire was as dull and drab as her suits. Not that it mattered to him what she wore so long as she was ready to work.

Kayla gathered her things, and then paused. "Before I leave, should I make plane reservations?"

He shook his head. "No need. We'll take my private jet."

Her pink lips formed an O but nothing came out. And for a moment, he let himself wonder what it'd be like to kiss those full, tempting lips. Not that he would, but he could imagine that one kiss just wouldn't be enough. Something told him that lurking beneath that proper and congenial surface was a passionate woman—

Again, he drew his thoughts up short. The last thing he needed was to notice her feminine qualities. He wasn't about to mix business with pleasure. No way.

CHAPTER THREE

FLUFFY CLOUDS FLOATED past the jet's windows.

They'd soon be touching down in Italy.

A giddy excitement bubbled up in Kayla's chest as she glanced across the aisle at Mr. Amatucci—er—Angelo. She still had a problem remembering to call him by his given name after referring to him as Mr. Amatucci for so long. Being on a first-name basis left her feeling unsettled—not exactly sure how to act around him. If anything, Angelo was even more quiet and reserved than before. Had he sensed her attraction to him?

Impossible. She hadn't said or done anything to betray herself. She smoothed a hand over her gray skirt. She was worrying for nothing.

Just act normal.

She glanced at her boss. "Do you know how long until we arrive?"

Angelo turned in his leather seat to look at her. "What did you say?"

"I was wondering how long we have until we land in Italy."

"Not much longer." His dark gaze dipped to the pen and paper in her lap. "Are you working?"

"I am." Her body tensed as she read over her scribbled notes for the Van Holsen account. She didn't have anything innovative enough to measure up to the Amatucci standard. "I thought this would be a good time to flesh out some ideas."

"And you like doing it longhand?"

"I think better that way." She'd never really taken the time to consider her creative process, but yes, now that she thought about it, she did always start with pen and paper. She didn't move to the computer until she had a fully functioning idea.

"Is that for the Van Holsen account?"

"Yes, I've been doing what you suggested and going with a nostalgic appeal."

"Good. Can I see what you've come up with so far?"

She glanced down at all of her scribbles and half thoughts. And then her eyes caught sight of his name scrolled out in cursive. Her heart clenched. *What in the world?*

She must have done it while she'd been deep in thought. Immediately, her pen started crossing it out. The last thing she needed was for her boss to think she had a crush on him. That would be the end of her career.

"I... I don't exactly have anything solid yet." She was going to have to be careful in the future of what she wrote down just in case Mr. Curious decided to peer over her shoulder.

"I could help you. Let me see what you have." He held out his hand.

She really didn't want to hand over her notepad, but what choice did she have if she wanted to stay in his good graces? She glanced down at the scratched-out spot and squinted. She could still see his name—all fourteen letters. But that was because she knew it was there. She ran the pen over it a few more times.

With great hesitation, she handed over the legal pad. Angelo's acute gaze skimmed over the page. Her palms grew moist. He took his time reading, but he paused as he reached the bottom. That was where she'd vigorously scratched out his name, almost wearing a hole in the page.

"I'm guessing that you've ruled out this idea?" He gestured to the blob of ink.

"Most definitely. It wouldn't have worked."

"Are you sure? Maybe you should tell me what it was,

and then we can see if there's any value in pursuing it?"
He sent her an expectant look.

"Honestly, it's not worth the effort. I was totally off the
mark with it." A man like Angelo, who could have a gorgeous model or movie star on each arm, would never be
interested in someone as plain and boring as herself.

He let the subject go and turned back to her notes while
she sat there realizing just how "off the mark" her imagination had wandered. No way was she going down that
romantic path again, even if it was paved with rose pet-
als. All it'd do was lead her into making a commitment—
having a family—everything she'd left behind in Paradise.
She wanted to be different—she wanted to be professionally successful. She needed to show everyone back in her
hometown that she'd made her dreams come true.

And then Angelo's gaze lifted to meet hers. She should
glance away but the intensity of his gaze held her captive.
Her heart raced. He didn't say anything, which was just as
well, because she doubted she could have strung two words
together. Had he figured out what she'd scribbled on the
page? *Please, not that.* But then again, he didn't look upset.
Instead, he looked like—like what? The breath hitched in
her throat. Was he interested in her?

He glanced away and shook his head. "Sorry about that.
Something you wrote down gave me an idea for the campaign, but then it slipped away."

Silly girl. What made her think he'd ever look at her that
way? And why would she want him to? It'd be the beginning of the end of her rising career—her dream.

Get a grip, Kayla.

"No problem." She held out her hand, willing it not to
shake. "If you let me have the pad back, I'll work on getting my thoughts more organized. Maybe we can discuss
them as soon as we get situated in Italy." She wasn't quite
sure where their accommodations would be since Angelo

had personally handled the travel arrangements, but she was certain they would be nice.

"Sounds good. Just because we're out of town doesn't mean we should fall behind on our work. I don't plan to be here long—just long enough to take care of some personal business. If we're lucky, perhaps I can wrap it up in a day or two."

What had happened to a week—maybe two? Disappointment assailed her. But it would be for the best. After all, it'd get her home sooner to make sure the ICL fund-raiser was moving along without too many snags. But she still couldn't shake the disappointment.

He'd missed this.

Angelo maneuvered the low-slung sports car over the windy roads of the Tuscany hillside toward his home in Monte Calanetti. He was grateful to be behind the wheel. It helped to center his thoughts. On the plane, he'd noticed his assistant in the most unexpected way. With her peaches-and-cream complexion, he'd been tempted to reach out and caress her smooth skin. But it was her green, almost-jade eyes that sparkled and hinted at so much more depth to the woman than he already knew—or would expect to know. The last thing he needed to do was get distracted by his assistant.

Actually, now that he'd noticed her—really noticed her—it was getting harder and harder to keep his mind on business around her. Perhaps bringing her on this trip wasn't his best decision, after all, but it was a necessity. He needed her help. He assured himself that, in the end, it would all work out as long as he stayed focused on the business at hand.

Thankfully, Kayla was just temporary help until his assistant returned from maternity leave. Then life would get back to normal. As far as he was concerned, that wouldn't be soon enough.

"This is wonderful."

The sound of Kayla's excited voice drew him out of his thoughts. He took his eyes off the roadway for just a moment to investigate what she found so fascinating, but he only saw vegetation. "Sorry. I missed it."

"No, you didn't. It's this. The long grass and the trees lining the roadway. It's beautiful."

What? The woman had never been outside of the city? He supposed that was possible. He honestly didn't know much about her other than her excellent work ethic. That, in and of itself, would normally be enough for him, but since they were traveling together, what would it hurt to know a little more?

"Is this your first time outside New York City?"

"I'm not a native New Yorker."

They had something else in common. Still, after all of those years living in New York, it was home to him now. He thrived on the constant energy that flowed through the city. He couldn't imagine living anywhere else. "Where does your family live?"

He could feel her curious gaze on him, but he didn't turn to her. "They live in a small town in Pennsylvania."

"So you really didn't move all that far from home."

"That's not what my parents think."

He glanced at her and saw she'd pressed her lips together in a firm line. Something told him that she hadn't meant to share that bit of information. But why? What else was she holding back?

"Your parents aren't crazy about the big-city life?"

There was a moment of hesitation as though she were trying to figure out how to answer him. "It's not New York so much as the fact that I'm not in Paradise anymore. They had my whole life planned out for me, but I rejected it."

"You must have had one of those chopper mothers I've heard about."

Kayla laughed. The sound was melodious and endearing. In that moment, he realized that he'd never heard her laugh before. He really liked it and hoped she'd do it more often, but for the life of him, he had no idea what he'd said to cause such a reaction.

"Do you mean a helicopter mom?"

He shrugged. "I guess. I knew it was something like that."

"My mom wasn't too bad. I know friends that had mothers who were much more controlling. But my mom is pretty good."

Wait. Something wasn't adding up. He pulled to a stop at an intersection. If he went straight ahead, it'd lead them up the hill to the village. But if he veered to the right, it'd take them to Nico's boutique vineyard—their childhood home.

Checking the rearview mirror and finding no traffic behind them, he paused and turned to her. "So if your mother is so great, why did you flee to the big city?"

Kayla shifted in her seat as though she were uncomfortable—or was it that he was digging too deep into personal territory? He knew what that was like—wanting to keep a firm lid on the past. But he couldn't help himself. There was just something about Kayla that intrigued him—and it went much deeper than her beauty. He was genuinely interested in her as a person.

Her voice was soft when she spoke, and he strained to hear. "I didn't live up to my parents' expectations."

That was so hard to believe. He was a very particular employer, and Kayla lived up to and in some areas exceeded his expectations. "Do they know what a wonderful job you've done at Amatucci & Associates?"

Her gaze widened. "You really think so?"

Angelo didn't realize he'd kept his approval of her work under wraps. Then again, he wasn't the sort of man to go on about someone's performance. Yet, in this moment, something told him that Kayla really needed to hear his evaluation of her performance.

"I think you've done an excellent job—"

"You do?" She smiled brightly and practically bounced in her seat before clasping her hands together.

"I do—"

A horn beeped behind them.

The interruption was a welcome one. This conversation was getting a little too emotional for his comfort. He thought for a moment that in her glee she might throw her arms around him. He didn't do hugs—no way—and certainly not with an employee. He couldn't—wouldn't—let the lines between them blur.

Angelo eased the car forward, focusing once again on the road and his destination. He urged himself to ignore the funny feeling Kayla's obvious excitement had given him. He trained his thoughts on the scene he'd be walking into at the vineyard. His fingers tightened on the black leather steering wheel.

On second thought, maybe he should have dropped Kayla off at the hotel before venturing out here. But he hadn't exactly been thinking straight—not since Nico had dropped the bombshell that their little sister was about to have a baby. Angelo was about to become an uncle. He wasn't sure how he felt about that. He'd worked so hard to distance himself from his family—from his emotionally charged parents and their chaotic marriage. But now that they'd moved, what excuse did he have to stay away from his birthplace—the home of his brother and sister?

"Is this the way to the village?" Kayla sat up a little straighter.

"No, this is the way to my brother's vineyard."

"Oh, how exciting. I've never visited a vineyard. I can't wait to see it. I bet it's beautiful like those magazine photos. Will we be staying there?"

"No." Angelo's tone was brusquer than he'd intended, but her endless chatter combined with his pending reunion had him on edge.

He chanced a glance her way and found her eyes had widened in surprise. He couldn't blame her, but how did he explain his family dynamics to her? Then again, why did he feel a need to explain his family at all?

"It'll be best if we stay at a hotel in the village. I'm not sure if the internet at the vineyard has been updated." There, that sounded like a valid reason for them to have some space between him and his siblings.

"Oh, I hadn't thought about that. I know the Van Holsen account needs to be updated as soon as possible. I already contacted the art department and let them know that a whole new strategy will be coming their way."

"Good. I want everything to move ahead without delay."

Whether he liked it or not, he'd been right to bring Kayla along on this trip. She was efficient and quite good at her job. Now, if only he could be just as professional and keep his mind from meandering into dangerous territory. However, the more time he spent around her, the more he found himself being anything but professional.

CHAPTER FOUR

THE CAR TURNED to the right and lurched forward. Kayla grabbed for the door handle. She had no idea that the vineyard would be so far out in the country, but then again, this was her first trip to Italy. In fact, other than one business trip to Canada, this was her first expedition out of the country.

"Welcome to Calanetti Vineyard."

Kayla glanced around, taking in the neat lines of grapevines. "Does all of this belong to your brother?"

"No. His vineyard is just a small portion of this land, but he produces some of the highest quality wine in the country."

"And you grew up here?"

"I did." Angelo pulled the car to a stop in front of a two-story villa. The home featured earth tones that blended in well with the land. "My brother will be expecting us. I phoned him from the airport."

As if on cue, the front door of the villa swung open and a man stepped out. Kayla did a double take—it was like looking at a slightly younger version of Angelo. The man approached the car wearing an easy smile. His eyes were dark brown like his brother's, but there was an easiness in them. They were quite unlike Angelo's dark and mysterious eyes.

When Nico opened the car door for her and held out his hand, she accepted his offer. Then she noticed the biggest difference of all. Instead of her stomach quivering with nervous energy in response to Nico's touch, she had no reaction at all. What did that mean? How could two men who looked so much alike have her reacting in such opposite ways?

It had to be that Angelo was her boss. That must be it. There was simply no other reasonable explanation for the electric charge that Angelo gave her every time she felt his gaze on her or when their fingers brushed as they passed papers back and forth.

"Benvenuta." Nico's voice carried a thick, warm Italian accent. When she sent him a puzzled look, he smiled. *"Scusi.* Welcome."

She smiled back, immediately liking Angelo's brother. "I'm so glad to be here."

"My brother doesn't bring many visitors home. In fact, you are the first. You must be special—"

"Nico, this is my assistant." Angelo frowned at his sibling.

Nico's dark brows rose and then a knowing smile pulled at his lips. "I hope my brother doesn't work you too hard while you're in Italy. There's so much to see. I'd love to give you a tour of the vineyard—"

"She doesn't have time for that stuff. She's here to work." Any hint of the easiness Angelo had displayed in the car was gone—hidden behind an impenetrable wall. "Now where is Marianna?"

"I don't know."

"What? Didn't you tell her that I was on my way?"

"I did." Nico folded his arms over his broad chest and lifted his chin. "I think that's the reason she left so early this morning without even bothering to grab a bite to eat. I haven't seen her since, but then again, I haven't looked for her, either."

"You let her walk away—?"

"What did you want me to do? Lock her in her room?"

"Maybe if you'd have done that a while ago, we wouldn't be in this mess."

Nico's arms lowered and his shoulders straightened. "You're blaming me for this?"

Angelo's body visibly tensed. "Yes...no. If only I'd have known something was wrong, I could have..."

"Could have what?"

Kayla's gaze darted between the two men who glared at each other. It was time to do something and fast. "This certainly is a beautiful place you have here." She acted as though she were totally oblivious to the torrent of under-currents. "Angelo told me you produce some of the finest wine in Italy."

At last, the brothers quit glaring at each other. Nico turned to her. "My brother got that much right. I'd be happy if you'd sample some while you're here."

"I'd be honored."

This palpable tension certainly wasn't what she'd been expecting for a family reunion, but then again, after over-hearing the heated conversation when Nico had phoned the office, she shouldn't be too surprised. She turned her atten-tion to her always-in-control boss, who looked as though he was about to lose his cool edge and have a meltdown. *Intriguing.* There was definitely a lot more to him than what she'd witnessed so far.

"I should have come back before now." There was a weary, pained toned to Angelo's voice. "I let the past keep me away."

Nico turned back to his sibling. "What happened to you was a long time ago. It wasn't right, but a lot has changed since then. You no longer have an excuse to stay away."

"But I still have a company to run. I don't have time to drop everything and travel halfway around the globe to check up on things. As far as I knew, everything was all right."

"Maybe if you didn't work all the time and bothered to call occasionally, you'd know how things were going around here."

Questions crowded into Kayla's mind—questions that were absolutely none of her business. But that didn't stop her from wondering what had happened to drive Angelo away from his family. He obviously loved them or he wouldn't have let his cool composure slide. And what caused him to keep his emotions under lock and key in the first place?

Angelo raked his fingers through his hair. "Maybe I should have called more."

"Yes, you should have."

The thud of a door slamming shut punctuated Nico's words. Kayla hesitantly glanced off in the distance as a young woman marched toward them. Her brown hair was wild and curly as it fluttered in the breeze. Her lips pressed into a firm line and her eyes narrowed in on the two men. This must be Marianna.

"Enough!" The woman came to a stop between Angelo and Nico. "You two are being ridiculous. Anytime you both want to quit with the overprotective-brother routine, we can talk."

Though she was at least a foot shorter than her brothers, Marianna certainly didn't hesitate to step between them. Something told Kayla that little sister wasn't a shrinking violet with these two as her brothers. She'd definitely have to be strong-willed. Silently Kayla cheered her on.

Angelo's broad chest puffed up before he sighed. When he spoke, his voice was much gentler. "Marianna, if only I'd known—"

"Stop." The young woman pressed her hands to her hips and pulled back her slender shoulders. "Neither of you are to blame for my choices."

Angelo's brows drew together in a formidable line. "But—"

"I'm not done." Her shoulders remained ramrod straight. "I'm a grown woman, if you hadn't noticed. But then again, you've been off in the States and missed the fact that I've grown up. Maybe if you'd spent more time here, you'd have realized this."

Kayla's heart went out to Angelo. He'd obviously made mistakes where his family was concerned, and they weren't shy about calling him out on it. In his eyes, she could see pain and regret. Beneath his hard, protective shell lurked a vulnerable man.

Angelo's stance eased and his head lowered. "I know I should have been here for you—"

"No. This isn't what I want." Marianna shook her head, sending her hair flying. "I don't need you feeling guilty. I need you to understand that I can make my own decisions."

"See, I told you," Nico piped in. "Trying to deal with her isn't as easy as it sounds."

Angelo turned to his brother. "Maybe if you'd have told me sooner—"

Nico's dark brows drew together in a formidable line. "Told you—I tried calling you but I always got your voice mail. And you didn't call back."

"I… I was getting around to it."

Nico shook his head in disbelief. "I'm glad to know where I fit on your list of priorities."

"You don't understand." Angelo rubbed the back of his neck. "You don't know what it's like to have a lot of people relying on you to produce cutting-edge promotions and other people looking to you for a paycheck. It's not as easy as it sounds to run a successful company."

Nico expelled a disgusted sigh. "And you think turning this place into a renowned boutique vineyard has been easy? Yet I still found time to call you."

"Your message never said it was important."

"Stop!" Marianna pushed Angelo back. "You aren't helping anything by coming here and fighting with Nico."

Angelo took a deep breath and blew it out. "I know I wasn't here when you needed me, but I'm here now. Let me help."

Kayla watched all of this in utter amazement. She never would have guessed her boss was capable of such a wide range of emotions. So then why did he strive at the office for such an unflappable persona? What was she missing?

Kayla was about to introduce herself to Marianna, when the young woman stared up at Angelo and said, "And I wish you weren't here now. Not like this. Not with all of the fighting." When Angelo's brows rose and his mouth opened but nothing came out, Marianna added, "I don't want to play referee." Her hand moved protectively to her still-flat stomach. "It isn't good for the baby."

Angelo and Nico looked at each other as though neither had considered how their fighting would stress their sister—their pregnant sister.

Marianna moved to look at both of her brothers. "I'm fully capable of taking care of myself."

Nico rolled his eyes. Angelo crossed his arms but refrained from saying anything.

"I hope you'll both give me some space."

Angelo's brows rose. "But first, we want to know the name of the father."

"That's none of your business."

Nico stepped forward. "It is our business if he thinks he's going to get our sister pregnant and then just walk away."

Marianna's face filled with color.

Angelo pressed his hands to his sides. "We deserve the right to speak to this guy. He needs to know that we expect him to step up and do his part—"

"And I expect you both to mind your own business." Marianna started for the house.

Enough was enough. The time had come to make a hasty exit. It was obvious that Marianna was in over her head and that her brothers were only making the situation worse.

When Angelo turned to follow his sister, Kayla moved swiftly in front of him. "I'm not feeling so good." It wasn't totally a lie—her stomach was in knots watching the Amatucci siblings squabble. "Could you take me to the hotel?"

Angelo's worried gaze moved from her to his sister to her. "Sure." He turned to Nico. "We need to talk more."

"I figured as much."

"I'll be back after we get settled."

Nico shrugged. "I'll be here. I can't speak for Marianna."

"I don't think she needs anyone to speak for her. She certainly does have a mind of her own. Even if it gets her in trouble."

"She always was strong-willed. I think she's a lot like Mama."

"Agreed."

At last the two had something they agreed on—their little sister's character. And now that things were on a good note, it was definitely time to say goodbye.

Kayla cleared her throat, hoping to gain Angelo's attention. When he didn't turn her way, she proceeded to say, "Angelo, are you ready to go?"

She'd have rather had a tour of the vineyard and stretched her legs, but not under these strained circumstances. She couldn't help but wonder if it was the situation with their sister that had them at odds or if they had a history of not getting along.

Angelo glanced her way. "It was a long trip. I suppose you would like to lie down for a bit."

"That would be nice." She turned to Nico, who was still eyeing his brother with obvious agitation. "It was so nice to meet you. I hope that we'll see each other again."

"I suppose that'll depend on my brother and whether he trusts you with me—"

"Nico. Enough." Angelo's voice held an obvious note of warning. "We'll be staying at the Hotel Villa Bellezza. If Marianna cools down, phone me."

Angelo quietly followed her to the car and opened the door for her. "I'm sorry you had to witness that."

"Don't be." She searched for words of comfort. "Families are messy. It's what happens when people love each other. And I saw a lot of love back there."

"You did?"

"Most definitely." She stepped past him and got in the car.

She'd never met anyone who could get under her boss's skin like Nico. The man appeared to have needling his big brother down to a fine art. There was so much more to the polished, successful businessman standing next to her than she'd ever imagined. And she was anxious to know more.

CHAPTER FIVE

KAYLA GRIPPED THE armrest tightly.

The line of cypress trees was no more than a blur as Angelo accelerated away from the vineyard. He didn't say a word as they zigzagged through the valley before starting their ascent up a hillside. The vegetation was so green and lush that she couldn't imagine there was a village, much less a five-star hotel, within miles of here.

"I need to apologize." Angelo's voice broke the awkward silence. "I didn't mean to have you witness our family drama."

"It's okay. I know how families can be." She couldn't help but want to know more about him and his family. "Your parents, do they live around here?"

He shook his head, keeping his eyes on the road. "They left the vineyard to us kids and moved to Milan. It was best for everyone."

Kayla wasn't sure what to say to that. Obviously there wasn't a close relationship between him and his parents. Did she even want to know why? It'd just move them further from boss and employee and into a new relationship—one that she didn't want to examine too closely.

Angelo downshifted for a curve. "I know that you come from a close-knit family, so it'd be hard for you to understand a family that functions better apart than together."

Kayla was surprised that he kept talking about his private life when she hadn't even asked him anything. It was as if these thoughts were pent up inside him, and he needed to get them out if he was to have any peace.

She searched frantically for words of comfort. "Every family is different. Not better. Not worse. Just different."

"But this is my fault." His palm smacked the steering wheel. "I shouldn't have left for New York to go to college. I should have found a way to stay here. Marianna was so young when I left, and my parents—well, they were so consumed with each other that they didn't have time to worry about anyone else."

"I'm sure they did their best."

He shook his head. "You don't know my parents. They are the most passionate people I know. And not in a good way. One minute they love each other and the next they are getting divorced. That's the end. They never want to see each other again. To say our childhoods were unstable is putting it mildly."

Kayla struggled to keep her mouth from gaping open. Her parents were the most mild-mannered couple. Their voices were rarely raised to each other, and they still gazed lovingly at each other like a couple of starstruck teenagers. Kayla knew they wanted her to experience the same sort of love and happiness. That's why she didn't hold it against them for trying to guide her life. It's just that she was different. There was so much more to life than love, marriage and babies. And she wanted to experience all of it.

Angelo cleared his throat, but his voice still rumbled with emotion. "I just couldn't take any more of their fighting and making up. It was so unnerving to never know if my parents were passionately in love or on the verge of calling their divorce attorneys. And there was no way I could take Nico with me—not that he'd have gone. He has this unbreakable tie to the vineyard—to the village. He never would have done what I did. And maybe he's right. Maybe if I'd stayed then Marianna wouldn't be alone and having a baby."

"It's not your fault." Kayla resisted the urge to reach out to him. "Your sister is a grown woman. She has to be allowed to make her own choices. Right or wrong. You couldn't have prevented this."

"But maybe if I'd been here, she'd have felt like she still had a family that loves her. Then she wouldn't have taken off on this trip of hers only to let some smooth-talking guy take advantage of her." Angelo's body noticeably stiffened.

"I'm fairly certain that no one could take advantage of your sister. She seems quite strong, like her brothers. She just needs some time to sort things out."

He sighed. "I'm sure she's plenty confused. And I suppose Nico and I did nothing to help by arguing. It's just that every time my brother and I get together, we disagree. We are very different. That's why I reserved us a suite at the hotel. I knew staying at the vineyard would just lead to more drama, and that's the last thing any of us need."

"But you two didn't argue at the end."

"That's because we both agree that Marianna needs both of us—whether she likes it or not."

"Good. Maybe you can build on that."

"Perhaps."

She decided that enough had been said for now on that subject. Angelo needed time to calm down. "Is the hotel far from here?"

"No. It's just at the rise of the hill." His voice had returned to its normal reserved, unemotional tone.

"Really. I never would have guessed. I can't wait to see the village." But if Angelo was serious about this being a productive trip, she wasn't sure that she'd get to see much of Italy. The thought dampened her mood. "Do you think I'll have some time to look around the village?"

He glanced at her before turning back to the road. "There really isn't much to see."

She'd beg to differ with him. Everything about Italy was special for this American girl. This was the biggest adventure of her life. How could he think this place was anything but special?

"I… I've never been here before. I was just hoping to sneak in some sightseeing."

"As long as you get your work done, I don't care what you do with your free time."

Oh, good!

As the car climbed the hill, Angelo pulled to the side for an older truck that was barreling toward them. Once back on the road, the car's tire dropped into a rut and bounced Kayla. The seat belt restrained her, but her bare thigh brushed against his hand as it gripped the gearshift. Heat raced up her leg, under her skirt and set her whole body tingling.

"Sorry about that." He quickly moved his hand back to the steering wheel.

Had he noticed their touch? Had it affected him, too? Was that why he'd moved his hand? Or was she just being ridiculous? Definitely being ridiculous. She knew when men were interested in her, and Angelo certainly wasn't. A frown pulled at her lips.

So why then did it bother her? Sure, he was the most handsome man she'd ever laid eyes on. But, he was her boss—the key to her career. She wouldn't—she couldn't—let some ridiculous crush get in her way after everything she'd sacrificed to get here.

Time to think about something else.

"I didn't have time to do any research before we left New York. What should I see while I'm here?"

He shrugged. "Honestly, there's nothing special about Monte Calanetti. It's just small and old."

"I'm used to small towns. I grew up in one. And there's always something special about them."

He glanced her way and his dark brow rose. "What was special about your town?"

"A number of things." She wasn't sure that she wanted to delve into this subject with him. She'd finally got past her homesickness. The way she'd done that was by not thinking of her hometown and what made it special.

"Such as?"

She shook her head. "Never mind."

Before he could question her more, she spotted what she thought was the edge of Monte Calanetti. "Are we here?"

"We are."

She stared out the windshield, not exactly sure what to expect. There was a tall wall. As they eased past it she found rustic buildings of earth tones similar in color to Nico's villa. People stopped and glanced their way as though trying to figure out if they should know them.

As more and more people turned to stare, Kayla couldn't hold back her curiosity any longer. "Why are they staring?"

He shrugged. "It must be the car."

"The car?"

"Yeah, you know because it's a sports car. They probably don't see many around here."

"Oh." She glanced over at him. Was he sitting up a little straighter? And was his chin tilted just a little higher? *Interesting.* "The village looks quite intriguing. And small enough to explore on foot."

Angelo didn't say anything. He just kept driving. And sadly he didn't offer her a guided tour. She forced herself not to frown. Then again, why should he bend over backward for her? She was, after all, merely an employee. They weren't even friends. Though little by little, she was getting to know Angelo better and better. In fact, she'd learned more about him in the past forty-eight hours than she had in the past two months while working as his assistant.

The car slowed as they eased through a wrought iron gate and up the short paved drive to a two-story building. The outside was plain but there was an elegance in its simplicity. Beneath a black awning, a bronze plaque off to the side of the front door read: Hotel Villa Bellezza. The place looked old but well kept. It reminded her of maybe a duke's grand house. She couldn't wait to check out the inside.

A young man in a black uniform rushed outside and opened her door for her. He smiled at her before his gaze moved to Angelo. The smile dimmed. She had the feeling that the young man had jumped to the wrong conclusion—that she and Angelo were a couple, here for a romantic tryst. Nothing could be further from the truth. But for the first time, she imagined what it might be like if Angelo were to look at her as a woman—a woman he desired. The thought rolled around in her mind at a dizzying pace.

Angelo moved to her side and spoke softly in her ear. "Are you okay?"

His voice drew her from her thoughts. She swallowed and hoped she succeeded in composing herself. "Yes."

"Are you sure? You're a little pale."

She patted his arm, not a good move as her fingertips tingled where they made contact. "I'm fine. Honest."

Or she would be, once she quit fantasizing about her boss. He obviously wasn't attracted to her. He saw her as nothing more than his temporary assistant, and that's the way it'd have to remain if she hoped to convince him of her talents.

While Angelo took care of registering them, she took in her surroundings. The modest exterior had not prepared her for the beauty of the interior. The floor was gleaming marble while the walls and ceiling were masterpieces of art with ornate parquet. Kayla had to force her mouth to remain closed instead of gaping open. She'd never stayed anywhere so fancy.

She couldn't even imagine how much this visit would cost Angelo. And the fact that he could afford to stay in a place such as this without even batting an eye impressed her. They sure didn't have anything like this back in Paradise. Wait until she told her mother and father about this.

CHAPTER SIX

THERE WAS NO time for fun and games.

Angelo didn't get to the top of his profession by taking time off. Now that they were settled into their suite and Kayla had rested for a bit, they needed to get back to work. As he waited for her to join him, he couldn't help but wonder what she made of his clash with his brother. He shouldn't have taken her to the vineyard. What had he been thinking?

Yet on the car ride here, she hadn't seemed to judge him. Instead, she'd acted as though she cared. It was as if she understood him. Her reaction surprised him. He wasn't used to letting people into his personal life. But from the moment he'd asked her to join him on this trip, the lines between personal and professional had become irrevocably blurred.

Kayla entered the common room between their bedrooms. Her auburn hair was loose and cascaded down past her shoulders. Her glasses were off and she was no longer wearing the drab gray business suit. Instead, she was wearing pink capris and a white cotton sleeveless top, which showed off her creamy shoulders and slender arms.

The breath hitched in his throat. Who was this gorgeous woman? And what had happened to his nondescript assistant?

"I hope you don't mind that I changed?"

Wow! All he could do was stare. It was as if she were some sort of butterfly who'd just emerged from a cocoon.

Kayla settled on the couch with her laptop. She gave him a strange look as though wondering why he had yet to say a word. The problem was he didn't know what to say. Ever since they'd left New York, the ground had been shifting under his feet. Now it was as though a fissure had opened up and he was teetering on the edge, scrambling not to get swallowed up.

She didn't appear to be too disturbed by his standoffishness, which was good. Before he took a seat anywhere near her, he had to get a hold on his rambling thoughts. Kayla wasn't just any woman. He couldn't indulge in a romantic romp with her, and then go about his life.

He was her boss and, more important, he couldn't afford to lose her because she was good—really good at her job. He'd already had ideas of promoting her, but he wasn't sure that she was ready to be advanced quite yet. He wanted to see how she handled the Van Holsen account, since he'd given her a lot of room to show him her stuff.

The tight muscles in his chest eased and he was able to breathe easier. Concentrating on work always relaxed him and put him back in his groove. Work was logical for the most part and it lacked emotions, again for the most part, depending on the client. But since he was the boss, he was able to hand off the more excitable clients to other account executives.

That was it. Focus on business and not on how appealing he found her. "How's the Van Holsen account coming?"

She glanced over the top of her laptop. "Thanks to your help, I think I've come up with some innovative ideas. Would you care to take a look?"

His gaze moved to the cushion next to her on the couch and his body tensed. He was being ridiculous. She wasn't the first beautiful woman that he'd been around. What in the world had got into him today? It had to be his return home. It had him feeling out of sorts.

Time to start acting like Angelo Amatucci, the man in charge. "Sure. I'll have a look."

He strode over to the couch and took a seat. Kayla handed over the laptop and their fingers brushed. Hers were soft, smooth and warm. A jolt of awareness zinged up his arm and the air hitched in his lungs. *Stay focused.* He didn't dare turn to look at her. Instead, he focused his gaze on the computer monitor.

He read over her ideas for the new fragrance campaign and was truly impressed. Not only had she taken his ideas and expanded upon them, but she'd also inserted some of her own. He loved her initiative. Kayla was exactly the kind of innovative person that he wanted at Amatucci & Associates. Talented people like Kayla were the assets that would keep his company one of the most sought-after advertising agencies in the world.

"This is really good." He turned to her. When her green gaze met his, the rest of his thoughts scattered.

"You really like it?"

He nodded. His line of vision momentarily dipped to her pink frosted lips before meeting her gaze again. He struggled for a nonchalant expression. "I think you've captured a touching nostalgic note with a forward-thinking view. This should capture both the new and old consumer."

Her tempting lips lifted into a broad smile that lit up her eyes. "Now we just have to hope the client will approve."

"I wouldn't worry about that. Send this along to the art department and have them start working on some mockups."

Her smile dimmed a bit. "You're sure about this?"

"Of course I am. Don't look so surprised. You don't think you got the position as my assistant just because you're beautiful, do you?"

Now why in the world had he gone and said that? But it was the truth. She was stunning. In fact, he was considering changing the dress code at the office. He really enjoyed this different look on her. Then again, if she looked this way in the office, he'd never get any work done.

Color bloomed on her creamy cheeks. "You think I'm beautiful?"

He stared back into her eyes longer than was necessary.

In that moment, his ability to speak intelligently was debatable. He merely nodded.

"No man has ever called me that."

At last finding his voice, Angelo said, "I'm having a hard time believing that."

"Steven was more matter-of-fact and sparing on compliments. It wasn't that he was a bad man. In fact, it's quite the opposite. He was really good to me. He just wasn't good with flowery words."

"This Steven, he's from Paradise, too?"

She nodded. "High-school sweethearts."

"The man must need glasses badly to have missed your beauty. Both inside and out. Is he still your boyfriend?" Part of Angelo wanted her to say yes to put a swift end to this surreal moment, but a much stronger part wanted her to be free.

"We…we broke up before I moved to New York."

The field was wide-open. Exhilaration flooded through Angelo. His hand reached out, stroking the smooth, silky skin of her cheek. The backs of his fingers skimmed down over her jaw, and then his thumb ran over the plumpness of her bottom lip. Her sudden inhale drew air over his fingers.

In her eyes, he noted the flames of desire had been ignited. She wanted him as much as he wanted her. And in that moment, he didn't want to think—he just wanted to act. He wanted to forget everything and enjoy this moment with the girl with wavy red hair.

His heart pounded as he leaned forward. He needed her and her understanding ways more than he imagined possible. Their lips met. He was a man who knew what he wanted and he wanted Kayla. Yet he fought back the urge to let loose with his mounting need. Instead, his touch was tentative and gentle. He didn't want to do anything to scare her away—not now that he had her exactly where he wanted her.

Kayla's lips were rose-petal soft. And when she opened them up to him, a moan grew deep in his throat. She tasted sweet like chocolate. He'd never been a fan of candy until this moment. Now he couldn't get enough of her sugary sweetness.

His arms wrapped round her curvy form, pulling her close. The gentle scent of perfume wrapped around them—the teasing scent that he hadn't been able to forget since that day in the office. It was as though she'd cast some sort of magical spell over him.

In the next instant, his phone vibrated in his pocket, zapping him back to his senses. He pulled back and Kayla's confused gaze met his. He couldn't blame her. He was just as confused by what had happened.

He held up a finger to silence her inevitable questions—questions for which he had no answers. Because there was no way he was falling for her. Getting involved with her—with anyone—meant dealing with a bunch of messy emotions. The last thing in the world he wanted to do was end up like his parents. Just the memory of their turbulent life had Angelo immediately working to rebuild the wall between him and Kayla. He just couldn't—wouldn't—subject anyone to such miserable instability.

Angelo glanced down at the screen to see his brother's name pop up. Hopefully his sister had confessed all. Angelo couldn't wait to confront the man who'd walked away from his responsibilities.

Angelo lifted the phone to his ear. "Nico, do you have a name yet?"

There was a distinct sigh. "Is this how you answer your phone these days? Too important for a friendly greeting before diving into the heart of the matter?"

Angelo's back teeth ground together. He quickly counted to ten, okay maybe only to five, before addressing his sibling. "Hello, Nico. What did Marianna say?"

"Nothing."

He was losing his patience. "But why did you call?"

"You and Kayla need to return to the villa. Now. I'll explain everything when you both get here." The line went dead.

Angelo slipped the phone back into his pocket. He turned to Kayla, whose face was still filled with color. "We have to go."

"What happened?"

"I don't know. That was Nico and he summoned us back to the villa. It must be Marianna. I just pray there aren't complications with the baby." Before they left he needed to clear the air about their kiss that never should have happened. "Listen, about the kiss, I crossed a line. I... I don't know what I was thinking."

A myriad of expressions crossed over her face. "It's forgotten."

He didn't believe her. "Can we talk about it later?"

"I'd rather not. There's nothing to say. Besides, you have more important things to deal with." She jumped to her feet and moved away from him. "You should get going. I'll be fine here."

"Nico requested you, too." Angelo held back the startling fact that he'd feel better facing this crisis with her next to him.

Kayla pressed a hand to her chest. "But why me?"

"I don't know. But we have to go."

"Okay. Just let me grab my shoes and purse." She rushed back to her room.

Angelo got to his feet and paced back and forth. Of course he was worried about his sister, but there was something else fueling his inability to sit still—Kayla's off-the-cuff dismissal of his kiss.

The women he was used to spending time with never brushed off his advances, though each of them knew his rules in advance—nothing serious. So why did that rule not apply here? Probably because Kayla was off-limits. She was his assistant. He couldn't forget that going forward—no matter how much his personal life spun out of control while in Italy.

From this point forward, Kayla was off-limits.

CHAPTER SEVEN

HER THOUGHTS RACED so fast that it unsettled her stomach.

Kayla stared out of the passenger window as she clasped her hands tightly together. Angelo expertly guided the rented sports car along the narrow, tree-lined road. How in the world had she lost control of the situation?

She inwardly groaned. As fantastic as that kiss had been, it couldn't have come at a worse time. Angelo at last had noticed her work and complimented her professionally. And what did she turn around and do, stare at him like some lovesick teenager—encouraging him to kiss her.

Sure, she was wildly attracted to him. What woman with a pulse wasn't? He was gorgeous with that short, dark hair, olive skin and dark, sensual eyes. But he was her boss—the man in charge of her professional future—her dreams.

She couldn't afford any more blunders. She had to remain aloof but professional. Surely it wasn't too late to correct things between them. At least he hadn't mentioned anything about sending her back to New York on the next plane, but then again they'd rushed out of the hotel so quickly that he didn't have time to think of it. His thoughts were on his sister.

Kayla sure hoped there wasn't anything wrong with Marianna. This was the first time Kayla had ever witnessed Angelo visibly worried. He obviously cared a great deal for his family though he never let on at the office—when he was working he was 100 percent professional—

So then what happened back there at the hotel?

Angelo pulled the car to a skidding halt in front of the villa. Before she could summon an answer to that nagging question, Angelo had her car door opened. She would figure it out later. Right now, she would offer her support in whatever capacity to Angelo's family.

Nico rushed into the drive. "About time you got here."

"We came right away." Angelo frowned at his brother. "What's the matter with Marianna?"

"Marianna?" Nico's brows drew together in a questioning look. "This has nothing to do with our sister."

"Then why in the world did you have us rush over here?" Angelo's voice took on a sharp edge.

Kayla breathed a sigh of relief. She had no idea what Nico wanted, but she was fully relieved that mother and baby were okay. However, she did have to wonder why Nico wanted her here? Was he hoping that she'd play referee?

Nico's eyes opened wide and his face became animated. "You are never going to believe this—"

"I might if you'd get to the point."

Nico smiled in spite of his brother's obvious agitation. "What would you say if I told you that I was just approached by representatives of Halencia? Monte Calanetti has just made the short list of locations for the royal wedding of Prince Antonio and Christina Rose."

Angelo rolled his eyes. "Nico, this is no time for joking around—"

"I'm not. I'm perfectly serious."

Kayla's mouth gaped open. A royal wedding. Wow! She really was in Europe because nothing like this ever happened back in the States. Wait until she told her family. They would never believe it.

Her gaze moved to Angelo. He still wasn't smiling. In fact, he didn't look the least bit excited about this news. She had absolutely no ties to this village and she was over-the-moon happy for them. So why was he so reserved?

Angelo pressed his hands to his trim waist. "You called us back here to tell us this?"

"Brother, you're not understanding. The royal family of Halencia wants us to make a pitch as to why Monte Calanetti should be the location for the soon-to-be king and his intended bride's wedding."

"And?"

Nico shook his head. "What aren't you understanding? This is where you come in. You and Kayla. This is what you two do for a living—pitch ideas, convince people to go with the products you represent. That's what we need."

Nico wanted Angelo and her to help? Really? For a royal wedding?

The breath caught in her throat as she held back a squeal of excitement. If she'd ever wanted a chance to stand out and gain a promotion, this was a prime opportunity. Plus, it'd mean continuing to work with Angelo. But once they got back to New York, away from this romantic countryside, things would go back to normal. Wouldn't they?

Surely they would. This project was huge. It was amazing. An honest-to-goodness royal wedding. She didn't even know where they'd begin, but she couldn't contain her excitement. She'd show Angelo how good an ad executive she could be. Just wait and see.

Pitch a wedding to royalty?

Angelo had never done such a thing. Weddings weren't his thing. He knew nothing about love and romance. He was highly unqualified for this project. But he wasn't about to admit any of this to Nico. No way. So how was he supposed to get out of this?

Nico smiled as he led them straight through the modestly decorated villa that still looked much the same as it did when he'd been a child. Once everyone was situated on the veranda with cold drinks, Nico turned to him. "So what do you think?"

"About what?"

"You know, coming up with a pitch for the village?"

Angelo wanted to tell his brother that he was too busy and that he couldn't possibly fit it into his schedule. He highly doubted his brother would hear him. Nico had selective hearing when he wanted something bad enough—like Angelo being a silent investor in the vineyard.

Angelo turned to Kayla to see what she thought about the idea, hoping she'd make some excuse to get them out of this situation. But her green eyes sparkled with excitement. How wrong could he have been to look to her for support? Was there a woman alive who didn't get excited about weddings? Or was it the part about pitching it to a real-life prince that had caught her full attention?

Angelo's gut tightened when he thought of Kayla being starstruck over the royal prince. He shrugged off the uneasy sensation. It was none of his concern. Besides, it wasn't as if she was attracted to him. She couldn't dismiss their kiss fast enough.

His jaw tensed as he recalled how easily she'd brushed off their moment. He could have sworn she'd been as into him as he was into her. It just showed how little he understood women.

He drew up his thoughts, refusing to dwell on the subject. In the meantime, Kayla had engaged his brother in light conversation about the vineyard and how it'd been their childhood home. Angelo looked around the place and was truly impressed by what his brother had done to bring this place back to life. It looked so different than when they were kids, when the place was dying off.

Angelo had actually thought that his brother was crazy for wanting to devote his time and money into reviving the vineyard, but with Nico's determination, he'd made a go of the place. In fact, this boutique vineyard might not produce a large quantity of wine, but what it did produce was of the finest quality. Angelo kept his private wine collection stocked with it. Calanetti wines impressed a great number of influential guests that he'd entertained.

The chime of Kayla's laughter drew his thoughts back to the moment. Nico was entertaining her with a tale from when they were kids. As the oldest, Angelo had always been put in charge of his siblings while his parents went out. But this one time, Angelo hadn't been paying attention and they'd sneaked off. What Nico failed to add, and what he probably didn't know, was that had been one of Angelo's scariest moments—not knowing what had happened to his brother and sister.

"Are you telling them about the royal wedding?" Marianna joined them. Her face was a bit on the pale side and there were shadows beneath her eyes.

Nico leaned back in his chair. "I just told Angelo about it. He's thinking it over."

Marianna turned to Angelo. "You have to think it over? But why? This will be the biggest thing you've ever done."

"You really want me to do the pitch?"

She nodded. "Please. It would be so wonderful for everyone. Couldn't you just this once help your family?"

Guilt landed squarely on his shoulders with the force of a full wine barrel. He owed his brother and sister this. It'd put Monte Calanetti on the map. And the benefits the village would reap from the royal wedding taking place here were countless.

But he was already fully obligated. And he couldn't do it all on his own. He'd need help. A good copywriter. His gaze strayed to Kayla. He'd already witnessed just how talented she was with words and images. He could easily imagine her taking on some more of his workload, allowing him time to work on the wedding proposal.

They'd have to work closely together—closer than ever. There was no way he'd let her loose with the company's most important clients. But would they be able to manage it after the kiss?

"So what do you say, Angelo?" Nico looked at him. "The village is all abuzz with the news, and you know that pitching a wedding isn't my area of specialty."

"Please Angelo, will you do it?" Marianna looked at him, openly pleading with him with her eyes.

He'd never been good at telling her no. And now that she was standing there carrying some stranger's baby— some man that his sister wouldn't even introduce to their family—his resistance to her plea was nonexistent. If playing host to a royal wedding made her happy, how could he deny it to her? The decision for once was quite simple.

"Okay. I'll do it."

"You will?" The words echoed around the patio.

"Why does everyone sound so shocked? It'll be good publicity for the firm." But that wasn't his reason for agreeing—it was to see the smiles on the two women in his life... and his brother.

Marianna launched herself into his arms. Warmth swelled in his chest. He may not have been here to protect her and watch over her as he should have been, but at least he could give her something to look forward to while she sorted out the rest of her life.

Marianna pulled back and sent him a watery smile. "Thanks."

He turned to Kayla. She looked like an excited kid on Christmas Eve. "How about you? Are you up for taking on some more responsibility?"

Kayla didn't waste a moment before uttering, "Definitely. Just tell me what needs done."

"Good." He turned to his brother. "It looks like you've hired yourself a team. I'll get started on the pitch as soon as we get back to New York."

"New York?" Nico's brows gathered together.

"Yes, that's where we work. I'll send through what I come up with, but it's going to take me a little time. I have a rush project that I—we—have to wrap up—"

"This can't wait. You have to get started on it right away."

Angelo didn't like the worried tone of his brother's voice. "Why? What haven't you told us?"

Nico got to his feet. "Does anyone need anything else to drink?"

Angelo knew a stalling tactic when he saw one. "Nico, spit it out. What is the catch?"

After Nico finished refilling Kayla's iced tea, he turned to his brother. "The catch is the pitch has to be completed in no more than three weeks' time."

"Three weeks." Angelo leaned back in his chair. "You sure don't give a person much time."

"And—"

"There's more?"

Nico nodded. "The presentation has to be given to the royal family at the palace in Halencia."

Nico sank down into his chair while Angelo charged to his feet. "This changes everything. I wasn't planning to stay in Italy for three weeks. Nico, don't you understand? I have a business to run."

"You're the boss. Can't you put someone else in charge while you're here?"

Angelo never sloughed off his work on other people. He stayed on top of things. Some people called him a control freak. He considered it the only way to keep the company on track. "That's not the point. There are certain things only I can do."

"The point is that when we need you, you're never here." Nico got to his feet and faced him. "Why should I have thought this would be any different?"

His brother's words were pointed and needled at his guilt. "That's not fair. I've lent you money for the vineyard—"

"This isn't about you writing out a check. I'm talking about you personally investing yourself—your time—in something that's important to your family."

Angelo turned to Marianna, looking for support, but she moved to Nico's side. When he sought out Kayla, she was busy studying her iced tea glass with such intensity that it was as if she'd never seen glassware before. He was alone in this. He knew what he should do, but it was so hard to just hand over the reins of the company he'd built from the ground up.

Three weeks was a long time to be away. And yet it wasn't much time to create a compelling campaign for a wedding—a royal wedding. It had just started to sink in what a big deal this really was for his brother and sister, and the village, plus it would be amazing for his company—that is if they won the pitch.

Angelo raked his fingers through his hair. Letting go of the reins at Amatucci & Associates went against every business instinct. Yet, he couldn't turn his back on his siblings again. "Okay. I'll stay."

Marianna turned to Kayla. "Will you stay, too?"

"Yes, Kayla," Nico chimed in. "Will you help my brother? I get the feeling that he won't be able to do it without you."

Kayla's eyes flashed with surprise. "I don't know that I need to stay in Italy to do it."

"It'd be most convenient," Marianna pointed out. "I'm sure Angelo will need your input. After all, we're talking about a wedding. And my brothers, well, they aren't exactly romantic."

"Hey!" Nico and Angelo protested in unison.

Both women burst out in laughter. Angelo supposed the dig was worth it as his sister's face broke into a smile. And when he turned to Kayla, the happiness reflected in her eyes warmed a spot in his chest. She was a very beautiful woman. Why, oh, why did it have to be now when they were practically attached at the hip that he truly realized his attraction to her?

When she caught him staring, the breath hitched in his throat. He should glance away, but he couldn't. He was in awe of her. Was it being away from the office that had him more relaxed about the proper conduct between employer and employee? Nonsense. He knew what he was doing. He could keep this together.

He gazed directly at the woman who took up more and more of his thoughts. "Well, don't keep us in suspense. Will you remain in Italy and lend a hand?"

CHAPTER EIGHT

THIS WAS A very bad idea.

But it was so tempting. How could she let such a rare opportunity pass her by?

Kayla worried her bottom lip. Though she wouldn't be working directly on the royal wedding, she'd be close at hand. Perhaps she could add an idea here and there. Oh, what she wouldn't give to actually work on the project itself. Yet, she understood with the magnitude of a royal wedding that only the best of the best would work on the project, and that meant Angelo.

But she was needed back in New York. The ICL fundraiser was quickly approaching, and seeing as it was her idea—it was her responsibility to make sure it went off without a hitch. However, she had put Pam, an associate at the after-school program, in charge while she was gone. And how much could possibly go wrong in three weeks?

"Please say you'll stay." Marianna looked so hopeful. "I could use someone on my side against my brothers, who think they know everything."

That sold her. Marianna could definitely use some help keeping her brothers in line while she figured out her next move. "Okay, I'll stay."

Everyone smiled except Angelo.

Aside from the fund-raiser, there was nothing waiting for her back in New York, not even a goldfish. When she wasn't at the office, she was at the after-school program helping kids with their homework followed by a game of dodgeball or basketball or volleyball. She wasn't very good at any of the games, but she gave it her best effort.

For the moment, she was giving herself permission to

enjoy Italy before she set to work. And this was the perfect place to start. She'd love to see more of the vineyard, and it'd give Angelo some private time with his siblings.

"Would you mind if I had a look around the vineyard?" Kayla's gaze met Nico's.

"My apologies. I should have offered to give you a tour earlier. I've had other thoughts on my mind—" his gaze strayed to his sister and then back to her "—with uh...the royal wedding."

"That's okay. I totally understand." Kayla got to her feet. "I've never been to a vineyard before. I'll just show myself around."

"Nonsense. Angelo can give you the grand tour while I make some phone calls and spread the good news. And make sure he shows you the chapel." Nico turned a smile to Angelo. "You can handle that, can't you, brother?"

Angelo's jaw tightened, but he didn't argue. Kayla took that as progress between the brothers. Not wanting to give Angelo time to change his mind, she set off for the vines, hoping Angelo would follow.

He did, and he proved to be quite an insightful guide. He explained to her the difference between a larger vineyard and this boutique vineyard. While Nico produced fewer barrels of wine—less than five thousand cases a year— it was carefully processed to the highest quality with the least amount of oxidation.

As much as the history and current production of wine interested her, it was the bell tower in the distance that drew her attention. She headed for the weathered building that sat on the other side of the wall that lined the edge of the vineyard. "Is this the chapel your brother mentioned?"

"Yes. Nico and I explored it as kids. We considered it our castle. I was the king and Nico was the daring knight fighting off dragons." Angelo smiled at the long-forgotten memory.

"You and your brother must have had a lot of fun."

"Now that I think about it, we did have some good times."

She smiled. "This looks like a great place for an adventure. Can we go inside the chapel?"

"It's nothing you'd be interested in."

"Sure I would." Her steps grew quicker as she headed for the opening in the wall that led to the little chapel. Maybe this was her chance to let Angelo know that she'd be more than willing to help with the wedding pitch—in fact, this was the opportunity of a lifetime. Now, how did she broach the subject with Angelo?

She stopped next to the four steps that led to two tall, narrow wooden doors. It looked as though time had passed it by. Okay so it needed a little TLC, but it had a charm about it that transcended time. "Your brother is so lucky to have this piece of history on his land. Imagine all of the weddings and christenings that must have taken place here."

"Technically it's not on Nico's land." Angelo pointed over his shoulder to the wall. That divides the vineyard. The other side is Nico's."

"So who owns this land, then?"

"This is Palazzo di Comparino. Its owner, Signor Carlos Bartolini, recently passed away. From what I understand, there's a young woman staying there now."

"You know this chapel gives me an idea—it'd be perfect for the royal wedding."

"I don't know." Angelo rubbed his chin. "It needs work."

She pulled open one of the doors and peered inside at the rows of pews. The place was filled with dust and cobwebs. "It's nothing that can't be done rather easily." This was her chance to put herself out there. "You know I could help you with the pitch."

Angelo didn't immediately respond. The breath hitched in her throat as she waited—hoping that he'd latch on to her offer. The experience from working on such a prestigious project had immeasurable potential, from a promotion at Amatucci & Associates to making her résumé stand out— head and shoulders above the rest.

"I don't think so. You'll have enough to do with the other accounts that need looking after." The disappointment must have filtered across her face because his stance eased and his voice softened. "I appreciate the offer, but I don't want you getting overwhelmed."

It teetered on the tip of her tongue to ask him if this had anything to do with the kiss, but she hesitated. She couldn't bring herself to tarnish that moment. The memory of how his eyes had devoured her before his lips had claimed hers still made her heart race.

If it wasn't the kiss, why was he turning away her offer of help? Was it just as he said, not wanting to give her too much work? Or did he feel she wasn't up to the task of working on something so important?

With the wind temporarily knocked out of her sails, she turned back to the villa. She wasn't giving up. She would show Angelo that she was invaluable.

What was the problem?

Two days later, Angelo paced around the hotel suite. He needed a fresh approach to the wedding. It had to be something amazing—something unique to Monte Calanetti that would appeal to a prince and his intended bride. But what?

He was stuck. This had never happened to him before. He inwardly groaned as his mind drew a total blank. This was ridiculous. He clenched his hands into tight balls. He had absolutely nothing. And that was so not like him.

He liked to think outside the box. He liked to push boundaries and experiment, but all he could think of was why would anyone would want to get married in Monte Calanetti? What special qualities did they see in the village for it to make the royals' short list?

He poured himself a cup of the now-lukewarm coffee.

The silence of the suite was getting to him. Kayla had cleared out early that morning, claiming she wanted some fresh air while she worked on the mock-ups for the Van Holsen account and answered emails. She'd been great about taking on additional responsibilities, allowing him time to brainstorm. Not that it was helping him much.

In fact, she'd done such an exceptional job that maybe he should see what she could do with this wedding stuff. After all, she was a girl, and didn't they all dream about their weddings?

Suddenly the image of Kayla in a white dress formed in his mind. His body tensed. As quickly as the image came to him, he vanquished it. She'd be a beautiful bride, but for someone else. He wasn't getting married—ever.

Determined to stay on point and to get her input on the wedding, he headed downstairs to the pool area. He opened the door and stepped outside, momentarily blinded by the bright sunlight. Once his vision adjusted, he glanced around, quickly locating his assistant. She was at a shaded poolside table. She lifted her head and smiled, but it wasn't aimed at him.

She wasn't alone. A young man stood next to her table. Angelo's gut knotted. He told himself that it was because she was supposed to be working, not flirting. His only interest was in her getting her work done in a timely fashion. But as the chime of her laughter carried through the gentle breeze, Angelo's mouth pulled into a frown.

He strode toward the table. Kayla didn't even notice him approach as she was captivated by the young man.

Angelo cleared his throat. "Hello, Kayla."

Both heads turned his way. Kayla's eyes opened wide with surprise. The young man drew himself up to his full height as though he was about to defend his right to be flirting with Kayla. The guy had no idea that Angelo had no intention of challenging his right to gain Kayla's attention. After all, it would be for the best if she was interested in someone—as long as it wasn't him. But that would all have to wait, because right now she was on the clock. And he needed her help.

Angelo used his practiced professional voice, the one that let people know that he meant business. "How's the Van Holsen account coming?"

"Uh, good. Dino was just asking about the royal wedding."

"He was?" Angelo stepped between Kayla and the young man. "What do you want to know?"

The young man glanced down, not meeting Angelo's direct gaze. "I... I was just curious if the rumor was true that they might pick Monte Calanetti for the wedding."

"It is. Is there anything else?"

Dino shrugged his shoulders. "I guess not."

"Good. Kayla has work to do now. If you'll excuse us."

"Uh, sure." Dino leaned to the side to look at Kayla. "I'll see you around."

"Bye."

Angelo took a seat next to Kayla. "It seems you've found yourself an admirer."

"Who? Dino?" She shook her head. "He was just interested in what I knew about the royal wedding, which wasn't anything more than he's heard through the grapevine. How's the pitch for the wedding coming?"

"Good." *Liar.*

He wasn't about to admit that he, Angelo Amatucci, couldn't come up with a dynamic pitch that would turn the prince's and his bride's heads. No way. What would Kayla think of him? No. Scratch that. He didn't want to know what she'd think. She'd probably laugh at him.

"I'm glad to hear it's going well. I know that I'm not the only one who's anxious for the pitch. Imagine a royal wedding. The whole world will be watching it and you'll have played a big part in it."

"Not a big part."

"You're too modest. You're like the village hero now."

Just what he needed was more pressure. He swallowed down his uneasiness. "You're assuming that the prince will choose this village, and that's a big leap."

"But why wouldn't they pick Monte Calanetti? From the little I've seen, I think it's a lovely village."

"That's just because you didn't grow up here."

Her green eyes widened. "You really didn't like living here?"

He shook his head, but he wasn't going to get into the details of his childhood or his strained relationship with his parents. Kayla had already been privy to more about his private life than anyone else ever. But something told him that his family secrets were safe with her.

Not in the mood to talk anymore about this village or dwell on the fact that he'd wasted two days without coming up with anything striking or fascinating, he decided to turn the conversation around. "How is the work going?"

CHAPTER NINE

COULD SHE PRETEND she hadn't heard Angelo?

Kayla had spent a large chunk of time at this poolside table. With most of the guests either off sightseeing or attending other engagements, it was a peaceful place for her to jot out more ideas for the Van Holsen account. But after going back and forth between the art department and the very demanding client, they were still missing the mark.

It didn't help that her ideas for the Van Holsen account had stalled. For the past half hour or so, she'd been jotting out ideas for the fund-raiser back in New York. The event was their last hope to keep the after-school program going for so many at-risk kids and it was weighing heavy on her mind. There were still so many details to iron out.

And as exciting as it was to be working with Angelo Amatucci on what could be the project to catapult her career, she couldn't forget the children. They were relying on her to make their lives a little better by raising money to keep their facility open.

"Kayla, did you hear me?"

The sound of Angelo's voice startled her back to the here and now. "Sorry. I just had a thought."

"About the account?"

She nodded. "It's coming along."

"Why don't you tell me what you have so far and we can work on it together?"

She glanced down at her closed notebook. "That's okay. I know you have more important things to concentrate on. I've got this."

Angelo's dark brows drew together. "Listen, I know that

things haven't exactly been right between us since, well, you know…the kiss. If that's still bothering you—?"

"It's not." Yes, it was. But not the way he was thinking. The kiss had been better than she'd ever imagined. And she knew that it could never happen again. She had too much on the line to risk it all by fooling around with her boss.

The truth of the matter was the pad of paper also contained her thoughts for the benefit concert. Angelo had a strict policy about not taking on charity accounts—he believed there were too many good causes and not enough time to help them all. Kayla couldn't understand his stance, but then again she'd never been in charge of a large company. Maybe there was more to it than what she knew.

The one thing she did know was that she couldn't let Angelo find out that she was organizing a fund-raiser while on this trip. She didn't want him to have a reason not to consider her for a promotion or worse yet to have her replaced as his assistant. She wasn't sure how he would handle the situation. In all of her time at Amatucci & Associates, she'd never witnessed anyone going against company policy. Angelo was a man no one wanted to cross.

"I'm just jotting out some ideas. Nothing specific yet." She caught herself worrying her bottom lip, hoping he wouldn't take exception to her not coming up with something more concrete. After all, they were on a timetable and the clock was ticking. "I spent the morning on the phone with the art department and Mrs. Van Holsen—"

His brows drew together into a formidable line. "Why didn't you get me?"

"I… I didn't want to disturb you. I'm supposed to be here to lighten your load."

He shook his head. "I can't spend all of my time on one campaign. That isn't fair to the other clients. I have to stay on top of everything. Next time you speak with a client, I expect to be in on the call. Understood?"

"Yes."

He let the subject go as he continued on with some other business items. "By the way, while I was on the phone with the office I mentioned that we'd been unavoidably detained in Italy, but I didn't go into specifics. I don't want any rumors starting up that we put off longtime clients in favor of this royal wedding pitch. I won't risk my company's reputation for something that is never going to happen."

Kayla's mouth gaped before she caught it and forced her lips together. "Is that really what you think?"

He nodded. "Pretty much."

"But why?"

"Well, I can't see what a royal couple would find so endearing about Monte Calanetti. I think everyone, including my brother and sister, are getting worked up over something that will never happen."

"I don't understand. If that's truly what you think then why go to all of the bother to delay your return to New York and work on a campaign that you're certain will fail?"

He shrugged. "It's an obligation that I owe them." He raked his fingers through his hair. "I owe it to Nico and Marianna—you know, for skipping out on them. For letting them fend for themselves with parents who were more wrapped up in their marital drama than worrying about their children."

"I'm sorry—"

"Don't be. I didn't tell you any of that so you'd feel sorry for me. In fact, I don't know why I mentioned it at all."

"I'm glad you did. I'd like to think that we've become more than coworkers." When she met his drawn brows, she realized that she'd said more than she should have. "I... I don't mean about the kiss. I just thought we might be friends, too."

A wave of relief washed over his face easing the stress lines. "I would like that."

"You would?"

Slowly he nodded, and then a smile tugged at his lips. "Yes, I would."

She couldn't help but smile back. She noticed how the worry lines bracketing his eyes and mouth smoothed. She'd never seen him look so worried before. Why would that be? He was amazing at creating winning pitches. He was amazing in a lot of ways.

Realizing that she was staring, she turned away, but by then, her heart was beating faster than normal. Images of the kiss they'd shared clouded her mind. She'd tried to put it out of her head, but the memory kept her awake late into the night. What had it meant? Had it meant anything? Because there was no way that a wealthy, successful businessman who could have his choice of women would fall for his assistant.

Kayla reached for a tall, cool glass of iced tea. "Would you like something to drink? I could go and get you something."

"Thanks. But I'm all right." He looked at her as though studying her. "Can I ask what direction you think the wedding pitch should take?"

"Really?" She sat up straighter. "You want my input?"

He nodded. "I thought you might have some ideas that I hadn't thought of."

"I do...have ideas, that is." She struggled to gather her thoughts.

"I'm listening."

She'd done a lot of thinking about this—probably too much, considering she hadn't even been invited to help with the royal pitch until now. "I'm thinking that regardless of whether they go big or small, they're going to want elements that play into an elegant yet traditional event."

"That's true. If they wanted a contemporary feel, they certainly wouldn't come to Monte Calanetti." He rubbed the back of his neck.

"What's bothering you?"

"I'm just trying to figure out why this village made the short list for the royal wedding. I mean, there's nothing special here. I've gone round and round with this, but I still have no answer. It's not like it has amazing history like Rome or the heartbeat of the nation like Milan or the stunning architecture of Venice. This is a little, old village."

"And it's tripping you up when you're trying to come up with a unique pitch."

Angelo hesitated as though he wasn't sure whether or not to confide in her. Then he sighed. "Yes, it's giving me a bit of a problem. No matter which way I go at it, I just can't find that special quality that will put Monte Calanetti head and shoulders above the other locations."

Kayla smiled and shook her head. "You just don't see it because you take this place for granted. It's your home, but to outsiders, it's something special."

His gaze met hers. "You think it's special?"

She decided a neutral stance was best. "I haven't made up my mind yet."

"Then how can you tell me that I'm blind to what's in front of me when you haven't even made up your mind?" His voice held a disgruntled tone.

She smiled, liking the fact that she could get past his polished persona and make him feel real genuine emotions. "I mean that I need to see the village." When he opened his mouth to protest, she held up her hand, stopping him. "And driving straight through it to get to the hotel does not count. It was more of a blur than anything."

"What are you saying?"

"I'm saying that tomorrow you and I will start exploring Monte Calanetti. You can tell me all about it. You know, the little things that a tourist wouldn't know—the parts that make the village special."

"Don't be too disappointed when it doesn't live up to your expectations."

"I think you'll actually end up surprising yourself."

His gaze narrowed in on her. "You really want to walk all through the village?"

She nodded. "If you want to come up with a winning pitch to make all of the citizens, not to mention your brother and sister very happy, you're going to have to see it differently."

"I'm not sure that's possible. But if you insist on it, I will give you the grand tour."

"I would like that."

"Now, if you'll excuse me, I promised to swing by my brother's villa. He wants to show me the latest improvements at the winery." He got to his feet. "Of course, if you'd like to accompany me, you're welcome."

Kayla glanced down at her rather sparse list of notes. "I think my time would be better spent here doing some research."

"You're sure?"

She nodded. "I am. But thank you for the invite."

The truth was, she and Angelo were getting along a lot better than they had in the office. She'd been working for him for weeks now and they'd only ever addressed each other with mister and miss, but now they were on a first-name basis. And then there was that kiss...er...no she wasn't going to think about it. No matter how good it was or how much she wished that he'd kiss her again—

Her thoughts screeched to a halt. Did she want him to kiss her again? She turned to watch his retreating form. His broad shoulders were evident in the linen suit jacket. His long, powerful legs moved at a swift pace, covering the patio area quickly.

Yes, she did want to be kissed again. Only this time she wanted him to kiss her because he wanted her and not because he was exhausted and stressed after a run-in with his siblings. But that couldn't happen. She needed this job.

A quick fling with her boss in the warm sunshine of

Tuscany wasn't worth throwing away her dreams—the rest of her life. No matter how tempting Angelo might be, she just couldn't ruin this opportunity.

And she couldn't return to Paradise as a failure.

CHAPTER TEN

WHY EXACTLY HAD he agreed to this?

The last thing Angelo wanted to do was take a stroll through Monte Calanetti. It was like taking a walk back through history—a history that he preferred not to dwell on. Still, he had to admit that having Kayla along would make the journey back in time a little more tolerable, but he still didn't see how it was going to help him create a winning pitch.

He paced back and forth in the hotel lobby, waiting for Kayla to finish getting ready for their outing. He'd also wanted to check with the front desk to make sure that extending their stay wouldn't be an issue.

"Mr. Amatucci, you're in luck." The concierge strode up to him. "We've just had a cancellation. And with a bit of juggling we've been able to keep you and your assistant in your suite of rooms." The young man, who was polished from the top of his short cut hair down to his spiffed-up dress shoes, looked quite pleased with himself. "Is there anything else I can do for you?"

"Actually there is." Angelo wasn't sure it was a good idea, but he decided that Kayla deserved a night out for being such a good sport. "I've heard that Mancini's is quite a popular restaurant."

"Yes, it is. We're so lucky to have had Raffaele Mancini return to the village. Mancini's is so popular that they only take reservations."

That's what Angelo suspected. "Would you mind making a reservation for myself and my assistant for tomorrow evening?"

The concierge's face creased with worry lines.

"Is there a problem?"

"Well, sir. They're usually booked well in advance."

Angelo wasn't used to being put off. Even in New York he didn't have a problem getting into the most popular restaurants. How in the world was it that he was being turned down in little old Monte Calanetti? Impossible.

"Do you know who I am?"

The young man's eyes opened wide, and then he nodded.

Angelo got the distinct impression that the young man didn't have a clue who he was or what power he wielded outside of the Tuscany countryside. He felt as though he'd stepped back in time, becoming a nobody who faded into the crowd. With his pride pricked, he gave the young man a pointed look. But he knew that he was letting his past get the best of him. He swallowed down the unwarranted agitation. Of course the young man didn't know him. The concierge wasn't much more than a kid.

Angelo decided upon a new approach. "Forgive me. My tone was uncalled-for just now. When you call for the reservations, tell them that the owner of Amatucci & Associates is requesting a table as we are considering including them in the pitch for the royal wedding."

Maybe he had put it on a little thick just now, but he wanted—no, he needed to prove to everyone including himself that he had far surpassed everyone's expectations of him—especially his father's. Angelo's gut churned at the memory of his father turning to him in anger and saying, *You'll never amount to anything.*

"Yes, sir." The concierge attempted a nervous smile. "I'll do that right away. I had no idea, sir—"

"It's okay." Angelo tipped the young man handsomely to make up for his brusqueness. "I just need you to know that this dinner is very important." But suddenly Angelo was no longer talking about business or proving himself to the villagers or even the royal wedding. His mind was on Kayla. He liked making her happy, and he was hoping this dinner would earn him another smile or two.

"I'll get right on it, sir."

"Thank you. I appreciate it."

Angelo moved over to the small sitting area in the lobby to wait for Kayla. Just about to reach for the newspaper to find out what was going on around the world, Angelo caught a movement out of the corner of his eye. Curious to see if it was Kayla, he turned.

His gaze settled on her slender form. He stood transfixed as he took in her beauty. Kayla's auburn wavy hair hung loose and flowed down over her shoulders. A pair of sunglasses sat atop her head like a hair band. Her face was lightly made up and her reading glasses were nowhere in sight. A sheer tan cardigan covered her arms while beneath was a lacy white tank top. She looked so stunning that all of the villagers would be too busy trying to figure out if she was a movie star to take any notice of him.

"Is everything all right with the suite?" She stopped next to him.

He swallowed hard and glanced away, telling himself to relax. This was still the same Kayla that he'd been working closely with for weeks. He gazed at her again, trying to see her as the levelheaded assistant that he'd come to rely on. Spending the day with her, leisurely strolling about was going to be a struggle. He just had to keep in mind that they had a mission to accomplish—a royal wedding to brainstorm.

"Angelo?" She sent him a concerned look.

"Um…sorry. Yes, the suite is ours for the duration."

She pressed a hand to her chest. "That's good. You had me worried for a moment there."

"Nothing at all to worry about. Are you ready for your grand tour?"

She smiled and nodded. "Yes, I am. I'm really looking forward to it."

Without thinking, he extended his arm to her. Surprise lit up her eyes but in a blink it was gone. She slipped her arm in his. He didn't know why he'd made the gesture. It just felt right. So much for the promise he'd made himself to remain professional around her. They hadn't even left the hotel and he was already treating her like...like... Oh, whatever.

Angelo led her out of the hotel into the sunshiny afternoon. He had to admit that it was nice to get away from the stress of the wedding pitch. The whole project had ground to a complete halt. He sure hoped this outing would refill his creative well. If nothing else, maybe it would help him relax so he could start brainstorming again.

He glanced over to find Kayla taking in their surroundings. "I thought we would walk since the village isn't far from here."

"Sounds fine by me. I've been cooped up in the hotel long enough. Back in New York, I'm used to doing a lot of walking."

"Really. Where do you walk?" He didn't know why but he was truly interested.

"I walk to the subway and then to the office. Sometimes, if the weather is right, I will duck out at lunch and stretch my legs."

"So you truly like to walk."

She nodded. "It sure beats eating like a bird. If you hadn't noticed, I do enjoy food." She rubbed her flat abs. "Especially pasta."

"Would you like to try some of the best Italian food in the region?"

"Definitely."

"Good. From what I've heard, you should be impressed with the restaurant I've chosen."

"Is it far from here?"

"Not at all. In fact, it's right here in Monte Calanetti. We have reservations for tomorrow night."

"I can't wait."

"Good. Consider it a date."

When her fine brows rose and her eyes glittered with unspoken questions, he realized he'd blundered. But he didn't take back the words. He liked the thought of having a friendly date with her.

They walked a bit before Kayla spoke. "What's it called?"

"Mancini's. It's an exclusive IGF-starred restaurant on the outskirts of the village. The chef is a friend of my brother's."

"This friend of your brother's, is he from around here?"

"Yes, he grew up here. After Raffaele achieved international success with his cooking, he returned to open his own restaurant. I suspect he was anxious to try running his own place, but I'm surprised he didn't start his business in one of the cities like Rome or Milan."

"Perhaps he just wanted to be home again. Have you really never considered moving back here?"

Angelo gave a firm shake of head. "Not even once."

"Don't you like it here?"

"It…it has a lot of memories. Not all of them good ones."

Angelo remembered how he'd been turned away from his home and told not to return. The buried memories came flooding back to him. The loud arguments between his parents. His brother and sister upset. And then there was the last time he came to his mother's defense. He'd experienced many a row with his father before that life-altering one—the one where his father threw him out of the house, telling him that he was old enough to make it on his own.

When Angelo had turned a pleading stare to his mother, she'd told him that he was a smart, strong young man and that it was time to make his way in life. That was when he'd had no choice but to follow his dreams. With the aid of his inheritance from his grandfather combined with his meager savings, he'd set out for New York.

Though he hated to leave his brother and sister, he didn't have a choice. His father was a stubborn man who wouldn't back down from an argument. And Angelo wasn't about to live any longer with his parents and their dysfunctional relationship. In fact, he hadn't even come back to Monte Calanetti to visit until his mother and father had moved to Milan. He had no intention of seeing his father again.

"I'm sorry. I didn't mean to upset you."

Kayla's voice drew him out of his thoughts. "What? Um…oh, you didn't."

She sent him an I-don't-believe-you look but said nothing more. They continued toward the village in silence. It felt so strange to be back here—when he'd left all of those years ago, he'd sworn that he'd never return. And he hadn't for a long time.

The truth was he missed his brother and sister. But he rarely made the journey home. It was too hard. There were too many unsettling memories lurking about, and he just didn't have the same draw to this place that his brother and sister did. He didn't understand Nico's need to cling to their heritage, not when there were so many adventures outside of Monte Calanetti to experience.

"This is beautiful." Kayla stood at the crumbling rock wall that surrounded the village, which was perched high upon a hill. "What an amazing view. What's with the wall?"

"The village is centuries old and used to be a stronghold against attacks."

"I couldn't imagine there being unrest here. I mean, did you ever see anything so peaceful?" There was a distinct note of awe in Kayla's voice. "There's something almost magical about it."

"I used to think that, too."

"You did?"

He nodded, recalling days of long ago. "I used to come to this spot when I was a kid." What he failed to mention is that he came here to get away from his parents' arguing.

"I'd pretend that I was the defender of the kingdom. Many sword battles took place where you're standing."

"Really? So you were Sir Lancelot?" She eyed him up as though imagining him in a coat of armor.

He was no knight—not even close to it. He'd just been a kid trying to escape the battlefield between his parents, but he didn't want to get into any of that. A gentle breeze rushed past them and he willed it to sweep away the unsettling memories. He didn't want the past to ruin this day.

"Look." She pointed to a flock of little birds as they took flight. They soared up into the sky, circled and swooped low before rising again. "Aren't they beautiful?"

He was never a bird-watcher, but he had to admire the symmetry of their movements. He couldn't help but wonder what else he'd been missing. His gaze strayed back to Kayla. How had he missed noticing how amazing she was both inside and out?

"And listen."

He did as she asked. "I don't hear anything."

"Exactly! There's nothing but the rustle of the leaves. It's so freeing."

Now that he could agree on. He'd been searching for quietness like this ever since he'd moved to New York, but he'd never been able to find it—until now. "It clears the mind."

"Good. We want clear heads when we tour Monte Calanetti." She turned and pointed off in the distance. "I just love the rows of grapevines. I wonder how they get the lines so straight."

"I'm betting if you were to ask Nico that he'd tell you anything you want to know about running a vineyard. He's very proud of his work."

"You mean all of that is Nico's land?"

Angelo nodded. "It has been passed down through the family. When my father couldn't make a go of it, they passed the land down to us kids. I was already working in New York and Marianna was too young, so Nico stepped up. He's worked really hard to rebuild the vineyard and make a name for the wine."

"Hardworking must be a trait of the Amatucci men."

"Some of them anyhow." His father wasn't big on work, which was evident by the poor condition of the vineyard when he'd handed it over to his children. "Come on. I thought you wanted to see Monte Calanetti."

"I do."

With Kayla's hand still tucked in the crook of his arm, Angelo took comfort in having her next to him. This was his first stroll through the village since that dreadful day when his father cast him out of their family home. These days when he returned to Italy, he either stayed in the city or at the villa. He just wasn't up for the curious stares or worse the questions about why he left.

As they strolled through the village, Angelo warned himself not to get too comfortable with Kayla. Soon this vacation illusion would end, and they'd be back in New York, where he'd transform back into Mr. Amatucci and she'd once again be Ms. Hill. Everything would once again be as it should.

CHAPTER ELEVEN

NEVER ONE TO lurk in the shadows, Angelo led Kayla into the center of Monte Calanetti. Their first stop was at the *caffè* shop. He'd never met a woman who loved coffee as much as Kayla. She savored each sip before swallowing. He loved to watch her facial features when she'd take her first sip—it was somewhere between total delight and ecstasy. He longed to be able to put that look on her face...and not with coffee...but with a long, slow, deep, soul-stirring kiss.

He'd given up the futile effort of fighting his lustful thoughts for Kayla. He couldn't lie to himself. He found her utterly enchanting. And as long as he stuck with his daydreams of holding her—of kissing her passionately—they'd be fine. It wasn't as if she could read his mind.

They stepped out of the shop and onto the busy sidewalk. As they started to walk again, he reminded himself not to get too caught up in having Kayla by his side. She was the absolute wrong person for him to have a dalliance with beneath the Tuscany sun. He was her escort—her friend—nothing more. He forced his thoughts to the quaint shops that offered such things as locally grown flowers and to-die-for baked goods. There was a little bit of everything. And he could tell by the rapt stare on Kayla's face that she was enthralled by all of it.

"Angelo, is that you?"

They both stopped at the sound of a woman's excited voice. Angelo glanced over his shoulder to see an older woman rushing toward them. She looked vaguely familiar.

"It is you." The woman couldn't be much more than five feet tall, if that. She beamed up at him. "I knew you'd come back."

It took him a moment, but then the woman's gentle smile and warm eyes clicked a spot in his memory—Mrs. Caruso. He hadn't seen her since he was a teenager. Back then, she'd had long dark hair that she kept braided over one shoulder. Now, her dark hair had given way to shades of gray, and instead of the braid, her hair was pinned up.

Kayla elbowed him, and at last, he found his voice. "Mrs. Caruso, it's good to see you."

"What kind of greeting is that?" She grabbed him by the arms and pulled him toward her. When he'd stooped over far enough, she placed a hand on either side of his head, and then kissed each cheek. "You've been gone much too long. You've been missed."

She pulled him back down to her and gave him a tight hug. He hugged her back. Heat warmed his face. He wasn't used to public displays of affection...no matter how innocent they might be. This would never happen back in the States. But then again, Monte Calanetti was a lifetime away from New York City, and the same rules didn't seem to apply here.

They chatted for a bit as she asked one question after the other about what he'd been doing with himself. The years rolled away as she put him at ease with her friendly chatter. The best part was that she really listened to him—as she'd done all of those years ago when he was a kid. Mrs. Caruso and her husband ran the local bakery. They'd never had any children of their own. Angelo always suspected that it wasn't from the lack of wanting or trying. Without little ones of her own, she'd doted on the kids in the village.

"You are going to do the royal wedding pitch, aren't you?" She smiled and clapped her hands together as though she'd just solved the world's problems.

"Nico asked me to work on it. My assistant and I just extended our stay here in order to work up a presentation for the royal family."

"Wonderful!" Mrs. Caruso beamed. "Now I'm more

certain than ever that the village will host the wedding. Everyone will be so grateful to both of you."

"I don't know about that—"

"You're just being modest. You always were." Mrs. Caruso's gaze moved to Kayla. "Now where are my manners? Angelo, introduce me to your girlfriend."

His girlfriend? Hadn't she heard him say Kayla was his assistant? His gaze moved from her to Kayla, who was smiling. Why wasn't she correcting the woman? Was she just being polite? Or should he be concerned that she was taking this friendly outing far too seriously?

"Hi, I'm Kayla." She held out a hand while Angelo struggled to settle his thoughts. "I'm actually Mr. Amatucci's assistant."

Mrs. Caruso's brows rose as her gaze moved back and forth between them. "I could have sworn that you two were— Oh, never mind me. I'm just so glad that you're both here to help with the wedding."

They promised to stop by the bakery soon and moved on down the walkway. He still didn't know why Mrs. Caruso would think they were a couple. Then he glanced down to where Kayla's hand was resting on his arm. Okay, so maybe from the outside the lines in their relationship appeared a bit blurred, but they knew where they stood. Didn't they?

He swallowed hard. "I'm sorry about back there with Mrs. Caruso jumping to conclusions about us."

"It's okay. It was a natural mistake."

A natural mistake? Wait. What exactly did that mean?

He glanced over at Kayla. "But you know that you and I…that we're, um…that nothing has changed. Right?"

She smiled up at him. "Relax. We're just two business associates enjoying a stroll through the village. It's a mission. We have to learn as much about this place as possible so that you can do some brainstorming about the pitch when we return to our suite."

She said all of the right things, but why did they sound

so wrong to his ears? Maybe he was just being hypersensitive. He took a deep breath and blew it out. "Exactly." Now he needed to change the subject to something a little less stressful. "Mrs. Caruso certainly seemed hopeful about the royal wedding."

"She did. It seems as if the whole village is buzzing with excitement about it."

"I just hope they don't end up disappointed."

She lightly elbowed him. "They won't be. You'll see to that."

At this particular moment, she had a lot more faith in his abilities than he did. "I don't know if I'm that good. This is just a small village and we're talking about a royal wedding—the sort of thing they write about in history books."

"And who better to sell the royal couple on the merits of Monte Calanetti?" She gazed up at him with hope in her eyes. "You just need to loosen up a bit and enjoy yourself."

"I am relaxed." As relaxed as he got these days.

She sighed and shook her head. "No, you aren't. Let down your guard and enjoy the sun on your face."

"Why is this so important to you?"

"Because I want you to really see Monte Calanetti and get excited about it." Her gaze met his and then dipped to his mouth. "I think if you're passionate about something it will show."

The temperature started to rise. He knew what she was thinking because he was thinking the same thing. He zeroed in on her inviting lips. He was definitely feeling passionate. Would it be wrong to kiss her again?

Someone bumped his shoulder as they passed by, reminding him that they were in the middle of the village. Not exactly the place for a passionate moment or even a quick peck. Besides, he couldn't give her the wrong impression. He didn't do relationships.

Before he could decide if he should say something,

Kayla slipped her arm in his and they started to walk again. They made their way around the piazza, taking in the various shops from a shoe boutique to a candy shop. Monte Calanetti offered so much more than he recalled.

Maybe it wasn't quite the small backward village he'd conjured up in his memory—the same village where he'd once got into a bit of mischief with harmless pranks. Those were the carefree days that he hadn't known to appreciate as they flew by.

"What are you smiling about?" Kayla sent him a curious look.

He was smiling? He hadn't realized his thoughts had crossed his face. "I was just recalling some antics I'd gotten into as a kid."

"Oh, tell me. I'd love to hear."

"You would?" He wouldn't think something like that would interest her. When she nodded, he continued. "There was this one time when I glued a coin to the sidewalk outside the market. You wouldn't believe how many people tried to pry it free."

Her eyes twinkled. "So you didn't always play by the rules."

He shrugged. "What kind of trouble did you get into?"

"Me? Nothing."

"Oh, come on, confess. There has to be something."

She paused as though giving it some serious consideration. "Well, there was this one time the neighborhood boys attached some fishing line to a dollar. It was similar to what you did. They'd lay it out in front of my parents' market, and when someone went to pick up it up, they'd tug on the line."

"See, I knew you weren't as innocent as you appeared."

"Hey, it wasn't me. It was them. I… I was just watching."

"Uh-huh." He enjoyed the way her cheeks filled with color. "It's good to know you have some spunk in you. That will come in handy in this business."

* * *

Kayla was in love—with the village, of course.

Brilliant sunshine lit up the heart of Monte Calanetti. The piazza was surrounded by a wide range of small shops to satisfy even the most discerning tastes. But it was the large fountain in the center of the village square that drew Kayla's attention. She tugged on Angelo's arm, leading them toward it.

The focal point of the fountain was a nymph draped in a cloak. She held a huge clamshell overhead. The sunshine sparkled and danced over the fine billowing mist from the continuous jets of water. Kayla stopped at the fountain's edge. She smiled, loving the details of the sculpture that included a ring of fish leaping out of the water.

"I take it you like the fountain." Angelo's deep voice came from just behind her. "You know there's a tradition that if you toss a coin and it lands in the shell, you get your wish."

Her gaze rose to the clamshell—suddenly it didn't look quite so big. "You'd have to be awfully lucky to get it all the way up there."

"Why don't you give it a try?"

"I… I don't think so. I was never good at those types of things."

Angelo held a coin out to her. "Here you go." His fingers pressed the money into her palm. "I made a wish once and it came true."

"Really?" She turned to him. "What was it?"

He shook his head. "You aren't supposed to tell your wish."

"But that doesn't apply if your wish has already come true. So, out with it."

The corner of his very inviting lips lifted. "Okay. I wished that someday I'd get to travel the world."

"Wow. It really did come true." She thought really hard, but was torn by what she should wish for. She could wish for the fund-raiser to be a huge success. Or she could wish for her promotion to ad executive. But fountains should be for fanciful dreams.

"Don't look so worried. Turn around."

She did as he said. The next thing she knew, his body pressed to her back—his hard planes to her soft curves. His breath tickled her neck. Her heart thumped and her knees grew weak. Thankfully he was there holding her up.

His voice was soft as he spoke. "You make the wish and I'll help you get the coin in the shell. Ready?"

She nodded. Together with their hands touching, they swung. The coin flipped end over end through the air.

Let Angelo kiss me.

Plunk! The coin landed in the clamshell.

"We did it!"

At that moment, Angelo backed away. "Did you ever doubt it?"

"I couldn't have done it without you." She turned around, hoping her wish would come true.

"Did you make your wish?"

Disappointment washed over her. Of course he wasn't going to kiss her. She'd let herself get caught up in the moment. That wouldn't happen again.

"We should keep moving." She turned to start walking. "We don't want to miss anything."

"Wait." He reached out for her hand. "Aren't you going to tell me what you wished for?"

"Um…no. I can't." When he sent her a puzzled look, she added, "If I tell you, it won't come true."

"Well, we wouldn't want that to happen."

Her hand remained in his warm grasp as they continued their stroll. Was it her imagination or was Angelo's icy professional persona melting beneath the Tuscany sun? She smiled. He was definitely warming up.

CHAPTER TWELVE

Simply *charming*.

At this particular moment, Kayla had no better word for it. And she wasn't just talking about the village. She gave Angelo a sideways gaze. Handsome, thoughtful and entertaining. "Quite a combo."

"What?"

Oops! She hadn't meant to vocalize her thoughts. "I... I was just thinking Monte Calanetti has quite an amazing combination of old-world charm and modern day functionality."

They meandered away from the fountain. On the edge of the piazza, they passed by a well that she was certain had seen its days of women gathering to fill their buckets. While waiting for their turn, she imagined they'd shared the happenings of the village—the historic form of gossiping around the water cooler. It was so easy to envision how things used to be. Something told Kayla that this village hadn't changed a whole lot over the years.

The sunshine warmed the back of her neck, but it was Angelo's arm beneath her fingertips that warmed her insides. She resisted the urge to smooth her fingers over his tanned skin. She was in serious danger of forgetting that he was her boss—the key to her future promotion.

As the bell towers rang out, Kayla stared at the cobblestone path that wound its way between the brick buildings. A number of the homes had flower boxes with red, yellow and purple blooms. There were also flowerpots by the various shaped doors painted in every imaginable color. In other places, ivy snaked its way along the bricks. This area was quite picturesque and made Kayla forget that she was in the center of the village.

A rustling sound had her glancing upward. She craned her neck, finding fresh laundry fluttering in the breeze. She couldn't help but smile. It was a lovely, inviting sight. But as much as she liked it, it was the man at her side that she found utterly captivating.

Angelo Amatucci might be icy cool in the office, but she'd found that once he thawed out, he was a warm, thoughtful man. Not that she was falling for his amazing good looks or his dark, mysterious eyes. Her priority was her career—the reason she'd left her home in Paradise. And she wasn't about to ruin her future by throwing herself at her boss.

She chanced a quick glance his way. But then again—

No. She pulled her thoughts up short. This wasn't getting her anywhere.

She was supposed to be touring Monte Calanetti to get ideas for the wedding pitch. If they were going to sell the royal couple on this location for the wedding, she needed to know as much about it as possible. And of what she'd seen so far, she loved it. This village and its occupants would give the wedding an old-world feel with lots of heart.

The villagers sent puzzled glances their way as though they should know who Angelo was but couldn't quite place his face. And then there were a few people that ventured to ask if he was indeed Angelo. When he confirmed their suspicions, he wasn't greeted with a simple hello or a mere handshake; instead, he was yanked into warm hugs. She could see the frown lines etched on his face, but to his credit he didn't complain. There were even a few tears of happiness from the older women who remembered him when he was just a young boy.

Angelo took her hand in his as though it were natural for them. Kayla liked feeling connected to him—feeling his long fingers wrapped around hers.

"I'm sorry about that." Angelo started walking again. "I didn't expect anyone to remember me."

"You must have spent a lot of time in the village as a kid."

"I did. It was my escape from the monotony of working around the vineyard." His jaw tensed and a muscle twitched.

"I take it that's why you let your brother have the run of Calanetti Vineyards?"

He nodded. "Nico is as passionate about the winery as I am with advertising. How about you? Do you have any brothers or sisters?"

Kayla shook her head. "My parents wanted more children, but that didn't work out. So with me being an only child, they heaped all of their hopes and dreams onto me."

"Hmm...sounds a bit daunting for one person."

"It is. That's why I had to leave Paradise."

"Somehow I just can't imagine life in Paradise could be such a hardship."

She shrugged. "It's great. The people are wonderful. It's the perfect place to raise kids."

"But you weren't ready for kids?"

The thought of taking on that sort of responsibility still overwhelmed her. "I have to figure out me first and accomplish some things on my own before I can be there 24/7 for others. And my parents, as much as I love them, didn't understand this."

"They wanted you to graduate high school and settle down."

She nodded. "They had it all planned out. I'd get married, have lots of kids and when the time came my husband and I would take over the family store."

"Doesn't sound so bad."

"No. It isn't. But I always had a dream of going to college and making a name for myself. I wanted to move to the city. I wanted to climb the corporate ladder. I wanted to—"

She bit off her last words. Heat rushed up her neck and warmed her face. She couldn't believe that she'd gotten so comfortable around Angelo that she'd just rambled on about her dreams. For a moment, she'd forgotten that she was talking to her boss.

Not good, Kayla. Not good at all.

She freed her hand from his. It was time she started acting like his employee, not his girlfriend. The time had come to get back to reality.

Angelo stopped walking and turned to her. "What aren't you saying? What do you want to do?"

"Um…nothing. It's no big deal. Let's keep going. I want to see the whole village." She turned to start walking again.

Angelo reached out, catching her arm in his firm grip. "Not so fast." She turned back, glancing up at his serious gaze. "Kayla, talk to me." His hand fell away from her arm. "I've told you all sorts of things that I don't normally share with people. I'd like to know what you were about to say and why you stopped. Surely by now you know that you can trust me."

Could she trust him? She supposed it depended on the subject. With her safety—most definitely. With her dreams—perhaps. With her heart— Wait, where had that come from?

"Kayla, what is it?"

She wasn't good at lying so that left her with the truth, but she didn't know how Angelo would take it. "I came to New York because I wanted…er… I want to be an ad executive."

His brows scrunched together. "And?"

She shrugged. "And that's it."

"That's what you didn't want to tell me?"

Her gaze moved to the cobblestone walkway. "It's just that I got comfortable around you and forgot to watch what I was saying."

"Oh, I see. Since I'm the boss, you feel like you have to screen what you say to me?"

She nodded.

"How about this? For the duration of this trip, I'm not

your boss. We're just business associates or how about friends? Would you like that?"

Her gaze met his and she found that he was being perfectly serious. "But what about when we return to New York?"

"Obviously things will have to change then, but for right now, I'd like to just be Angelo, not Mr. Amatucci. I'd forgotten what it's like just to be me again."

"And I like you calling me Kayla." Her gaze met his. Within his eyes she found a comforting warmth. "Consider yourself a friend."

He held out his hand to her. She accepted it. A shiver of excitement raced up her arm. They continued to stare deep into each other's eyes, even though it was totally unnecessary. She knew she should turn away. She knew that it was the proper thing to do with her boss. But as he'd just pointed out they were friends—for now.

His voice grew deeper. "I couldn't think of a better friend to have."

Her heart fluttered in her chest. What had just happened?

Angelo turned and tucked her hand back in the crook of his arm. Why did it suddenly feel as though their relationship had just taken a detour? How would they ever find their way back to just being boss and employee now?

Monte Calanetti is a diamond in the rough.

Had that thought really just crossed his mind?

Before he'd left the hotel a few hours ago, he'd envisioned Monte Calanetti as he had when he was a child— suffocating with its traditional ways and its resistance to growth and to modernization. But somehow, with Kayla by his side, he'd seen the village from a different perspective —he'd seen it through her very beautiful, very observant eyes. With her passion and romantic tendencies, she might just be the key he needed to pull this wedding pitch together. But did he dare ask for her help?

Sure, she had talent. He'd witnessed it firsthand with the Van Holsen account. But did he trust her with a project that was so important to his family? After all, his brother and sister, not to mention the entire village, were counting on him to represent them properly to the royal couple. But how was he supposed to do that when he kept hitting one brick wall after the other?

They walked some more before Kayla turned to him. "Thank you for showing me your hometown. I love it."

"Really?" He failed to keep the surprise from his voice.

"Of course I do. How could you not? Not only that but it has the most delicious aromas and it's so peaceful." Just then two scooters whizzed by them. "Okay, so it isn't totally peaceful."

"You'll get used to them. Scooters are very popular around here."

A couple more scooters zoomed down the road causing Kayla to step into the grass. She took a moment, taking in her surroundings. "Is this where you went to school?"

Angelo glanced at the back of the building off in the distance. The years started to slip away. "Yes, it is."

"I bet you were a handful back then."

As a young kid, he'd been the complete opposite of the way he is now. "I believe the word they used was *incorrigible*."

Now why had he gone and admitted that? Letting down his defenses and opening up about his past would only lead to confusion and misunderstandings, because sharing was what people did when they were getting serious. And that wasn't going to happen. He refused to let it happen. No matter how ripe her lips were for a kiss. Or how her smile sent his pulse racing.

"You probably picked on all of the girls and pulled on their ponytails."

He shook his head. "Not me. I didn't have time for girls, not until I was a bit older."

"And then I bet you broke a lot of hearts."

He wasn't sure about that, but there was one girl, Vera Carducci, and he'd had the biggest crush on her. He hadn't thought of her in years.

"See. I was right." Kayla smiled triumphantly.

"Actually, I was the one who got dumped."

"That's so hard to believe—"

"It's the truth." Why did he feel the need to make Kayla believe that his life was far from idyllic? What was it about her that had him letting down his guard? He had to do better. He couldn't let her get too close. It'd only cause them pain in the end.

Kayla walked over to a tree in the school yard. Her fingers traced over the numerous carvings from initials to hearts. "Was this the kissing tree?"

He nodded, suddenly wishing they were anywhere but here.

"I bet your initials are here…somewhere." Kayla's voice drew him back to the present. "Want to point me in the right direction?"

"Actually, they aren't here."

Her eyes opened wide. "Really? I thought for sure that you would have been popular with the girls."

He shrugged, recalling his fair share of girlfriends over the years. But he'd never kissed them here. Not a chance.

"Surely you stole a kiss or two." Her gaze needled him for answers.

"Not here."

"Why not?"

Oh, what did it matter if he told her? It wasn't as if there was any truth to the legend. It was all a bunch of wishful thinking.

"There's some silly legend attached to the tree that says whoever you kiss here will be your soul mate for life."

Kayla's green eyes widened with interest. "Really? And you don't believe it?"

He shook his head. "It's just an old wives' tale. There's nothing to it."

"And yet you've made a point not to kiss anyone here." She stepped closer to him. "If you don't believe in such superstitions, prove it."

His pulse kicked up a notch. Why was there a gleam in her eyes? Was she challenging him? Did she really expect him to kiss her here?

Instead of the idea scaring him off, it actually appealed to him. His gaze dipped to her lips. Kayla was the only woman he had ever contemplated kissing here—wait, when did that happen? He gave himself a mental jerk, but it didn't chase away the tempting thought.

What was it about Miss Kayla Hill that had him wishing there were such things as happily-ever-afters instead of roller-coaster relationships? He'd had so much turbulence in his life that he couldn't stand anymore. But Kayla was different. She had a calming presence.

This wasn't right. He should make it perfectly clear that he was no Romeo, but the way she kept staring at him, challenging him with her eyes, filled him with a warm sensation. He didn't want it to end. What would it hurt to let her remain caught up in her romantic imaginings?

Without thinking about the pros and cons of what he was about to do, he dipped his head and caught her lips with his own. Her lips were soft and pliant. He wrapped his arms around her slender waist and pulled her to him. She willingly followed his lead. Her soft curves pressed to him and a moan swelled deep in his throat. How in the world was he ever going to let her go? He'd never felt anything this intense for anyone—ever.

He wanted to convince himself that it was because she was forbidden fruit—his assistant. But he couldn't buy that. There was something so special about her that he couldn't diminish the connection with such a flimsy excuse. He knew as sure as he was standing there in a lip-lock with her that if their situation were different and he wasn't her boss that he'd still desire her with every fiber of his body.

His mouth moved over hers, slow at first. Yet when she met him move for move, the desire burning in him flared. Her mouth opened to him and she tasted sweet like the sun-ripened berries she'd sampled back in the village. He'd never tasted anything so delectable in his life. He doubted he'd ever experience a moment like this again.

There was something so special about Kayla. It was as though no matter what he did, she could see the real him. But could she see his scars, the ones that kept him from letting people get too close?

Her hands slid up over his shoulders and wrapped around the back of his neck. Her touch sent waves of excitement down his spine. He wanted her. He needed her. But his heart and mind were still guarded.

If he let her get any closer, she'd learn of his shame—of his ultimate pain—and then she'd pity him. Pity was not something that he could tolerate. He was Angelo Amatucci. A self-made man. He needed no one's sympathy. He needed no one.

Anxious to rebuild that wall between them, he braced his hands on her hips and pushed her back. Her eyes fluttered open and confusion showed in them.

"We should head back to the hotel. I... I have work to do."

Disappointment flashed in her eyes. "Oh. Okay."

He retraced their steps. "I have a conference call this afternoon."

Kayla fell in step beside him. He should say something. Explain somehow. But he didn't know what to say because that kiss left him utterly confused by the rush of emotions she'd evoked in him. Somehow, some way, she'd sneaked past his well-placed barriers and with each smile, each touch, she was getting to him. That wasn't part of his plan.

Unable to decide what to do about his undeniable attraction to his assistant, he turned his attention to something much less stressful—the village. For the first time, he saw its charms. Kayla had opened his eyes to everything he'd blocked out, from the amazing artisans, to the detailed architecture, to the warm and friendly people. He had so much to work with now. The pitch would be amazing if he could pull it all together, even though he was still unsure about the wedding aspect.

Still, Monte Calanetti had some of the best food in the world. It was sure to impress even the royal couple. And to be truthful, he was quite anxious to try Raffaele's restaurant—if the rumors were anything to go by, it was out of this world.

Although his desire to go to dinner had more to do with Kayla than the food. He hungered for more of her melodious laugh and her contagious smiles. Though he shouldn't, he'd come to really enjoy her company.

As productive as they were, working as a team, he was enjoying getting to know her on a personal level. After all, it wasn't as if this thing, whatever you wanted to call it, would carry over to New York. He'd make sure of it. But what would it hurt to enjoy the moment?

CHAPTER THIRTEEN

ANGELO SWIPED HIS key card and opened the suite door for Kayla. When she brushed past him, he noticed the softest scent of wildflowers. He inhaled deeply, enjoying the light fragrance as he followed her into the room, wishing he could hold on to her delicate scent just a little longer.

When she stopped short, he bumped into her. He grabbed her shoulders to steady her. She turned in his arms and gazed up at him with those big luminous green eyes. His heart pounded in his chest.

"Wasn't the afternoon wonderful?"

Was it his imagination or was her voice soft and sultry? And was she looking at him differently? Or was it that he wanted her so much that he was projecting his lusty thoughts upon her?

He swallowed down the lump in his throat. "Yes, it was a really nice day."

"Thank you so much for spending the day with me. I promise to pay you back." She stood up on her tiptoes and leaned forward.

She was going to repeat their kiss. His heart pounded. His brain told him that it shouldn't happen, but his body had other thoughts. He started to lean forward—

Buzz. Buzz. His phone vibrated in his pocket, breaking the spell.

He pulled back. After retrieving the phone from his pocket, he checked the screen. "It's the conference call. I have to take it. Can we talk later?"

He moved to his room to take the call in private. He actually welcomed the interruption. It gave him time to figure out how to handle this change of dynamics with Kayla.

The phone call dragged on much longer than he'd anticipated. When he finally disconnected the call, he found Kayla was still in the suite working on her laptop.

He cleared his throat and she glanced up, but her gaze didn't quite reach his. "Sorry about the interruption."

"No problem." Her voice didn't hold its normal lilt. She lifted her reading glasses and rested them on her head.

As much as he'd like to pretend that the kiss hadn't happened, he couldn't. It was already affecting their working relationship and that was not acceptable. "I need to apologize. That kiss...back at the tree, it shouldn't have happened. You must understand that it can't happen again."

"Is that what you really want?"

"Yes. No. I don't know." He raked his fingers through his hair. "Maybe I was wrong about this. Maybe it'd be better if you flew back to New York."

"What?" She jumped to her feet. Her heated gaze was most definitely meeting his now.

"This isn't going to work between us." He glanced away, knowing he'd created this problem. "We can't keep our hands off each other. How are we supposed to concentrate on all of the work we have to get done?"

She stepped up to him and poked him in the chest. "You're not firing me. I won't let you—"

"Wait. Who said anything about firing you?" He wrapped his hand around her finger, fighting off the urge to wrap his lips around it. "Certainly not me. You are very talented. Do you honestly think that I'd sack you over a kiss or two—kisses that I initiated?"

"Then what?" She pulled her finger from his hold as though she'd read his errant thought. "You don't think you can keep your hands to yourself around me?"

"Yes... I mean, no." He absolutely hated this feeling of being out of control—of his emotions or whatever you called it ruling over his common sense. "You confuse me."

"How so?" Her gaze narrowed in on him. When he didn't answer her, she persisted. "Tell me. I want to know."

He sighed. "It's nothing. Just forget I said anything."

"What is this really about? It has to be about more than just a kiss."

His gaze lifted and met hers head-on. How could she understand him so well? No other woman had ever seen the real him—they'd always been more interested in having a good time. But then again, he'd gone out of his way to hook up with women who didn't have serious, long-term plans where he was concerned.

His strong reaction to Kayla was due to a lot more than just the kiss. She made him feel things—want things—that he had no business feeling or wanting. And the way she'd moved him with that passionate kiss hadn't done anything to settle him. It had only made him want her all the more. What was up with that? He'd never desired a woman with every single fiber of his being. Until now.

Kayla stepped closer and lowered her voice. "Angelo, I think we've grown close enough on this trip that you can talk to me and know that it won't go any further. Tell me what's eating you up inside."

He knew what she was after—the secrets of his past. But was he ready for that? Did he have the courage to peel back those old wounds? Was he ready to deal with her reaction? Could he stand having her think less of him?

The answer was a resounding no.

Angelo inhaled a deep breath and blew it out. He wasn't prepared to open that door. It wasn't as if they were involved romantically. They didn't have a future, just the here and the now.

But there was something else...

He needed her—well...er...her help. He couldn't do this wedding pitch alone. The admission twisted his gut in a knot. He was not a man accustomed to reaching out to others.

He made a point of being the man handing out assign-
ments, making suggestions and overseeing operations. He
was never at a loss for how to accomplish things—especially an advertising pitch. This was supposed to be his
area of expertise—his specialty.

What was wrong with him? Why couldn't he come up
with a solid pitch? And what was Kayla going to think of
him when he made this request? Would she think less of
him?

Wanting to get it over with, he uttered, "I need your assistance."

"What?" Her brow creased. "Of course I'll help you.
That's what I'm here for." She took a seat on the couch.
"What do you need?"

His gaze met hers briefly, and then he glanced away.
"I... I'm having issues with this pitch. Weddings and romance aren't my thing." That much was the truth. He
avoided weddings like the plague—he always had a prior
business engagement. "I thought maybe you'd have some
experience with them."

"Well, um... I have a bit of experience." Her cheeks took
on a pasty shade of white.

"You don't look so good. I'll get you something to drink."

"You don't have to wait on me. I can get it."

She started to get up when he pressed a hand to her
shoulder. "I've got this."

He retrieved a bottle of water from the fridge and poured
it in a glass for her. This was his fault. He'd had her gal-
livanting all around Monte Calanetti in the sun. She must
have worn herself out.

He moved to her side and handed over the water. "Can
I get you anything else?"

She shook her head. "Thanks. This is fine."

He sat down beside her as she sipped at the water. "I'm
sorry if I pushed you too hard in the village. I should have
brought you back here sooner—"

"No, that's not it. The visit was perfect. I wouldn't have changed anything about it." She sent him a smile, but it didn't quite reach her eyes.

"I don't believe you. There's something bothering you." He stopped and thought about it. "And it started when I mentioned the wedding pitch. Do you feel that I'm expecting too much of you?"

"That's not it." She placed a hand on his knee. The warmth of her touch could be felt through his jeans. "I'm just a bit tired."

"Are you sure that's all it is? It doesn't have anything to do with your broken engagement?"

Her eyes widened. "That's been over for a long time. I've moved on."

Moved on? Surely she wasn't thinking those kisses—that they'd somehow lead to something. He swallowed hard and decided it was best to change topics. "Have you made many friends since you moved to New York?"

"I haven't had much time. But I made a few at the after-school program." She pressed her lips together and turned away.

He was missing something, but he had no idea what that might be. "What do you do at this after-school program?"

She shrugged. "It's no big deal. So what can I do to help you with the wedding pitch?"

"Wait. I'd like to hear more about this program. What do you do? And how do you have time?" It seemed as if she was always in the office working long hours without a complaint.

"I do what is necessary. It all depends on the day and how many volunteers show up. Sometimes I help with homework and do a bit of tutoring. Other times I play kickball or a board game."

"You do all of that on top of the overtime you put in at the office?"

"It's not that big of a deal." She toyed with the hem of her top. "I don't have anything waiting for me at home, so why not put my spare time to good use?"

"You shouldn't dismiss what you do. There are very few people in this world who are willing to go out of their way for others. It's impressive."

Her eyes widened. "You really think so?"

"I do. Why do you seem so surprised?"

"It's just that at the office you've banned employees from taking on charitable accounts."

"It has to be that way." He raked his fingers through his hair. "There are only so many hours in the workday. I write out enough checks each year to various organizations to make up for it."

Kayla nodded, but she certainly didn't seem impressed. Uneasiness churned in his gut. Maybe she would be more understanding if she knew the amount of those checks.

"I'm sure those organizations appreciate the donations."

Guilt settled over him. What was up with that? It wasn't as if he didn't do anything. He just couldn't afford the time to take on more accounts—especially for free. He was still working on growing Amatucci & Associates into the biggest and the best advertising firm. Speaking of which, he needed to get moving on this pitch. Time was running out before his trip to Halencia.

"I need to ask you something."

She reached for the glass of water. "Ask away. Then I need to go check my email. I'm waiting on some responses about the Van Holsen account."

He shook his head, thinking this was a bad idea. "Never mind. You have enough to deal with."

She arched a thin brow at him. "You can't back out now. You have me curious."

He just couldn't admit to her that he had absolutely no direction for the pitch. Three wasted days of jotting down ideas and then realizing that they were clichéd or just plain stupid—certainly nothing that he would present to the royal family.

"If it doesn't bother you—you know, because of your broken engagement—I wanted to ask you some wedding questions."

She reached out and squeezed his hand. "I appreciate you watching out for my feelings but talking about weddings won't reduce me to tears. I promise. Let's get started."

His gaze met hers and his breath caught in his throat. He was going to have to be really careful around her or he just might be tempted to start something that neither of them was ready for. And once he got something started with her, he wasn't sure he'd ever be able to end it when reality crashed in around them.

CHAPTER FOURTEEN

THIS IS IT!

At last, it was her big break.

Kayla grinned as she sat by the pool the next day. She could hardly believe that at last her plans were all coming together. If only she could keep her attraction to Angelo under wraps. Was that even possible at this point?

Who'd have thought that the wish she'd made at the fountain would actually come true?

Angelo had kissed her—again.

Her eyelids drifted closed as her thoughts spiraled back to their amazing day beneath the Tuscany sun. The day couldn't have gone any better. She'd always treasure it. And then there had been that mind-blowing, toe-curling kiss—

"And what has you staring off into space with a smile on your face?"

Kayla glanced up to find Angelo gazing at her. "Um… nothing. I… I mean I was thinking about the wedding."

"How about the Van Holsen account? We don't want to forget about it."

"Of course not. I've sent out the new concepts to the art department."

"Good." He took a seat next to her. "You know if you're having problems you can talk to me?"

Was he referring to personal problems? Or business ones? Since they'd arrived in Italy the lines had blurred so much that she wasn't sure. But she decided that it was best for her career to take his comment as a purely professional one.

"I understand." She smoothed her hands down over her white capris. "And so far the accounts are all moving along.

I should have some drafts back from the art department this afternoon to run by you."

"Sounds good. Can I see what you've come up with so far for the royal wedding?"

She pushed her notebook over to him. "Go ahead."

The seconds slowly passed as his gaze moved down over the first page. "But this is all about Monte Calanetti." He shoved aside the pages. "There's nothing here about the wedding itself. Nothing sentimental or romantic."

Oh, boy.

This was not the start she'd imagined. She swallowed a lump in her throat. To be honest, she wasn't ready to present her ideas to him. They were only partial thoughts— snippets of this and that.

She'd have to think fast on her feet if she wanted him to keep her on this account, because she wasn't about to let this opportunity slip through her fingers. She leveled her shoulders and tilted her chin up, meeting his frown. "I think the main focus should be all about the location."

"You do?"

She nodded. "The royal couple have already been taken by the village's charm." Kayla lowered her voice and added, "I was taken by it, too. It'd be the perfect backdrop for a wedding. And that's the part I think we should exploit."

Angelo's eyes widened and he was quiet for a moment as though considering her words. "What issues do you have with basing the pitch on the wedding itself? You know with all of the pomp and circumstance. We could even throw in a horse-drawn carriage for good measure."

Kayla smiled, loving the idea of six white horses leading a shiny white carriage with gold trim. And then her imagination took a wild turn and there was Angelo next to her in the carriage. Her insides quivered at the thought. Then, realizing that she was getting off point, she gave herself a mental jerk.

"We don't know anything about what the bride wants for the actual ceremony. But we need to show them that no matter whether it is a big, splashy affair, which seems most reasonable considering it's a royal wedding, or whether they want something smaller and more intimate, that Monte Calanetti can be quite accommodating."

Angelo leaned back and crossed his arms as he quietly stared at her. He was taking her suggestions seriously. She inwardly cheered. Not about to lose her momentum, she continued. "No matter what the size of the ceremony, we need to show them that we are willing to work with the bride. We need to show them that the whole community will come together to make it a day that neither of them will ever forget."

"So you think our approach should be two-pronged, showing the village both as intimate and accommodating."

Kayla nodded. "The tour you gave me was a great start. But if we are going to sell the royals on the virtues of this village, I think we need to dig deeper."

Angelo nodded. "Sounds reasonable. What do you have in mind?"

Before she could continue, her phone vibrated on the table. She'd turned off the ringer, not wanting to bother anyone else who was around the pool.

"Do you need to get that?" Angelo's gaze moved from her to the phone.

"Um...no."

Angelo cocked a brow. "It could be the office."

"I already checked my voice mail and sorted everything that needs attention." She wanted to get back to their conversation, but he kept glancing at her phone. Knowing he wasn't going to let up on this subject until he found out why she was so hesitant to answer, she grabbed her phone and checked the ID. Just as she'd suspected, the call was from the States but it wasn't the office—it was Pam, the woman handling the fund-raiser while Kayla was in Italy.

"It's nothing urgent." Kayla would deal with it later.

"Are you sure?"

"I am." This wasn't Pam's first call of the day nor would it likely be her last.

Why was Angelo looking at her that way? It was as though he could see that she was holding something back. And the last thing Kayla needed was for him not to trust her. Because this royal wedding was the opportunity of a lifetime. She planned to grasp it with both hands and hold on tight. Having Angelo make her an official part of this pitch would be the validation she needed to show her parents that she'd made the right decision with her life. At last, they'd be proud of her and her choices.

"Okay." He waved away the phone and grabbed for her notebook again. "You need to add more detail to these notes."

"I will, but I was thinking we need to visit each of the establishments in the village again. I could write up very specific notes about their specialties—things that will be hard to find elsewhere—items that the village is especially proud of."

His eyes lit up. "And I know exactly where we'll start."

"You do?" She smiled, knowing he liked her ideas. "Where?"

"Mancini's. You did bring something pretty, formal— Oh, you know what I mean."

"A little black dress?"

"Yes, that will do nicely. We have reservations at seven. Consider it a research expedition during which I want to hear more of your thoughts."

Her mounting excitement skidded to a halt upon his assurance that this evening would be all about business. She didn't know why she should let it bother her. This is what she wanted—for things to return to a business relationship. Wasn't it?

* * *

Time flew by far too fast.

A week had passed since their dinner at Mancini's. Angelo had been quite impressed with the service and most especially the food. What Raffaele was doing spending his time here in the countryside was beyond Angelo. The man was a magician in the kitchen. He could head up any restaurant that he set his sights on from Rome to New York. Although, it was lucky for Angelo, because Mancini's award-winning menu was going to be the centerpiece of the pitch.

Angelo stood in the middle of the hotel suite. He really liked what he saw. His gaze zeroed in on Kayla. They'd had a couple of tables brought in. The room had been rearranged so that the area loosely resembled an office more than a relaxing, posh hotel room. And it seemed to be helping them to stay on track.

Feeling the pressure to get this right, Angelo had relented and had Kayla pass along some of their other accounts to his top ad executive. Their attention needed to be centered on the wedding, especially since he'd already lost time spinning his wheels. One of the accounts they had retained was Victoria Van Holsen's account. The woman simply wouldn't deal with anyone but himself or Kayla. Victoria, who was quite particular about who she dealt with, had surprisingly taken to Kayla's sunny disposition. It seemed no one was immune to Kayla's charms—him included.

There was so much more to Kayla than he'd given her credit for when he'd hired her as his temporary assistant. Sure, her résumé had been excellent and her supervisors had nothing but glowing reports about her. Still, he was so busy rushing from meeting to meeting, cutting a new deal and approving the latest cutting-edge promotion that he never had time to notice the girl behind the black-rimmed glasses and the nondescript business suits.

While in Italy, he'd witnessed firsthand her passion for her work. She invigorated him to work harder and dig deeper for fresh ideas to top her own, which was nearly impossible as she came up with ideas for the wedding that never would have crossed his mind. To say she was a hard worker was an understatement. She was amazing and it wasn't just her work ethic that fascinated him.

Her smile lit up his world like the golden rays of the morning sun. And when he would lean over her shoulder, he'd get a whiff of her sweet, intoxicating scent. It conjured up the image of a field of wildflowers in his mind and always tempted him to lean in closer for a deeper whiff.

Then there were times like now, when she was concentrating so hard that her green eyes grew darker. She lifted her hand and twirled a long red curl around her finger. He noticed that she did this when she was unsure of something. He wondered what was troubling her now.

He moved closer. "Need some help?"

She glanced up with a wide-eyed stare as though she'd been totally lost in her thoughts. "Um…what?"

This wasn't the first time she'd been so lost in her thoughts that she hadn't heard him. "I said, would you like some help?"

"Sure. I was contemplating the piazza. I'm thinking it should play a prominent part in the wedding processional."

Her words sparked his own imagination. They made a great couple…um, team. He couldn't remember the last time he'd felt this invigorated. "How about having a horse-drawn carriage circle the fountain, giving the villagers a chance to cheer on the future queen?"

"I don't know. The bride will be a bundle of nerves. I don't know if she'll want to spend the time waving at people—"

"Sure she will."

Kayla sent him a doubtful look. "What would you know about weddings?"

"Nothing." His jaw tightened. And he planned to keep it that way. "You're forgetting one important thing."

"And what's that?"

"The villagers are the part that makes the village special."

A smile eased the worry lines on her face. "I'm glad you were paying attention while on our tour. And if the bride is willing, I think the villagers should play a prominent role in the festivities."

"And along the route there could be large royal flags waving in the breeze—"

"No. That's too impersonal." Her eyes sparkled. "What if we hand out small complimentary flags to the onlookers to welcome the newest member of the royal family?"

Angelo paused as he considered the idea. "I like it. It'll be a sea of color."

"I also think the chapel should be included in the pitch." Before he could utter a word, she rushed on. "The place is so beautiful. Sure it needs some work, but it has such a romantic feel to it. Just imagine it filled with roses— No, make that lilies. And the glow of the candles would add to the magic. Can't you just imagine it all?"

"No." He didn't believe in magic or romance. They were just fanciful thoughts. "I can't imagine anyone wanting to get married in such a dump—"

"It's not a dump!"

He ignored her outburst. "Besides, you're forgetting that I talked to the new owner and she wants nothing to do with the wedding."

"And that's it...you're just giving up? She could change her mind."

What was Kayla getting so worked up for? He wasn't making up these problems. "The chapel is crumbling. We are not putting it in the pitch. The royal couple would laugh us out of the room if we presented it—"

"They would not." Her words were rushed and loud. "They'd love its charm."

His muscles tensed. He hated conflict. "We're not using it!"

Her fine brows drew together as she crossed her arms. "You're making a mistake!"

He wasn't used to people challenging his decisions and they certainly didn't raise their voice to him. This argument was ending now. "This is my company—my decision! We're not including the chapel." When she went to speak, he added, "End of story."

She huffed but said nothing more.

For a while, they worked in an uncomfortable silence. He kept waiting for Kayla to rehash their disagreement, but she surprised him and let it go. He didn't know how much time had passed when they started to communicate like normal again.

Angelo rubbed his jaw. "Perhaps our best option is to take all of these photos and do a workup of each setting. We can have sketches made up of how each wedding scenario would work. Nothing sells better than letting the client see it with their own eyes. I'll have the art department start on it right away. They'll be on solid overtime until our meeting with the happy couple."

"You never said— Where is the meeting? At Nico's villa?"

"No. The meeting is in Halencia. It's an island not far from here."

"Oh, how exciting. You must be nervous to be meeting a real prince and his bride."

"Me? What about you?"

"What about me?"

"You're part of this team. You'll be going, too. I hope you have something in your suitcase suitable for a royal meeting. If not, perhaps you can find an outfit or two in the village."

Kayla's mouth gaped open and he couldn't help but chuckle. She looked absolutely stunned. Surely she didn't think that he'd put her to all of this work and then leave her behind. He was never one to take credit for another person's work, and he wasn't about to start now. Kayla deserved this honor.

But he sensed something else was on her mind. He could see the subtle worry lines marring her beautiful complexion when she didn't think he was looking. He had no doubt she was still smarting over his unilateral decision to scrap the chapel proposal. She had to accept that he knew what he was doing.

Just then a cell phone vibrated, rattling against the tabletop. Not sure whose phone it was, Angelo headed for the table in time to witness Kayla grabbing her phone and turning it off without bothering to take the call. She'd been doing it a lot lately.

He cleared his throat. "You know, just because I'm here doesn't mean you can't take a phone call from home now and then."

She shook her head. "It…it was nothing."

"Are you sure about that? I get the distinct feeling that the call was definitely something."

"I told you it's nothing important." Her voice rose with each syllable. "Why are you making such a big deal of it?"

"I just thought it might be important."

Her gaze didn't meet his. Her voice was heated and her words were rushed. "It's nothing for you to worry about. Besides, we have work to do."

He'd never witnessed Kayla losing her composure— ever. What was wrong with her? And why wouldn't she open up to him?

"Kayla, if you need a break—"

"I don't." She ran her fingers through her long red curls before twisting the strands around her fingertip. "Can we get back to work?"

His jaw tightened. These heated exchanges reminded him of his parents, and not in a good way. Kayla had just reinforced his determination to remain single. He wanted absolutely nothing to do with a turbulent relationship.

"Work sounds like a good idea." He turned to his laptop. Before he could even type in his password, Kayla softly called out his name. In fact, her voice was so soft that he was sure he'd imagined it. He glanced over his shoulder to find her standing next to him.

Her gaze was downcast and her fingers were laced together. "I'm sorry for snapping. I didn't mean to grouch at you. I... I—"

Before she could go any further, he uttered, "It's okay. We're both under a lot of pressure, working night and day to get this pitch perfected."

Her eyes widened in surprise. "Thanks for understanding. It won't happen again."

He didn't doubt that she meant it, but he was a realist and knew that blowups happened even in the best of relationships. So where did they go from here?

When he didn't immediately say anything, she added, "The phone call was a friend. I'll deal with it later."

Not about to repeat their earlier argument, he let her comment slide. "Then let's get back to work. We have the menu to work into the layout."

He didn't miss the way she played with her hair—the telltale sign she was nervous. Oh, that call was definitely something important. All of his suspicions were now confirmed. So what could be so important that it had her jumping for the phone, and yet she refused to take the call in front of him? A boyfriend? But she'd already stated categorically that she didn't have one, and he believed her.

So what had her nervous and fidgeting with her hair? What didn't she want him to know? And why was he more concerned about her blasted phone calls and mysterious ways than he was about this presentation that was quickly approaching?

He really needed to get his head in this game or Monte Calanetti would lose the pitch before they even gave their presentation in Halencia. But with Kayla so close by it was difficult at times to remember that she was here to work and not to fulfill his growing fantasies.

Moonbeams danced upon the window sheers as Kayla leaned back in her chair. They'd been working on this pitch night and day, trying to make it beyond amazing. A yawn passed her lips. Not even coffee was helping her at this point.

"You should call it a night." Angelo stared at her over the top of his laptop. "I've got this."

Not about to let him think she wasn't as dedicated to this project as he was, she said, "If you're staying up, so am I."

He sent her an I-don't-believe-you're-so-stubborn look. "If you insist—"

"I do." She crossed her arms. Even that movement took a lot of effort.

He arched a brow, but he didn't argue. "How about we take a break? I'm starved."

"Sounds good to me, but I don't think there's any room service at this hour."

"Who needs room service? There's still half of a pizza in the fridge."

"Oh. I forgot."

In no time, Angelo warmed them each a couple of slices in the microwave in their kitchenette. After handing her a plate, he moved to the couch. "Sorry, I can't provide you anything else."

"This is plenty. It reminds me of my college days. Leftover pizza for breakfast was a common staple in the dorms."

Angelo leaned back, kicked off his loafers and propped his feet up on the coffee table. There was no longer any boss/employee awkwardness between them. Being closed up in a hotel suite, no matter how fancy, left no room for cool distances. In fact, they'd shared some passionate disagreements over the pitch, which only led them to better, outside-the-box ideas. But it was far too late for any passionate conversations—at least the professional ones.

"I'm surprised your parents let you go to college." Angelo's voice roused her from her exhaustion-induced fantasy.

"Why?"

"Because they had your life planned out to be a wife, to be a mom and to take over the family business. Why spend the money and time on an advanced degree if you weren't going to use it?"

The fact that Angelo Amatucci, star of Madison Avenue, was truly interested in her life sent her heart fluttering. "It was hard for them to object when I won an academic scholarship. Plus, they knew I had my heart set on earning a degree. My guess is they thought I'd go, have fun with my friends for a few years and eventually realize my place was with them in Paradise." Her gaze met his. "Didn't your parents expect you to return to Italy after you graduated college?"

He glanced away as he tossed his plate of half-eaten pizza onto the table. "My family is quite different from yours. Their expectations weren't the same."

"I have a hard time believing that, after seeing how much your brother and sister miss you. Maybe you can slow down and fly here more often."

"I don't know." He rubbed the back of his neck. "I'd have to find someone to help with the special accounts— someone the clients would trust."

"Do you have anyone in mind?"

His steady gaze met hers, making her stomach quiver.

"I have an idea or two. And how about you? Is Amatucci & Associates just a stepping-stone for you? Do you have other plans for your future?"

"I'm exactly where I want to be."

His gaze dipped to her lips and then back to her eyes. "That's good to know. I want you here, too." He glanced away. "I mean at the company. You've become really important to me." He cleared his throat. "To the company. You know, it's really late. Let's call it a night and pick up where we left off tomorrow. You know, with the pitch."

Kayla sat there quietly as her normally calm, composed boss tripped and fell over his words. She wanted to tell him to relax because she liked him, too—a lot. The words teetered on the tip of her tongue when he jumped to his feet and moved across the room to shut down his computer.

Disappointment settled in her chest. Shouting her feelings across the room just didn't seem right, nor did she have the guts to do it. And by the rigid line of his shoulders, he wasn't ready to hear the words. She had to accept that the fleeting moment had passed—if it had truly been there at all.

She tried to tell herself that it was for the best. Taking a risk on revealing her feelings to Angelo was putting all of her hopes and dreams on the line, but she wasn't much of a gambler. She liked sure bets. At the moment, the odds were really good that she'd gain a promotion if they pulled off this royal pitch. And that's what she needed to focus on—not on the way Angelo's intense gaze could make her stomach do a series of somersaults.

CHAPTER FIFTEEN

THIS COULDN'T BE HAPPENING.

Two days before Angelo's private jet was scheduled to sweep them off to the Mediterranean island of Halencia, Kayla received yet another phone call from Pam. However with Angelo hovering so close by and forever checking over her shoulder to see the progress she was making with their pitch, she couldn't answer the call. No way. No how.

Kayla sent the call to voice mail before returning to the email she was composing. But a thought had been nagging at her that perhaps after their talk Angelo might have changed his stance on the company doing some charity work. There were so many worthy causes out there that really could use the power of Amatucci & Associates to make a difference. And she wasn't just thinking of her beloved after-school program.

There were countless other organizations that were worthy of a helping hand. Perhaps it was worth a shot. What was the worst that could happen? He would tell her to drop the subject and get back to work? Because surely at this point he wouldn't fire her, would he?

"You've done a really good job with this pitch." And she meant it. Angelo was very talented and creative. If he weren't, he wouldn't be at the top of his game. "It might be a nice idea if you'd considered implementing a charity program at the office. I know a lot of people would be willing to help—"

"No."

Just a one-word answer? Really? Kayla tried to accept it as his final word, but she was having problems swallowing such a quick dismissal. Why did he have to be so close-minded? Was he that worried about his bottom line?

She stared at him. How was it possible that the same man who had escorted her around the village and had shared some of his childhood memories with her could be opposed to helping charities? There had to be something more to his decision.

Maybe if she understood, she could change his mind—make him see that charities needed his special kind of help. Not everyone was gifted in getting the word out in so many different capacities from tweeting to commercials and radio spots. Not to mention that Angelo had an army of contacts in Hollywood willing to help him when needed.

"Why are you so opposed to the idea of helping out charity organizations?"

"You just aren't going to let this go, are you?"

She shook her head. How could she be honest with him about what had her distracted when she knew that it would put her job in jeopardy? Maybe if she understood his reasons, it would bridge the divide. "Explain it to me."

He raked his fingers through his hair and pulled out a chair next to her. "When I came to the States, I was alone. I didn't know anyone. And I'll admit that it wasn't easy and there were a few scary moments."

This certainly wasn't the explanation that she was expecting, but she liked that he was opening up to her, little by little. "I can't even imagine what that must have been like for you. I mean, I moved to New York City and I didn't know a soul here, but I was only a car ride away from my family. You practically moved halfway around the world."

"I didn't have a choice." His lips pressed together into a firm line as though stopping what was about to come out of his mouth.

"What do you mean?"

"Nothing. It's just that when I was in school, I got caught up in the football team and my dream of graduating college started to fade into the rearview mirror. Now granted, that isn't the same as working for a charitable organization, but

I learned a valuable lesson—if I wanted to be the best at whatever I decided to do, I had to commit myself 100 percent. I couldn't let myself get distracted."

Was that happening to her with the fund-raiser? Was she spreading herself too thin? Was she trying to cover too many bases?

She didn't want to accept that she was setting herself up to fail. He had to be wrong. "Couldn't you have done both in moderation?"

"You're not understanding me—I had to succeed—I had to be the best to get anywhere in New York City. Competition is fierce and if I failed, I couldn't go home."

"Sure you could have—"

"You don't know what you're talking about." His intense stare met hers, warning her not to delve further into that subject. "The point is that I know what happens when people become distracted for any reason—no matter how good the cause. They lose their focus. Their ambition dwindles. And that can't happen to Amatucci & Associates. I hate to say it, but it's a cutthroat business. If we lose our edge, the competitors will swoop in and steal away our clients."

Between the lines she read, if she lost her edge—if she didn't give 100 percent—she'd lose her dream. She'd fail and return to Paradise with her tail between her legs. Her stomach twisted into a queasy knot.

She clasped her hands together. Knowing all of this, there was no way she was about to confess to Angelo that she was spending every free moment handling a fund-raiser that seemed to hit one snag after the next. He'd think she wasn't dedicated to her career—that couldn't be further from the truth.

She cleared the lump from the back of her throat. "And that's why you compromise and write generous checks each year to the various organizations?"

He nodded. "I didn't say I wasn't sympathetic. But the office policy stands. End of discussion."

She was more than happy to change subjects, and he'd touched upon one that she was most curious about. "And your parents—"

"Are not part of this discussion."

They might not be, but that didn't mean that she didn't understand a whole lot more about them now. At last, the pieces of his family life started to fall into place. She had wondered why they weren't at the villa to greet Angelo. Nor were they around to help their daughter cope with her unplanned pregnancy. There was definitely discord, and it must run quite deep if Angelo still wasn't ready to broach the subject.

Something told her that he'd closed himself off from that part of his life and focused on his business not so much because he was worried about losing focus, but rather because he found his business safe. It lacked the ability to wound him the way family could do with just a word or a look. That was why he was so cold and professional most of the time. It was his shield.

That was no way to live. There was so much more in life to experience. And she desperately wanted to show him that…and so much more.

But how was she to help him if he wasn't willing to open up?

"Help! I don't know what to do. Everything is ruined."

Kayla's heart lurched at the sound of Pam's panicked voice. She gripped the phone tightly and reminded herself that Pam tended to overreact. Things with the ICL fundraiser had been going pretty well. Ticket sales were still lagging but the radio spots were helping. What could be wrong now?

"Pam, slow down."

"But we don't have time."

"Take a deep breath. It can't be as bad as you're thinking."

"No, it could be worse." Pam sniffled.

Okay. What had happened this time? Did Pam lose another file on her computer? Or misplace the phone number for the manager of the headline band? Pam did blow things out of proportion.

"Pam, pull yourself together and tell me what happened." While Kayla hoped for the best, she steeled herself for a catastrophe.

"They canceled."

Kayla sat up straight, knocking her empty water glass over. Surely she hadn't heard correctly. "Who canceled?"

"The band." Pam started to cry again.

Impossible. "The band quit?"

"Yes! What are you going to do?" She hiccupped.

"But they can't just quit. We have an agreement—a contract."

"That…that's what I said. They said there was a clause or some sort of thing in there that let them back out."

Kayla rubbed her forehead. This couldn't be happening. What was she supposed to do about it all the way in Italy?

"I… I just can't do this anymore. Everyone is yelling at me." The sniffles echoed across the Atlantic. "I can't."

Oh, no. She couldn't have Pam backing out on her, too. "Calm down." Kayla's hands grew clammy as she tightened her hold on the phone. "You can't quit. The kids are counting on us. We can't let them down."

"But what are you going to do? You have to fix this. I can't."

Kayla wanted to yell that she didn't know but that the whining wasn't helping anyone. "I don't know yet. What did the band say was the problem?"

"They got a contract with some big band to be the opening act on a cross-country tour. They leave before the concert."

It'd certainly be hard to compete with a national tour.

Most likely this was the band's big break and Kayla's heart sank, knowing that wild horses couldn't hold them back. And to be honest, she couldn't blame them. This was what they'd been working toward for so long now. But none of that helped her or the fund-raiser.

Kayla struggled to speak calmly. "Just sit tight. I'll think of something."

"You know of another band that can fill in at the last minute?"

She didn't have a clue where to find a replacement. In fact, she'd totally lucked into that first band. A friend of a friend knew the band manager, who liked the idea of free publicity. Where in the world would she locate another band?

"I need time to think." Kayla said, feeling as though the world was crumbling around her.

"But what do I tell people?"

"Tell them that we'll have an announcement soon."

Kayla ended the call. Her mind was spinning. She didn't know how she was going to save the event. The enormity of the situation was only beginning to settle in. With no headline act, there was no point. The tickets would have to be refunded. The Inner City League after-school program would cease to exist.

All of those at-risk kids would be turned away.

No! She refused to fail them. Visions of Gina's smiling face, Patrick's pout when she didn't have time to throw the ball with him and Lilly's anxious look as she'd handed Kayla a new drawing filled her mind. And there were so many more faces—all counting on her to come through for them.

Something splashed her hand. Kayla glanced down to see a tear streak down the back of her hand. She lifted her fingers and touched her cheek, finding it damp. At that moment, she heard the door to the suite open. She took a deep calming breath and dashed the back of her hands across her cheeks.

"I'm back." Angelo's deep voice echoed through the large room. "Did I miss anything?"

Talk about a loaded question. "Um…no." She struggled to sound normal as she kept her back to him. She blinked repeatedly and resisted the urge to fan her overheated face. "Nothing much happened around here."

"You were right about approaching my brother." He paused. "Kayla?"

"Yes."

"Is there a reason I'm talking to the back of your head?"

She shook her head. "I'm just finishing up an email."

"Do you want to hear this?"

"Um…yes. Of course. I can do two things at once."

There was an extended pause as though he was deciding if she were truly interested or not. "Well, I asked Nico for permission to offer up his vineyard as one of the sites for the wedding. The photographer from the village is stopping by tomorrow to take some professional photos."

"I'm glad the meeting went smoothly between you and your brother. What about the new owner of the neighboring vineyard? What did you say her name was?"

"Louisa something or other." He rubbed the back of his neck. "I talked to her about using her vineyard, since it's larger than Nico's place, but she was adamant that she wants absolutely nothing to do with the wedding."

"Really? How odd."

"Not as odd as this."

"What do you mean?" Kayla hated putting on this pretense, but she knew that he would never abide her splitting her work hours between the royal wedding and a charity event. He'd already made that abundantly clear.

"You won't face me and there's something off with your voice." His approaching footsteps had her body tensing. He knelt down next to her. He placed a finger beneath her chin and turned her face to his. "Now tell me, what's got you upset?"

His voice was so soft and comforting. All she wanted to do in that moment was lean into his arms and rest her face in the crook of his neck. She wanted to feel the comfort and security of his strong arms holding her close. She wanted him to tell her that everything would be all right— that they would work together to find a solution.

But none of that could or would happen. Angelo would never understand how she'd knowingly gone behind his back to work on this fund-raiser instead of focusing solely on the royal wedding. She'd never be able to justify her actions to his satisfaction.

"I'm fine." Her gaze didn't meet his.

"You're not fine. Not by a long shot." As though he'd been privy to her thoughts, he reached out and pulled her to him.

She shouldn't do this. It wasn't right. But her body had other thoughts and willingly followed his lead. Her cheek pressed against the firmness of his shoulder and she inhaled the spicy scent of his cologne mingled with his male scent. It was quite intoxicating.

Her eyes drifted closed and for a moment she let go of everything. The silent tears streamed down her cheeks. She took comfort in the way Angelo's hands rubbed her back. It wove a spell over her and relaxed muscles that she hadn't realized were stiff.

"I'm sorry for working you too hard."

She dashed her fingers over her cheeks and pulled back. "You aren't making me work this hard—I want to do it. I want to do everything to make our pitch stand out."

He ran his hands up her arms, sending goose bumps racing down her skin. "But not to the point where you've worn yourself to a frazzle. Look at you. You've gotten yourself all worked up."

She shook her head. No matter how much she wanted

to open up to him, she couldn't. They only had two days until they had to catch a plane to Halencia, and they still didn't have a completed pitch. And what they had didn't sparkle. And it didn't scream "pick me." There was something missing, but she just couldn't put her finger on it. And now, add to it the problem with the fund-raiser and she was at a total loss.

"Kayla, if you won't talk to me, how can I help?"

Her gaze met his, and she saw the worry reflected in his eyes. "You can't."

"Why don't you give me a chance?"

He just wasn't going to let this go. His eyes begged her to open up to him—to trust him. But she couldn't give up her dream of being the sort of person that Angelo Amatucci would want as an ad executive—she'd given up everything to follow this dream. She couldn't return to Paradise and face her parents as a failure.

"The truth is I... I have a headache." And that wasn't a lie. The stress of everything had her temples pounding.

He studied her for a moment as though weighing her words. "Did you take anything for it?"

"I was about to, but I hadn't made it there yet."

Angelo nodded as though he knew what needed to be done. "Go lie down on the couch and rest—"

"But I have stuff that needs done—"

"Later. Right now, you're going to rest. I'll get some medication for you."

His thoughtfulness only made her feel worse—about everything—most especially that she couldn't open up to him. She was certain that he would have some amazing suggestion that would save the fund-raiser, but she just couldn't risk everything she'd worked for. Instead, she'd have to pray for a miracle.

CHAPTER SIXTEEN

HE WAS AS ready as he would ever be.

Angelo kept telling himself that, hoping it would sink in.

As the royal limo ushered them through the streets of Halencia toward the palace, Angelo stared out the window. Mounting tension over this meeting had his body stiff. This sort of reaction was unfamiliar to him. Usually he was calm, cool and collected. He was the expert when it came to marketing. But ever since he'd let his guard down around Kayla, he'd lost that cool aloofness that he counted on when doing business.

She'd gotten past his defenses and had him connecting with his emotions. He just hoped he hadn't lost his edge—the confidence needed to execute a pitch and sell the buyer on his—er—their ideas.

The flight had been a short one as Halencia was just a small island nation not far off the coast of Italy. Angelo had noticed how Kayla kept to herself, working on her computer. He had no idea what she'd been working on because at that point the pitch had been locked in. They had the talking points nailed down and the graphics were in order. He'd made sure to include what he considered the key element—a sample menu from Raffaelle's restaurant. All combined, he hoped this pitch would clinch the royal couple's interest.

Kayla had even insisted on bringing along some of the baked goods for the royal couple to sample. They were fresh baked that morning and delivered to their hotel suite. He'd tried to taste them, but Kayla had smacked his hand away with a warning glance. Everyone in Monte Calanetti was excited and more than willing to do their part to help.

But Kayla had him worried. She'd been so quiet on the flight here. And now as she leaned against the door of the limo with her face to the window, the bubbly woman who toured Monte Calanetti was gone. He didn't recognize this new person.

He cleared his throat. "Are you feeling all right?"

Kayla turned to him, the dark circles under her eyes were pronounced. His gut tightened.

She smiled, but her lips barely lifted at the corners. "Sure. I'm fine."

He wasn't going to argue the point when it was obvious that she was anything but fine. "You did an excellent job preparing the pitch."

She shrugged. "I don't know. I guess it all depends on what the royal couple says."

He shook his head. "It doesn't matter whether they chose Monte Calanetti or not for the wedding, I know for a fact that you went above and beyond for this project." He hated how his praise seemed to barely faze her. She'd worn herself out and he'd been so busy trying to tie up all of the loose ends for this pitch that he'd failed to notice.

On the flight to Halencia, he'd been mulling over how to recognize Kayla's tremendous effort. He decided to share part of it with her now. "And when we get back to New York, you'll be rewarded for your accomplishments not only with the royal pitch but also with the success of the Van Holsen account."

Her eyes widened. "Really? I… I mean thank you."

Before she could say more, her phone buzzed. She swiped her finger over the screen and frowned. Her fingers moved rapidly over the touch screen as her frown deepened.

Even Angelo had his limits. Work could wait. They were almost at the palace and having her upset was not going to be a good way to start their meeting with the royal couple. He reached out and snagged her phone from her.

She glanced up and her mouth gaped open. Then her lips pressed together into a firm line and her gaze narrowed.

She held out her hand. "It's important."

"It can wait."

"No, it can't."

The car slowed as they eased through the gates leading up the drive to the palace. "We're here. Forget the rest of the world and enjoy this adventure. It isn't every day you get a royal invitation to a palace."

Kayla turned to the window as they wound their way up the paved drive lined with statues and greenery. It was very prestigious and yet it wasn't overly pretentious. In fact, he found it quite a fitting reflection of their nobility. He just hoped that they'd find the prince and his bride to have the same unassuming demeanor.

When the palace came into view, Angelo was taken by surprise at the enormity of it. The palace stood three stories high and appeared to be a large square with towers at each corner. The outside was painted a sunny yellow while the numerous windows were outlined in white. Grand, sweeping stairs led the way to a large patio area with two enormous doors in the background that granted access to the palace.

There weren't that many things in life that still took Angelo's breath away, but he had to admit that this palace was an amazing piece of architecture. And with the abundance of greenery and bright flowers, it was definitely like stepping into paradise. He couldn't even imagine what it must be like calling this place home.

The car swung up the drive and stopped right in front of the palace. To one side was a garden with a fountain in the center. It was quite inviting. He could easily imagine taking Kayla for a stroll through it after dinner as the setting sun cast a watermelon hue over the sky. They'd stop to admire a flower and she'd turn to him. The breeze would rush through her hair as her gaze would meet his. Then his attention would move to her lips. No words would be necessary as they'd lean into each other's arms.

"Angelo, this is amazing."

Kayla's voice jerked him from his daydream, which was in fact amazing. "Um…yes. This is quite beautiful."

"Is this your first visit?"

"It is. I've never done business in this part of the world before." Though he had done business in a great many other countries.

As beautiful as the grounds were, Angelo's attention was drawn back to Kayla. He had plans for her. A surprise after their big presentation. At first, he'd been hesitant, but now, seeing how weary she was, he was certain that he'd made the right decision. He just hoped she would relax long enough to enjoy it.

He still had the feeling that she was keeping something from him—something that was eating at her. But what was it? Was she worried that he'd make another move on her?

The thought left him feeling unsettled. Granted, he wasn't that good at reading women. They were forever a mystery to him, but he'd swear that she was into him and his kisses. She'd come alive in his arms. He was certain that he hadn't imagined that. So then, what had her putting an unusually big gap between them in the limo?

He was impressive.

Kayla sat in one of the plush chairs in the palace's state room. Instead of taking a closer view of the ornate ceiling with large crystal chandeliers, the red walls with white trim, the huge paintings of historical figures or the priceless statues on pedestals, her entire attention was focused on Angelo as he stood in the front of the room in his freshly pressed navy suit and maroon tie. Every inch of him looked as if he'd just stepped off the cover of a men's magazine. He was definitely the most handsome man she'd ever laid her eyes on.

And his presentation was truly impressive. If this didn't sell the royal couple on the benefits of holding the royal wedding in Monte Calanetti, then nothing would. Angelo's talk was informative while containing bits of entertainment. Sure, he'd gone over it with her back in Italy, but somehow here in front of the royal prince and his bride, it seemed so much more special—more dynamic.

"Monte Calanetti offers a variety of services from a world-renowned chef to the most delicious bakery." Angelo moved off to the side while Kayla started the slideshow presentation on a large high-definition screen. "You can see here an overview of the village—"

With the slideshow up and running, Kayla's thoughts spiraled away from the presentation she knew verbatim. Instead, she was amazed by the man making the presentation. Though he didn't have the best one-on-one people skills, he was truly amazing when he was selling an idea. His voice was strong, sure and unwavering. His tone was cajoling. And his posture was confident but not cocky. No wonder he was the best in the business.

So then how in the world was he so inept when it came to dealing with people—people like his family? People like her? Why did he have to make it so tough to get close to him?

Why couldn't he let his guard down and take a chance on love like the crown prince and his Cinderella bride? Kayla's gaze moved to the soon-to-be couple, envious that they seemed to have it all—success, stability and most of all love.

But as they sat there surrounded by their staff, Kayla didn't see any telltale signs of love. There were no clasped hands. No loving gazes when they thought no one was looking. No nothing.

Kayla gave herself a mental jerk. She was overthinking things. Of course they were being all businesslike. This was their wedding—a wedding that would have all of the world watching. That had to be their focus right now.

Still, there was something that nagged at her about the couple, but she brushed it off. Whatever it was—bridal nerves or such—it was absolutely none of her business. She had enough of her own problems.

He'd nailed it.

Angelo wore an easy smile. The presentation had gone without a hitch. Everything had fallen into place just as he'd practiced it over and over again with Kayla in their hotel suite. He had a good feeling that Monte Calanetti would be in serious contention for the site of the royal wedding.

After the slideshow presentation was over, Angelo asked, "Are there any questions?"

"Yes." The bride, Christina Rose, sat up straight. "I didn't see anything in your presentation about the chapel. I'm particularly interested in it."

Angelo's gut knotted. He'd been wrong. His gaze sought out Kayla. He was certain that she'd be wearing an I-told-you-so look. But her chair was empty? Where had she gone? The next thing he knew Kayla was standing next to him. What in the world?

"Hi. I'm Kayla." She sent him an I've-got-this smile. "The chapel is my part of the presentation."

He moved away and went to take a seat. What in the world did Kayla have up her sleeve? He thought they'd settled this back in Monte Calanetti—no chapel presentation. His back teeth ground together as he remembered that call had been his.

Angelo leaned back in his chair while Kayla put photos of the chapel up on the screen with a pitch that he'd never heard before, but it sounded like music to his ears. So the little minx had gone behind his back and done exactly what he'd told her not to do.

And he couldn't be happier.

After Kayla finished her short presentation, the bride

spoke up again. "The chapel—you mentioned that it had just switched ownership—the new owner—have they approved the use of it for the wedding?"

Seriously? That had to be the first question. Kayla's gaze momentarily strayed to him. He had no help to offer her, but he was anxious to see how she handled the question.

Kayla laced her fingers together. "At this moment, we have not obtained a release for the use of the chapel." The bride's face creased with frown lines. That was definitely not a good sign. "Knowing the chapel is of particular interest to you, we will make it a priority to secure its use for the wedding."

The young woman's eyes lit up, but she didn't say anything as she glanced over at the crown prince. He didn't speak to Kayla, either, but rather conversed softly with his advisors, who had a list of questions.

Kayla handled the inquiries with calm and grace. Angelo couldn't have done any better. She certainly was full of surprises, and he couldn't be happier having her by his side.

It wasn't until much later that Angelo walked with her toward their rooms. This was their first chance to talk privately since the presentation. As they strolled along the elegant hallways, Kayla waited anxiously to hear Angelo's thoughts on how she'd handled her part of the meeting. She hoped he wasn't too upset about her ignoring his dictate about the chapel.

Angelo stopped and turned to face her. "Stop looking so worried. You did an excellent job today."

"I did?"

He nodded. "I owe you an apology for not listening to you and a thank-you for being so prepared."

"Really? Even though I didn't do what you said?"

He gazed deep into her eyes. "I think you have excellent instincts and the courage to follow them. You've got what it takes to have a very bright future."

In her excitement, she threw her arms around him. He had no idea how much she needed this one perfect moment.

Coming back to earth, she grudgingly let go of him and stepped back. "Thank you for the opportunity."

"You earned it. And you did well by knowing all of the answers to their questions. And you took notes of things that particularly interested them. I couldn't have done any better."

"You really mean that? You're not just saying these things to make me feel better."

He chuckled. "Did anyone ever tell you that you don't take compliments well?"

She shrugged. "I guess I'm still wound up."

"We make a great team."

It was the first time he'd ever referred to them in that manner and she liked it. She really liked it. More than that, she liked him a lot—more than was wise. But that didn't stop her heart from pounding in her chest when he gazed deeply into her eyes.

He was going to kiss her—again. She should turn away. She should pretend she didn't know that he was interested in her. But her body had a will of its own, holding her in place. She knew that nothing good would come of it, but she wanted him to kiss her more than she wanted anything in that moment.

Angelo turned and continued down the hallway. The air that had been caught in her lungs rushed out. What had happened? It took her a second to gather her wits about her, and then she rushed to catch up to him.

They continued on in silence until they stopped outside her bedroom door. He turned to her again. "Thank you for everything. If I had done this alone, I wouldn't have stood a chance of winning their favor. You were my ace in the hole."

His gaze caught and held hers.

"I… I was?"

He nodded and stepped closer. "How could anyone turn you down?"

Her heart pitter-pattered harder and faster. She didn't want this moment to end—not yet. It was her very own fairy tale. "Do you want to come inside?"

He tucked a loose curl behind her ear. Then the back of his fingers grazed down her cheek. "I don't think that would be a good idea. We're expected at dinner with the royal couple. It wouldn't look right if we were late."

The hammering of her heart drowned out her common sense. Because when he was looking at her that way and touching her so sweetly, all she could think about was kissing him—

She lifted up on her tiptoes and pressed her lips to his. He didn't move at first and she wondered if there was some way that she had misread the situation. But then his arms wrapped around her and pulled her hard against him. She'd been here before, but it never failed to excite her. He was thoughtful, sweet and kind. Nothing like her boss at the office. This was a different side of him, and she found him utterly irresistible.

Angelo braced his hands on her hips, moving an arm's length away. "We need to stop now or we are never going to make it to that dinner."

"Who needs dinner?" There was only one thing she was hungry for at that moment and she was staring at him.

"Don't tempt me." He smiled at her. "I don't think that would help our pitch." He pressed a kiss to her forehead and proceeded down the hallway to his room.

In that moment, Kayla felt lighter than she had in days. Suddenly anything seemed possible. Maybe she'd given up on the fund-raiser too soon. She pressed a hand to her lips. Perhaps everything would work out in the end, after all.

She sure hoped so.

CHAPTER SEVENTEEN

"I DON'T UNDERSTAND."

Kayla's gaze narrowed in on Angelo as they stood beneath the crystal chandelier in the marble foyer. He'd been acting mysterious ever since they'd given their pitch to the royal couple the day before. Was it the kiss? It couldn't be. He hadn't been distant at the royal dinner. In fact, he'd been quite attentive—even if the evening hadn't ended with any more kisses.

"Trust me." His dark eyes twinkled with mischief. "You will understand soon enough."

"It'd be easier if you'd just tell me where we're going. If this has something to do with the pitch, you should tell me. I would have brought my laptop. Or at least I could have grabbed my tablet."

"You don't need it." He took her hand and guided her out the door, down the palace steps and into an awaiting limo. "Trust me."

"But how do I know if I'm dressed appropriately. The only formal clothes I have with me I wore yesterday for the pitch and then the dinner with the royal couple. I thought that we'd be leaving today."

"I've delayed our departure."

He had? She didn't recall him mentioning anything to her. Then again, she'd been so caught up in her thoughts lately that she might have missed it.

"Don't worry. I ran it past your boss." He winked at her. "He's fine with it."

"He is, huh?" She wondered what Angelo was up to and why he was in such a good mood. "But why aren't we flying back to Italy? I thought you'd be anxious to wrap things up there before we return to New York."

"It can wait."

She had absolutely no idea where they were headed. The curiosity was eating at her. But the driver knew. She turned to the front to ask him.

"Don't even think of it," Angelo warned as though he knew exactly what she intended. "He's been sworn to secrecy."

Her mouth gaped open. Angelo really did know what she was thinking. Thankfully he didn't know everything that crossed her mind or else he'd know that she'd gone against his express wishes and worked on the fund-raiser during work hours.

And worst of all, her efforts were for naught. She'd reached out to everyone she could think of, but she had yet to come up with another big-name band on such short notice. But ever the optimist, she wasn't canceling the event until the very last minute. There just had to be a way to help the kids.

"Hey, no frowning is allowed."

She hadn't realized that her thoughts had transferred to her face. "Sorry. I was just thinking of all the work I should be doing instead of riding around with you."

"You'll have plenty of time for work later. In fact, when we return to New York I imagine that you'll have more work than you'll ever want."

She sent him a quizzical look. Was he trying to tell her something?

"Quit trying to guess. You aren't going to figure out our destination."

The car zipped along the scenic roadway. Angelo was totally relaxed, enjoying the terrific view of the tranquil sea. But she couldn't relax. Not yet. Not like this. Not with the fate of the fund-raiser hanging over her head.

Kayla desperately wanted to ask Angelo for help, but she just couldn't bring herself to trust him, knowing his adamant stance on such matters. But if she didn't ask Angelo for help, what did that say about their relationship? Did it mean what they'd shared meant nothing?

The thought left a sour taste in her mouth. The Angelo she'd got to know so well here in Italy put his family above his own needs even at the risk of one of his most important accounts. But that was his family? And she was what?

She had absolutely no answer.

Realizing that he was still holding her hand, her heart thumped. She was certainly more than his assistant—but how much more?

He turned to her. Their gazes caught and held. Her heart started to go *tap-tap-tap*. Oh, yes, she was definitely falling for her boss.

But what would happen when this trip was over? What would their relationship be like when they returned to the reality of their Madison Avenue office? Or worse yet, what if he found out that she'd been working on the fund-raiser instead of devoting all of her attention to her work?

"Relax. Everything will be okay." Angelo raised her hand to his lips and pressed a gentle kiss to the back of her hand.

Her stomach shivered with excitement. Throwing caution to the wind, she uttered, "When you do that, relaxing is the last thing on my mind."

"In that case…" He pulled her close and with her hand held securely in his, he rested his arm on his leg. His voice lowered. "You can get as worked up as you like now."

His heated gaze said a hundred things at once. And all of them made her pulse race and her insides melt. He wanted her. Angelo Amatucci, the king of Madison Avenue, was staring at her with desire evident in his eyes.

If she were wise, she would pull away and pretend that none of this had happened. But her heart was pounding and her willpower was fading away. She'd been resisting this for so long that she was tired of fighting it—tired of denying the mounting attraction between them.

Maybe this thing between them wouldn't survive the harsh glare of the office, but that was days away. They were to remain in Italy until the royal couple had all of the inquiries answered and their decision made. In the meantime, what was so wrong with indulging in a most delightful fantasy?

Once again, Angelo seemingly read her mind—realizing that she'd come to a decision. He turned to her and leaned forward. His lips were warm as they pressed to hers. Her eyes drifted closed as her fingers moved to his face, running over his freshly shaved jaw. His spicy aftershave tormented and teased. It should be illegal for anyone to smell so good. A moan bubbled up in the back of her throat.

The car stopped, jostling them back to the here and now. Angelo was the first to pull away. Disappointment coursed through her. Her eyes fluttered open and met his heated gaze.

"Don't look so disappointed. There will be time for more of this later." He smiled and her discontentment faded away. "Remember, I have a surprise for you."

"Did I forget to tell you that I love surprises?"

He laughed. "I was hoping you would."

She glanced out her window, finding nothing but lush greenery, flowers and trees. She struggled to see around Angelo, but with his arm draped loosely around her, she couldn't see much.

"I can't see." She wiggled but his strong arm kept her next to him—not a bad place to be, but she was curious about their location. "Where are we?"

"My, aren't you impatient? You'll soon see."

She couldn't wait. Though she still had problems to resolve, for just this moment she let them shift to the back of her mind. She might never have this kind of experience again, and she didn't want to miss a moment of it. And it had nothing to do with the surprise that Angelo had planned for her.

It had everything to do with the man who could make her heart swoon with those dark, mysterious eyes.

Mud. Seriously.

Angelo frowned as he sat submerged in a mud bath. He felt utterly ridiculous. This was his first trip to a spa, and though he'd set up the appointment for Kayla, he'd thought he might find out what he was missing. After all, Halencia was known for its world-renowned spa. It ought to be renowned for the exorbitant prices and, worse yet, the cajoling he had to do to get an appointment at the last moment. He'd finally relented and name-dropped—the prince's name certainly opened up their schedule quickly. But it had been worth it when Kayla's face lit up.

He glanced sideways at her as she leaned back against the tub's ledge with her eyes closed. Her long red wavy hair was twisted up in a white towel, safe from this muck. She definitely wasn't the prim-and-proper girl that he'd originally thought her to be when he'd hired her as his temporary assistant. No, Kayla definitely had a bit of a naughty, devil-may-care attitude. And that just intrigued him all the more.

"I'm sorry." Angelo didn't know what else to say. "I guess I should have done more research before making the reservations, but we were so pushed for time with the royal pitch that it just slipped my mind."

Kayla lifted her head. "It's really no problem. I'm enjoying myself."

"But how was I to know that they would set us up for a couple's spa day?"

Her eyes lit up. Her smile stretched into a grin and her eyes sparkled with utter amusement.

"Hey, you aren't inwardly laughing at me, are you?"

"Who? Me? No way." She clutched her bottom lip between her teeth as her shoulders shook.

He wasn't used to being the source of entertainment, but she certainly seemed to be enjoying herself. He supposed that made it worth it. Although, when he'd found out what was involved in the deluxe package, he did think that she was going to balk and walk away. But he'd been worried for no reason.

Kayla wasn't shy. In fact, she could be quite bold. The memory of her in hot pink lacy underwear before she'd stepped into the mud had totally fogged up his mind. Although, when he'd had to strip down to his navy boxers, he'd been none too happy. How could he have overlooked the need to bring swimsuits? Talk about taking down each other's defenses and getting down to the basics.

"What are you thinking about?"

He turned to Kayla, finding her studying him. "Nothing important. So, are you enjoying your trip?"

"Definitely. But…"

"But what?"

"I get the feeling that you aren't enjoying it. Why is that? Is it because of your sister's situation?"

He shrugged. "I suppose that has something to do with it."

"What else is bothering you? I'd think after being gone for so long that you'd be happy to be back in Italy."

"And you would be wrong. Returning to Monte Calanetti and interacting with my siblings and villagers is one of the hardest things I've ever had to do."

She arched an eyebrow and looked at him expectantly.

Why had he opened his mouth? He didn't want to get into this subject. It would lead to nothing but painful memories. And he couldn't even fathom what Kayla would think of him after he told her the truth about his past—about how he ended up in New York.

She reached out her hand and gripped his arm. "You know that you can talk to me. Openness and honesty are important to a relationship—even a friendship or whatever this is between us. Besides, I'm a really good listener."

Even though they were submerged in this mineral mud

stuff, her touch still sent a jolt up his arm and awakened his whole body. After telling himself repeatedly that she was off-limits, he wanted her more with each passing day. He turned and his gaze met hers.

She was the most beautiful woman he'd ever laid his eyes on and it wasn't just skin-deep. Her beauty came from the inside out. She was kind, thoughtful and caring. She was everything he would ever want in a woman—if he were interested in getting involved in a serious relationship.

But he wasn't. He jerked his gaze back to the large window that gave an amazing view of the Mediterranean Sea, but it wasn't the landscape that filled his mind—it was Kayla. She consumed far too many of his thoughts.

"Angelo, talk to me." Her voice was soft and encouraging.

For the first time in his life, he actually wanted to open up. And though his instinct was to keep it all bottled up inside, he wondered if that was the right thing to do. Maybe if Kayla, with her near-perfect home life, were to see him clearly she wouldn't look at him with desire in her eyes.

But could he do it? Could he reveal the most horrific episode in his life? More than that, could he relive the pain and shame?

He gazed into Kayla's eyes, finding compassion and understanding there. He swallowed hard and realized that perhaps he had more strength than he gave himself credit for. Though taking down his ingrained defenses to expose the most vulnerable part of himself would be extremely hard, he firmly believed it would be for the best. If it would put an end to this thing between him and Kayla, how could he hold back?

He cleared his throat. "Remember when I told you that I left Italy to go to school in the States?"

She nodded. "It's the bravest thing I've ever heard. I couldn't have done it—"

"But the thing is… I didn't do it because I wanted to."

Her brows drew together. "What are you saying?"

"My father and I didn't get along and that's putting it mildly." Angelo's body tensed as his mind rolled back in time. "My parents have always had a rocky relationship. On and off. Divorcing and remarrying." He shook his head, chasing away the unwelcome memories. "It was awful to listen to them."

He stopped and glanced at Kayla, whose expression was one of compassion. And then she did something he didn't expect. She reached over, grabbed his arm again and slid her hand down into the mud until she reached his hand. She laced her fingers tightly around his and gave him a big squeeze.

He exhaled a deep breath and continued. "My father is not a small man and he can be quite intimidating. When I'd had enough and my mother needed help with his temper, I... I'd step between them. My father did not like that at all."

"You don't have to tell me this."

"Yes, I do." He'd started this and he was going to see it through to the end. "It didn't matter what I did, it was never up to my father's expectations. I don't think there was anything I could have done to please him. And by the time I graduated school, I was done trying. And he was done trying."

"One day he blew up at me for not doing something in the vineyard. His bad mood spilled over to my mother— this was one of their good periods, so she didn't want to ruin things with him. When I tried to intervene between him and her by trying to soothe him, my father...he...he threw me out."

Kayla's fine brows rose. "But surely he calmed down and let you back in."

Angelo shook his head as he stared blindly out the window. Suddenly he was back there on that sunny day. His father had pressed a meaty hand to Angelo's chest, sending him stumbling out the front door. His mother's expression was one of horror, but she didn't say a word—not one thing—to contradict her husband. Instead, she'd agreed with him. Angelo's hurt had come out as anger. He'd balled up his hands and lifted them, taunting his father into a fight. But his father had told him that he wasn't worth the effort. How did a father do that to his son? How did he turn his back on him?

Angelo blinked repeatedly. "He told me that I was worthless and that I would never amount to anything. And then he told me to never darken his doorway again. He closed the door in my face."

"But your mother—"

"Wanted to make her husband happy. Don't you get it? Neither of them...they...didn't want me." His gut tightened into a knot and the air caught in his lungs as he fought back the pain of rejection.

This is where Kayla would turn away—just like his parents. She would know he was damaged goods. Not even his own parents could love him. He couldn't face Kayla. He couldn't see the rejection in her eyes.

"So you just left?" Her voice was soft.

He nodded. "I wasn't about to go back."

"But you were just a kid."

"I was man enough to make it on my own. I didn't have a choice. I couldn't live with him after that. And he didn't want me there. Nico brought my clothes to me, and with the money I'd saved from odd jobs over the years and my inheritance from my grandfather, I left. If it wasn't for Nico and Marianna, I'd have never looked back."

"And this is why you avoid serious relationships?"

He shrugged. "There isn't any point in them. The relationship will fail and somebody will get hurt. It's best this way."

"Best for who? You? You know that not everyone will treat you like your parents."

Suddenly he turned to her. His gaze searched her eyes. What was she saying?

Her warm gaze caressed him. "You can't keep yourself locked away from love because you're afraid. Some things are worth the risk."

She is worth the risk.

He leaned over and dipped his head, seeking out her lips. Every time he thought he'd learned everything there was to know about Kayla, she surprised him again. What did he ever do to deserve her?

He deepened the kiss. She responded to his every move. Her heated touch was melting the wall of ice inside him that he used to keep everyone out. Every second with their lips pressed together and their fingers intertwined was like a soothing balm on his scarred heart.

He needed her. He wanted her. He…he cared oh, so much about her.

A person cleared their throat in the background. "Do you need anything?"

Yeah, for you to leave.

Fighting back a frustrated groan, Angelo pulled back. If it wasn't for their attendant, he might have continued that kiss to its natural conclusion. Yes, he'd have definitely followed her into the shower and finished it.

In what seemed like no time, they were ushered from the mud bath into a shower and then into a private Jacuzzi. Angelo didn't know what to do with his hands. Well, he knew what he wanted to do with them, but with their attendant floating in and out, those plans would have to wait for later. For now, he stretched his arms along the rim of the tub and pulled her close to him. He just needed to feel that physical connection.

"Are you enjoying yourself?" He just had to be sure.

"This is perfect. Thank you."

"Well, not quite perfect. I did overlook the need for swimsuits." The heat of embarrassment crept up his neck.

"And miss seeing you in your boxers?" She waggled her brows at him. "I think it worked out perfectly."

"But you had to ruin your...um, clothes. They're all stained now."

"Oh, well. It was worth the sacrifice."

"Don't worry. I'll make sure to replace your...things." Why did he get so tripped up around her? It wasn't like him. But then again, everything was different when he was around Kayla.

"Will you be picking them out yourself?" Her eyes taunted him.

"Sure. Why not?"

"Do you have much experience with women's lingerie? And exactly how will you know what sizes to get?"

Boy, this water was starting to get hot—really hot. "Fine." His voice came out rough, and he had to stop to clear his dry throat. "I'll give you the money and you can get what you need."

She grinned at him. "I never thought of you as the kind to take the easy way out."

He had the distinct feeling there was no winning this conversation. No matter which way he went, he was doomed. "I'll make you a deal."

"Oh, I like the sound of this. Tell me more."

"We'll go together. I'll pick them out, but you have to promise not to wear them for anyone else."

Her eyes widened and then narrowed in on him. "Why, Mr. Amatucci, are you hitting on me?"

"I must be losing my touch if it took you this long to fig- ure it out." He didn't even wait for her response before his head dipped and he caught her lips with his own.

Their relationship was unlike anything he had known previously—he never tired of Kayla. In fact, he missed her when she wasn't next to him. And her kisses, they were sweet and addicting.

What was wrong with him? He never acted like this.

And he never took part in flirting. He never had to. Normally women gravitated to him and things were casual at best. But with Kayla it was different—he was different. He barely recognized himself. It was as if he'd let down his shield of Mr. Angelo Amatucci, Madison Avenue CEO, and could at last be himself.

However, Kayla had taught him that a relationship didn't have to be turbulent like his parent's relationship. She'd opened his eyes to other possibilities. She'd shown him through her patience and understanding that, with openness and honesty, things didn't have to be kept bottled up inside until they exploded.

She hadn't been afraid to voice her disagreement over ideas for the wedding pitch. Nor had she been shy about vocalizing her objection to his no-charity-projects rule at the office. And though he hadn't agreed with her on some of the things, he'd been able to communicate it without losing his temper. Was it possible that he wasn't like his parents? Or was Kayla the key to this calm, trusting relationship?

He wasn't sure what it was, but the one thing he was certain about was that he wanted to explore this more—this thing that was growing between them.

When their attendant entered the room, they pulled apart. Disappointment settled in his chest. But the thought of picking up where they'd left off filled him with renewed vigor. This wasn't the end—it was just the beginning.

"I just have one question." Kayla gave him a puzzled look. "What exactly are we supposed to wear when we leave here? Please don't tell me that we're going commando."

He burst out laughing at the horrified look on her face.

"Hey, this isn't funny."

"Relax. I have another surprise waiting for you."

The worry lines on her face eased. "You do? Aren't you a man of mystery today?"

"I try."

"So tell me what it is."

He shook his head. "Just relax and let the water do its magic. You'll learn about your next surprise soon enough."

CHAPTER EIGHTEEN

CINDERELLA.

Yep, that's exactly how Kayla felt as she stepped out of the limo. Her nails were freshly manicured, her face was done up by a makeup artist and her hair was swept up with crystal-studded bobby pins. And that was just the beginning.

Angelo had surprised her with a gorgeous navy blue chiffon dress. Wide satin straps looped over her shoulders while a pleated bodice hugged her midsection. The tea-length skirt was drawn up slightly in the front while the back of the skirt flirted with her ankles. The thought that Angelo had picked it out for her and that it fit perfectly amazed her.

And there was lingerie—she wasn't even going to ask how he got all of her sizes right. Heat tinged her cheeks. Some things were best left unknown. Her silver sandals, though a bit tight, looked spectacular. And he'd even thought to present her with a sparkly necklace and earrings. The man was truly Prince Charming in disguise.

She looped her hand through the crook of his arm as he escorted her into a very posh restaurant. Tall columns, a marble floor and white table linens greeted them. Palms grew in large urns. The soft lighting and instrumental music made the ambience quite romantic. When the maître d' led them to the back of the restaurant and out a door, she wondered where they were going.

She soon found them standing on the terrace overlooking the Mediterranean Sea. A sweet floral scent filled the air. Kayla glanced up to find a wisteria vine woven through an overhead trellis. The beautiful bunches of delicate purple flowers were in full bloom. Lanterns hung from chains and gave off a soft glow. The whole setup was just perfect for a first date—this was a date, wasn't it?

Her gaze strayed to Angelo. What exactly had been his intention in giving her this magical day? Suddenly she decided she didn't want to analyze it—she just wanted to enjoy it.

The maître d' stopped next to a table by the railing. The view was spectacular, but even that word didn't cover the magnificence of the sight before her. The sea gently rolled inland, lapping against the rocks below the balcony. The glow of the sinking sun danced and played with the water, sweeping away her breath. She didn't know such a beautiful place existed on earth.

"If this is a dream, I don't want to wake up."

Angelo smiled at her. "Trust me. I'm having the same dream and I have no intention of waking up anytime soon."

"You have made this a day I'll never forget."

"Nor will I."

She continued to stare across the candlelit table at Angelo, who was decked out in a black tux that spanned his broad shoulders—the place where'd she'd been resting her head not so long ago. Even his dark hair was styled to perfection. Her fingers itched to mess up the thick strands while losing herself in another of his kisses. But that would have to wait until later. It would be the sweetest dessert ever.

The maître d' presented the menus and explained the wine list to Angelo before walking away. Everything sounded delightful.

Angelo peered over the menu at her. "I hope you brought your appetite."

She nodded, eating him up with her eyes. This was going to be a very long dinner.

However much Kayla wanted to throw caution to the wind, there was still a small hesitant voice in the back of her mind. And try as she might, it was impossible to ignore. She'd worked so hard to get to where she was at Amatucci & Associates—did she really want to jeopardize her dreams? And worse yet, if she did continue to thrive there, would she always wonder if her flourishing was due to the fact that she'd had a fling with her boss?

"Did I tell you how beautiful you look?" The flickering candlelight reflected in his dark eyes as he stared across the table at her.

"You don't look so bad yourself."

"You mean this old thing?" He tugged on his lapel. "I just grabbed it out of the back of my closet."

His teasing made her laugh. Maybe she'd worry about all of the ramifications tomorrow. "Is it possible that we never have to go back to New York? Couldn't we just live here in this little piece of heaven and never let the moment end?"

"Mmm... I wish. I've never enjoyed myself this much. But we can make the most of our time here." His eyes hinted at unspoken pleasures that were yet to come. "You know if we weren't in public and there wasn't a table separating us, I'd finish that kiss we started back at the spa."

Her stomach shivered with the anticipation. "Then I guess I have something more to look forward to."

"We both do."

Like Cinderella swept away in her carriage...

The limo moved swiftly over the darkened roadway back to the palace. All Kayla could remember of the dinner was staring across the table at her date. Angelo had presented one surprise after the other, and somewhere along the way, she'd lost her heart to him.

She didn't know when her love for him had started. It was a while back. Maybe it was when she first witnessed how much Angelo cared about his family. Or maybe it was when he'd given her a tour of his village and told her about pieces of his past—finally letting down that wall he kept between them. Then somewhere, somehow, Angelo Amatucci had sneaked into her heart.

Kayla loved him wholly and completely.

The revelation shook her to her core. Part of her wanted to run from him—from these feelings. They had the power to destroy everything she'd built for herself back in New York. But how did she turn off the powerful emotions that Angelo evoked in her? And did she want to?

Just a look and he had her heart racing. Her body willingly became submissive to his touch. And she reveled in the way he'd looked at her back at the spa. He had no idea that her insides had been nothing more than quivering jelly when she stripped down to her undies. But when his eyes had lit up with definite approval and then desire, her nervousness was quickly forgotten.

In his eyes, she saw her present and her future. She saw a baby with Angelo's dark eyes and her smile. Startlingly enough, the thought didn't scare her off. In fact, she liked it. Maybe it was never the idea of a family that frightened her, but rather she'd had her sights set on the wrong man.

"Hey, what has you so quiet?" Angelo reached out and pulled her to his side.

"Nothing." *Everything.*

"I hope you had a good day."

"It was the best." She turned her head and reached up, placing a kiss on the heated skin of his neck. There was a distinct uneven breath on his part.

His fingers lifted from her shoulder and fanned across her cheek. "No, you're the best."

They both turned at once and their lips met. There was no timidity. No hesitation. Instead, there was a raw hunger—a fiery passion. And it stemmed from both of them. Their movements were rushed and needy. Their breath mingled as their arms wrapped around each other. Reality reeled away as though it was lost out there in the sea.

Right now, the only thing Kayla needed or wanted was

Angelo. If they were to have only this one moment together, she wanted it to be everything. She wanted memories that would keep her warm on those long lonely winter nights back in New York.

Angelo moved his mouth from hers. His hands held her face as his forehead rested against hers. His breathing was ragged. "I don't want to leave you tonight."

She knew her response without any debate. "I don't want you to go."

For once, she was going to risk it all to have this moment with the man she loved—even if he didn't love her back.

The limo pulled to a stop at the foot of the palace's sweeping white stairs that were lit with lanterns trailing up each side. Angelo didn't follow protocol. He opened the door before the driver could make it around the car. Angelo turned back and held out his hand to help her to her feet.

With both of them smiling like starstruck lovers, they rushed up the steps and inside the palace. Brushing off offers of assistance from the staff, hand in hand they swiftly moved to the second floor. They stopped outside her bedroom door and Angelo pulled her close. His mouth pressed to hers. He didn't have to say a word; all of his pent-up desire was expressed in that kiss.

When he pulled back, he gazed into her eyes. "Are you sure about this?"

She nodded and opened the door. She'd never been so sure about anything in her life. She led the way into the room. This would be a night neither of them would ever forget.

CHAPTER NINETEEN

WHAT IN THE world had he let happen?

Angelo raked his fingers through his hair, not caring if he messed it up or not. He'd already messed things up bigtime with Kayla. In the bright light of the morning sun, he stood on the balcony of his suite in the royal palace. He'd woken up in the middle of the night after a nightmare—a nightmare he'd thought he'd done away with long ago.

After leaving Italy, he'd had nightmares about his father turning him out—of his father throwing his clothes out in the drive and telling him that he was not welcome there ever again. In his dream, and in real life, his mother had cried, but she didn't dare go against her husband's wishes even if it meant sacrificing one of her own children.

But last night his nightmare had been different. It was Kayla who'd turned him away. She'd told him that she never wanted to see him again. He'd begged and pleaded, but she'd hear none of it. Her face had been devoid of emotion as she slammed the door in his face. With nowhere to go, he'd walked the dark streets of New York. When a mugger attacked him, Angelo had sat up straight in bed. His heart had been racing and he'd broken out in a cold sweat.

Angelo gave his head a firm shake, trying to erase the haunting images. Of course, he knew that he wasn't going to end up homeless, but he also knew that the dream was a warning of looming trouble. If his own parents could turn him out, why couldn't Kayla? How could he risk getting close to her, knowing how unreliable relationships could be? After all, his own parents were quite familiar with the divorce courts as they broke up and got back together on a regular basis. Angelo's chest tightened.

The only thing he could do was end things with Kayla—quickly and swiftly. There was no way to put the genie back in the bottle, but that didn't mean that they had to continue down this road—no matter how tempted he was to do just that. He couldn't put his tattered heart on the line only to have it shunned again. The price was just too high.

A knock at his door alerted him to the fact that their car was waiting to take them to the airstrip. It was time to return to Italy. More than that, it was time to face Kayla. He didn't know what to say to her—how to explain that everything they'd shared was a big mistake.

By the time he made it downstairs, Kayla was already in the car. Not even the clear blue sky and the sight of the beautiful gardens could lighten his mood. He was in the wrong here. Things had spiraled totally out of control yesterday, and it had been all his doing.

"Good morning." He settled in the seat next to her, making sure to leave plenty of room between them.

Her face was turned away. "Morning."

That was it. The only conversation they had as his luggage was loaded in the rear. Time seemed suspended as he waited for the car to roll down the driveway. This was going to be a very long trip back to Italy. And a very quiet one.

It wasn't until they were on his private jet and airborne that he realized ignoring the situation wasn't going to make it go away. They still had to work together.

"We need to talk."

Kayla turned to him. "Funny you should pick now to talk."

"What's that supposed to mean?"

"It means that you didn't have time to talk last night. You had one thing on your mind and now that you've gotten it, you want to give me the big kiss-off."

"Hey, that's not fair. I didn't set out to hurt you. You were as willing for last night as I was."

"You didn't even have the decency to face me this morning. You slunk away in the middle of the night."

"That's not true." Not exactly. "I couldn't sleep and I didn't want to wake you up." The truth was that he'd never gone back to sleep after that nightmare. He just couldn't shake the feeling of inevitable doom.

She eyed him up. "So then I jumped to the wrong conclusion? You weren't trying to get away from me?"

The hurt look in her eyes tore at him. This was all about him, not her. She was wonderful—amazing—perfect. He just wasn't the guy for her. But how did he make that clear to her?

He got up from his seat and moved across the aisle and sat beside her, still not sure what to say. Somehow, someway he had to say the right words to make her realize that she was amazing, but they just weren't going to have more than they'd shared yesterday.

He resisted the urge to pull her into his arms and kiss away the unhappiness written all over her face. Instead, he took her hand in his. "Kayla, you are the most wonderful woman I have ever known. And yesterday was very special. I will never ever forget it—"

"But you don't want to see me again." She jerked her hand away.

"No—I mean yes." He blew out a breath. "I'm not the man to settle down into a serious relationship."

"Is that what you tell all of your women?"

"No. It's not." She eyed him with obvious disbelief reflected in her eyes. "I'm telling you the truth. I never let anyone get this close to me."

She crossed her arms. "Then why me? Why did I have to be the one that you let get close only to reject me after one night?"

Frustration balled up in his gut—not at her, at himself for being unable to explain this properly. He'd been a scared young man with no one to turn to for help. Thank goodness for his inheritance or else he never would have been able to make it in the States. But did either of his parents care? No. Did they ever write or phone? No. Not until he'd made it on his own did he hear from his mother—she was marrying his father again and she wanted him to be there. Angelo didn't bother to respond. The only family he acknowledged these days was his brother and sister.

He didn't need a romantic relationship. Love was overrated. His business gave him happiness and a sense of accomplishment—that was all he'd ever need.

And somewhere along the way, he'd stumbled upon his explanation to Kayla. "You have to understand that for years now the only thing I've had to count on in my life was my career, and then it was my business. I've put everything I am into it—"

"But what does that have to do with me—with us?"

He reached out as though to squeeze her arm, but when her eyes widened, he realized that he was making yet another mistake and pulled back. "One of the reasons that Amatucci & Associates was able to grow so rapidly into a top advertising firm is that I gave it 110 percent of my attention—to the point of spending many nights on the couch in my office."

Her eyes grew shiny and she blinked repeatedly. "So what you're saying is that your company is now and will always be more important to you than me."

Is that what he was saying? It sure sounded much harsher when she said it. His gut twisted in a painful knot, knowing that he couldn't be the man worthy of her heart.

"You have to understand. I'm losing my edge. I fumbled this wedding pitch. If it wasn't for you, it would have been a disaster. The thing is I don't fumble accounts. I always maintain my cool. I keep my distance so that I am able to view projects objectively. But since we've been in Italy—since that first kiss—I haven't been able to maintain a professional distance. I've been all over the place, and that can't happen—I can't lose focus. It's what keeps me ahead of my competitors."

He did his best work when he relied on his head and not his heart. It was all of the talk about romance and weddings that had him thinking there was something between him and Kayla. That was all. Exhaustion and too much talk of love.

"I really need to work now." Kayla's voice was icy cold and dismissive.

"Do me a favor." He wanted to say something to lighten her mood.

"Depends."

"Remind me to stay far, far away from any other accounts where there's a wedding involved."

She didn't smile. She didn't react at all. Her head turned back to her computer.

He felt compelled to try again to smooth things over. Was that even possible at this point? "Is there anything I can help you with?"

Her narrowed gaze met his straight on. "You've helped me quite enough. I can handle this on my own. I'm sure you have something requiring your objective view and professional distance."

He moved back to his seat on the other side of the aisle. The fact that she was throwing his own words back in his face hurt. But he deserved it and so much more. He'd lost his head while in Halencia and now Kayla was paying the price.

For the rest of the flight, Kayla didn't say a word, and though he longed for her understanding—he had to accept that it was too much for her to take in. There was a part of him that wasn't buying it, either. It was the same part of him that couldn't imagine what his life was going to be like without her in it.

He leaned back in his seat, hearing the wheels of the plane screech as they made contact with the tarmac. Instead of returning to Italy, he longed to be in New York—a return to a structured, disciplined work atmosphere.

Back at the office there'd be no cucumber waters with sprigs of mint and the most adorable woman dressed in nothing more than a white fluffy robe that hid a lacy hot pink set of lingerie. His mouth grew dry as he recalled how Kayla had stared at him over the rim of her glass with those alluring green eyes.

He drew his thoughts to a sharp halt. He reminded himself that his regular PA should be returning from her maternity leave soon—real soon. If he could just keep it together a little longer, his life would return to normal. But why didn't that sound so appealing any longer?

It doesn't matter.

Kayla kept repeating that mantra to herself, wishing her heart would believe it. Three days had passed since she'd woken up alone after a night of lovemaking. How could Angelo just slip away into the night without a word? Did he know how much it would hurt her? Did he even give her feelings any consideration?

It doesn't matter.

Today was the day they learned whether their royal wedding pitch had been accepted or not. Kayla replayed the presentation in her head. She couldn't help wondering—if she hadn't been so distracted by the problems with the fundraiser and with her growing feelings for Angelo could she have done more? She worried her bottom lip. For months and months, she'd done everything to be the best employee, and now that it counted, she'd lost her focus. She'd let herself fall for her boss's mesmerizing eyes, devilish good looks and charms.

It doesn't matter.

Dismissing their time together was his choice. Why should she let it bother her? She didn't need him. She squeezed her eyes shut, blocking out the memories of being held in his arms—of the tender touch of his lips. How could such a special night go so terribly wrong? Had she totally misread what Angelo had been telling her?

None of it matters!

She had important work to do. Angelo had just departed for his brother's villa to speak to him about their sister. Kayla had declined his stilted offer to take her with him. She may have made a mess of things with Angelo, but there was still time to pull together the after-school program fund-raiser.

Kayla focused on the email she was composing to the manager of another New York City band. She could only hope they had a cancellation because the most popular bands were booked well into the future. With her name typed at the bottom, she reread it, making sure it contained plenty of appeals to the man's generous side. After all, who could possibly turn down a group of needy kids? She sure couldn't. Once she was certain there weren't any typos, she pressed Send, hoping and praying that this appeal to the Spiraling Kaleidoscopes would turn things around.

Her thoughts immediately turned to her faltering career at Amatucci & Associates. She grabbed frantically for some glimmer of hope that there was a way to get back to their prior boss-employee relationship. But every time Angelo looked at her, her heart ached and her mind went back in time to those precious moments they'd spent together, wondering if any of it was real.

Ending things now was for the best. It was all of this talk about a wedding that had filled her head with these ridiculous romantic notions. And after working so closely with Angelo these past few weeks, it was only natural that she would project them onto him. The truth was that she wasn't ready to fall in love with him—or anyone. She didn't want to settle down yet. She still had her dreams to accomplish and her career to achieve.

A message flashed on the computer screen. She had a

new email. Her body tensed and she said a silent prayer that it would be good news.

She positioned the cursor on the email and clicked, opening the message on to the screen:

To: Kayla Hill
From: Howard Simpson
RE: Spiraling Kaleidoscope Booking
Thanks so much for thinking of us for your fund-raiser. I am sorry but we are already booked solid for that weekend, in fact, we're booked for the month. Next time consider booking well in advance.

The backs of Kayla's eyes stung. She continued to stare at the email, wishing the letters would rearrange themselves into an acceptance letter, but they refused to budge. This was it. She was out of ideas and out of time. No other band at this late date was going to be available.

Another email popped into her inbox.

To: Ms. Kayla Hill
From: Ms. Stephanie Dyer, Public Relations, Paper Magic Inc.
RE: ICL after-school program fund-raiser
It has recently come to our attention that the fund-raiser no longer has a headline performer. And it is therefore with great regret that we will have to pull our sponsorship...

Her vision blurred. She'd made a mess of everything. And she had no idea how she was ever going to face the children of the after-school program and tell them that she'd let them down—that the doors of the center were going to close.

Just then the door of the suite swung open. It must be the maid. Kayla swiped a hand across her cheeks and sniffled.

She was a mess. Hopefully the cleaning lady wouldn't notice. And if she did, hopefully she wouldn't say anything.

"I'll just move out of your way." Kayla closed her laptop, preparing to move down to the pool area to work.

"Why would you have to get out of my way?"

That wasn't the maid's voice. It was Angelo's. He was back. But why?

When she didn't say a word, he moved to her side. "Kayla, what's the matter?"

She didn't face him. "I... I thought you were the maid."

"Obviously, I'm not. I forgot my phone so I came back. I didn't want to miss a call from the royal family about the pitch."

"Oh, okay." She kept her head down and fidgeted with the pens on the table.

"Kayla, look at me."

She shook her head.

"Kayla." He knelt down next to her.

Oh, what did it matter? She lifted her face to him. "What do you need?"

"I need you to explain to me what's wrong." The concern was evident in the gentleness of his voice. "I thought we had everything worked out between us."

"Is that what you call it?" He really wanted to know? Then fine. She'd tell him. "I call it ignoring the big pink elephant in the middle of the room."

But that wasn't the only reason she'd been crying. It seemed in the past few days that everything she cared about was disintegrating.

"Kayla, talk to me."

His phone chimed. Saved by the bell so to speak. He checked the caller ID and then held up a finger for her to wait. He straightened and moved to the window, where he took the call.

This was her chance to escape his inevitable interrogation. She didn't know where she would go. Suddenly gelato sounded divine. So what if she was wallowing in her own misery? She deserved some sugary comfort—until she figured out what to do next.

She moved to her room to splash some water on her face, repair her makeup and grab her purse. When she was ready to go, there was a knock at her door. She knew it was Angelo. She sighed. Why couldn't he just leave well enough alone?

"Kayla, we need to talk."

CHAPTER TWENTY

"No, WE DON'T." Kayla moved to the door and swung it open. "Not unless it's about work. Other than that we have nothing to say."

Frown lines bracketed Angelo's face. "Did I hurt you that much?"

She glared at him. He really didn't expect an answer, did he? "Please move. I'm on my way out."

He moved aside and she passed by. She'd reached the exterior doorknob when he said, "Kayla, that was the prince's representative on the phone."

That stopped her in her tracks. Her heart pounded in her chest. *Please don't let the wedding fall through, too.* She turned and scanned Angelo's face. There were no hints of what had transpired on the phone.

"And..."

"The royal couple is steadfast in their decision that the chapel must be a part of the wedding. The bride was totally taken with the place. From what I understand that's the reason Monte Calanetti was placed on the short list."

"Did you try again to talk Louisa into letting them use it?"

His face creased with worry lines. "I did. And no matter what I said, she wanted no part of the wedding."

Kayla worried her bottom lip. This wasn't good. Not good at all. "This is all my fault. I shouldn't have let the royal couple believe we could deliver something that we obviously can't."

"It's not your fault. I thought that Louisa would change her mind. What I don't understand is why she's so adamant to avoid the royal wedding. Aren't all women romantics at heart?"

"Obviously not. And it's my fault. Everything is falling apart because of me."

Kayla's chin lowered. How could this be happening? Instead of helping everyone, she was about to let them all down. Most of all, she was about to let down the man she loved—correction, the man she worked for.

Angelo stepped up to her and grabbed her by the shoulders. "I've had enough of the riddles. There's more going on here than the royal wedding. I want to know what it is. Let me help you."

Her heart wanted to trust him. It wanted to spill out the problems so that they could work together to solve them. Perhaps it was time she let go of her dream of being an ad executive at Amatucci & Associates.

The price for her career advancement was far too steep. In her haste to escape her home and make a name for herself, she feared that she'd lost a part of herself. Now she realized that deep down where it counted, she still had the same principles that she'd been raised with. Her caring hometown and loving family had shown her what was truly important in life.

And the fact was she could never be happy as an ad executive, knowing she'd stepped over other people's hopes and dreams to get there. It was time to put her faith in Angelo's kindness and generosity.

She needed his help.

Why wouldn't she let him in?

Why did she insist on refusing his help?

Then Angelo remembered how their night of lovemaking had ended. His jaw tightened as he recalled how badly he'd handled that whole situation. No wonder she didn't trust him. If the roles were reversed, he'd feel the same way. But he couldn't give up. He couldn't just walk away and leave her upset.

"I know you don't have any reason to trust me, but if

you'll give me a chance, I'd like to help." His tone was gentle and coaxing. "I did my best for Nico and Marianna when they asked me—"

"But they are family. And...and I'm, well, just an employee."

His thumb moved below her chin and tilted her face upward until their gazes met. "I think you know that you're much more than that."

It was in that moment the air became trapped in his lungs. In her worried gaze he saw something else—something he hadn't expected to find. And it shook him to his core.

He saw his future.

It was in that moment that he realized just how much she meant to him.

He, the man who was intent on remaining a bachelor, had fallen head over heels, madly, passionately in love with his assistant. She was everything he'd been trying to avoid. Excitable, emotional and compassionate. The exact opposite of the cool, collected businessman image he'd created for himself.

The how and the when of these emotions totally eluded him. The startling revelation left him totally off-kilter and not sure what to say or do next. All that kept rolling through his mind was...

He, Angelo Amatucci, loved Kayla Hill.

"Angelo, what is it?"

"Um...nothing. And don't try changing the subject. We were talking about you and what has you so upset."

She breathed out an unsteady breath. "It's the emails."

"What emails? From the office?"

She shook her head. "Emails from the band's manager and the sponsors. Everyone's pulling out and...and it's in shambles—"

"Whoa. Slow down. I think we better take a seat and you need to start at the beginning."

Once seated on the couch, everything came bubbling to the surface. She told him about how she was involved with the after-school program. It came out about how the program was about to lose their lease unless they could come up with money to cover a hefty increase in the lease. And then she told him that she was heading up a fund-raiser—a big fund-raiser.

In fact, he'd heard about the fund-raiser. It was all over the radio and the papers. At the time, he'd been surprised his company hadn't been approached for a donation, but now he knew why.

"And this fund-raiser, you've been organizing it while you were here in Italy?"

She nodded. "I didn't have a choice."

So this is what she'd been hiding from him. "And you didn't think to mention it?"

"I thought about it." His mouth opened to respond but she cut him off. "And don't you dare blame this on me. I tried." Her voice rose and her face filled with color. "Every time I mentioned helping a charitable organization, you didn't want any part of it. Me not telling you before now is as much your fault as mine. I couldn't risk my job."

His voice rose. "You thought I'd fire you?"

She shouted back. "Wouldn't you have? Correction, aren't you going to now that you know?"

What he wanted to do was leave. Kayla was loud, emotional and making him extremely uncomfortable. She had him raising his voice—something he avoided at all costs. In that moment, he had flashbacks of his parents' endless arguments. He refused to end up like them.

He started for the door. The walls started to close in on him.

"Where are you going?"

"Out." His head pounded.

"And my job?"

"I don't know." He honestly didn't. He was torn between

his newfound feelings for her and the fear that they'd end up miserable like his parents. The pain in his temples intensified.

He stormed out the door, covering as much ground as he could cover with no destination in mind. He just had to get away from the arguing.

Over the years he'd worked so hard to control as much of his life as possible—keeping it the exact opposite of his emotional, turbulent parents. And then in one afternoon, he found himself back exactly where he'd started—in the middle of a heated relationship. That was unacceptable. His home and his office were kept orderly and on an even keel. Everything was how he wanted it—so then why couldn't he control his own traitorous heart?

CHAPTER TWENTY-ONE

HAD SHE BEEN FIRED?

Impossible.

But she was resigning from Amatucci & Associates effective as soon as she completed this one final task. Kayla sat across from Louisa Harrison on her patio. The Tuscany sun beamed bright overhead, but Louisa had the white table shaded by a large yellow umbrella. The woman was quiet, reserved and poised. Not exactly the easiest person to get to know.

"Thank you so much for taking the time to see me." Kayla fidgeted with the cup of coffee that Louisa had served just moments ago.

"I'm new here so I don't get much company."

Kayla gazed up at the huge palazzo. "Do you live here alone?"

Louisa nodded.

"You must get lonely in this big place all by yourself." Kayla pressed her lips together, realizing she'd once again said too much. "Sorry. I shouldn't have said that. Sometimes I don't think before I speak."

"It's okay. Most people probably would get lonely." Louisa played with the spoon resting on the saucer. "I moved here to get away from the crowd in Boston."

So Louisa wanted to be alone—perhaps that was the reason for her refusing to host a royal wedding that would bring a huge crowd of onlookers, not to mention the press. So was Louisa an introvert? Or was there another reason she preferred a quiet atmosphere?

First, Kayla had to build some friendly bridges. Hopefully she'd do a better job of that going forward. She genuinely liked Louisa. And she felt sorry for the woman, being so secluded from life.

And then a thought struck Kayla—if she wasn't careful and didn't stop pushing people away, she might end up alone just like Louisa. First, she'd shoved away her ex because she just didn't share his vision of the future. And now, there was Angelo, who had given her one amazing opportunity after the next. And how did she repay him but by having an utter meltdown.

She hadn't spoken to him since he'd stormed out of their suite that morning. He'd never returned. And she'd been so busy losing her cool that she never did get to ask him for help with the fund-raiser.

At the moment, though, she had to focus on Louisa. "You know, we have something in common. I'm new here, too. Except I'm not staying. I'm only here on a business trip with my boss, Angelo Amatucci."

Louisa's cup rattled as she placed it on the saucer. "I met Mr. Amatucci. I suppose he sent you here to convince me to change my mind about the royal wedding?"

Kayla could hear the obvious resistance in Louisa's voice. She'd have to tread lightly if she were to learn anything. "Actually, he didn't send me. He doesn't even know I'm here."

Louisa's eyes widened. "Then why have you come?"

"I need to be honest with you. I am here about the use of the chapel."

Louisa's mouth pressed together in a firm line and she shook her head. "I haven't changed my mind. I told Mr. Amatucci numerous times that I wouldn't agree to it."

"But I was wondering if there was something we could do to make the idea acceptable to you. The fact of the matter is this event could really help the village's economy. And the royal couple is adamant about using the chapel. If it's not available, they'll move on to the next village on their list."

Surprise reflected in the woman's eyes. "It's really that important?"

Kayla nodded. "I haven't lied to you so far. I need you to believe me now."

Louisa's light blue gaze met hers. "I do believe you. As much as I'd like to help, I just can't do it."

Kayla leaned forward. "If you tell me the problem, maybe I can find a way around it."

"I… I just can't have all of those people and reporters poking around here."

Something told Kayla that Louisa had spent more time in front of the paparazzi's cameras than she preferred. Her sympathy went out to the woman, but there had to be a compromise. "What if I make it my personal mission to ensure that you aren't photographed or even mentioned in the press coverage?"

Louisa's eyes opened wide. "You can do that?"

"Remember, we are dealing with royalty here. They have far-reaching hands. I'll let them know about your stipulation, and I'm sure they'll be able to handle the press."

There was a moment of silence. "If you're sure. I suppose it'd be all right."

Kayla resisted the urge to reach out and hug the woman, not wanting to scare her off. Instead, she leaned forward and squeezed Louisa's arm.

"Thank you." Kayla sent her a smile. "Now, if you don't mind, I'd love to hear more about your plans for this place. It's absolutely beautiful here."

Kayla sat back and sipped her coffee. She was happy that she could provide Angelo with this parting gift. With her resignation already typed up on her laptop, it was time for her to print it out.

That evening, Angelo had plans to dine with his brother and sister. While he was off having some family time, she would catch a plane home. Her moment beneath the Tuscany sun was over, and it was time to face the harsh reality of being jobless and heartbroken.

CHAPTER TWENTY-TWO

THIS HAS TO WORK.

Angelo sat in the back of a limousine outside Kayla's apartment. He'd been trying to call her ever since he'd found her resignation letter and the hotel suite empty, but she wasn't taking his calls. He'd just arrived in New York earlier that day after wrapping things up in Italy. Thanks to Kayla, Monte Calanetti was hosting the royal wedding.

He'd have left earlier but he couldn't. Nico and Marianna had been counting on him to stay until the royal decree was announced. Now that he and his siblings had achieved a peaceful relationship, it was as if they were truly a family again—something Angelo hadn't known how much he'd missed. And though Marianna still refused to divulge the name of the father of her baby, she knew without a doubt that both he and Nico were there for her—to support her no matter what decision she made about her future.

He'd returned to New York with orders from his brother and sister to track down Kayla and sweep her off her feet.

Since she'd been gone, he'd had time to realize how black-and-white his life was without her in it. He'd overreacted when he realized that he loved her. But now that he'd come to terms with the depth of his emotions, he hoped what he had planned was enough for her to give him—give them—a second chance.

Thanks to Kayla's very helpful assistant, who was a romantic at heart, he and Pam had secretly been able to piece the fund-raiser back together. And Kayla had been notified that a very special sponsor would be sending a car to escort her to the event.

He hated waiting. It seemed like forever since he'd last

laid his eyes on her. He wanted to march up to her apartment and beg her forgiveness, but he couldn't take the chance that she'd slam the door in his face. Worst of all, she'd end up missing her big night at the fund-raiser. He couldn't let that happen.

Instead, he'd stayed behind in the limo and sent up his driver with instructions not to mention that he was waiting. He needed a chance to talk to Kayla face-to-face. There was so much that he wanted to say—to apologize for—but he still hadn't found the right words.

The car door swung open and Kayla slid in the car next to him. She wore the navy dress he'd given her for their date in the Mediterranean. It hugged all of her curves and dipped in just the right places. It left him speechless that any woman could look so good.

When her gaze landed on him, her eyes opened wide. "What are you doing here?"

"What does it look like?"

Her gaze scanned his dark suit. "It looks like…like you're set for a night on the town."

"And so I am."

"Well, it can't be with me. I'm quite certain that it goes against your rules to date an employee."

"Ah, but what you're forgetting is that you're no longer an employee of Amatucci & Associates." He sighed. "We need to talk."

"Now's not the time. I have a fund-raiser to attend. Alone." She reached for the door handle, but before she could open it, the car started moving.

"And it looks like I'm your ride."

Her gaze narrowed in on him. "Angelo, there's nothing left to say. You said it all back in Tuscany."

"Not everything. Why did you quit without even talking to me?"

"First, I have a question for you. I thought it was strange when an internationally acclaimed rock band wanted to play for our fund-raiser on short notice. No one would tell me how Slammin' Apples heard about our need for help. Now I know. It was you, wasn't it?"

He wasn't so sure by the tone of her voice if this was going to go his way or not. "I was the one who called in a favor or two to have the band show up tonight."

"That isn't just any band. They are amazing. They've won national awards."

Angelo was going to take this all as a good sign. "I'm glad that you are pleased."

Her brows gathered together. "I didn't ask for your help."

"Kind of like how I didn't ask for your help with gaining permission from Louisa to use the chapel."

She shrugged. "I don't quit in the middle of projects."

He hoped this news would thaw her demeanor. "And thanks to you, Monte Calanetti is the official host of the royal wedding."

"Really?" A big smile bowed her lips and eased her frown lines. "I mean, I'm really happy for them."

"I knew you would be. Nico and Marianna send along their sincerest thank-yous." This was his chance to fix things. "I'm sorry about what was said in Tuscany. I never ever meant for you to quit. I need to make things right. You're far too talented to let go."

The light in her eyes dimmed. He'd obviously not said the right thing. For a man who made his fortune coming up with just the right words to turn people's heads and convince them to buy certain products or ideas, why was he messing this up so badly? Why couldn't he find the words to tell Kayla what she truly meant to him?

And then he knew what it was—what was holding him back. He was afraid that she wouldn't feel the same. He didn't want her to close the door on him as his parents had done so many years ago.

But still, he had to do it. He had to put himself out there if he ever wanted to win Kayla back. And that was something he most definitely wanted. After their month in Tuscany —he couldn't imagine another day without Kayla's sunny smile or her beautiful laugh.

Yet before he could sort his thoughts into words, the car pulled to a stop. Without waiting for the driver, Kayla swung the door open.

"Kayla, wait."

Without a backward glance, she faded into the sea of people waiting to get into the convention center. Though he rushed to get out of the car, by the time he did so she'd vanished—lost in the excited crowd.

He'd lost his chance to speak his piece. Maybe showing her how he felt would be better. He just hoped that his other surprise worked, because he just couldn't lose her now, not after she'd shown him that there was a different way to live—one with love in it.

CHAPTER TWENTY-THREE

Kayla's heart ached.

She bit down on the inside of her lower lip, holding in the pain. Her legs were on automatic pilot as they kept moving one after the other, weaving her way through the throng of people. She didn't have a particular destination in mind. She just needed to put distance between her and Angelo before she crumbled in front of him.

After all they'd shared, how could Angelo look at her and see nothing more than an Amatucci & Associates asset? Was that truly all she was to him? The thought slugged her in the chest, knocking the breath from her.

And the sad thing was, for the longest time that's what she thought she'd wanted—Angelo to look at her and see her for all of her creative talent. But now things had changed—they'd changed considerably. Now she wanted him to see oh so much more—to see the woman that loved him with all of her heart.

After passing through security, she made her way to the front of the hall where the stage was set up. The kids of the ICL after-school program rushed up to her.

"Ms. Hill." Her name was repeated in chorus.

"Hi." With so many happy, smiling faces looking at her, it was like a temporary bandage on her broken heart. She forced a smile to her lips. "Is everyone here?"

"Yeah!"

The parents made their way up to her, shaking her hand and thanking her. She wanted to tell them that she hadn't done this, that it had been Angelo, but every time she opened her mouth to explain someone else thanked her.

And then her parents stepped in front of her. Her mother's eyes were misty as she smiled at her and her father looked at her. "You've done us proud."

They drew together into a group hug—something she'd grown up doing. No matter how old she got, some things didn't change.

Kayla pulled back. "But what are you two doing here?"

"Honey—" her mother dabbed at her eyes "—you don't think that we'd miss this after the invitation you sent."

Invitation? That she had sent? Something told her that Angelo had orchestrated this, too. Suddenly she wasn't so upset with him. For him to listen to her and give her this chance to show her parents what she'd accomplished while in New York touched her deeply. She wished he was around so that she could apologize for overreacting in the limo. More than that, she wanted to thank him.

The lights dimmed and one of the security guards approached her. They guided her through the barrier, around the stage and up a set of steps. When she stepped on the stage, she was awed by the number of people in the audience. She wondered if Angelo was out there somewhere or if he'd given up and gone home. The thought of him giving up on her left her deeply saddened.

Oh, boy. This wasn't good. She couldn't think about Angelo. Not here. Not now. She had to keep it together for all of the excited faces in the audience who were counting on her to pull this off. She'd made it this far—just a little longer.

And then as if perfectly timed, pink-and-silver balloons fell from the ceiling, scattering across the stage. *What in the world?*

The head of the outreach program stood at the microphone. Mr. Wilson was an older gentleman who'd already raised his family. Now he and his wife spent their time helping the children enrolled in the program.

"Kayla, join me." He turned to the audience. "Everyone,

please give the mastermind behind this amazing event a round of applause."

The clapping and cheers were unbelievable. And it would have been so much better if Angelo was standing next to her—after all, he'd been the one to save the fund-raiser. Not her.

As she peered at the countless smiling faces, her gaze connected with Angelo's. Her heart picked up its pace. What was he still doing here?

When quiet settled over the crowd, Mr. Wilson continued. "Kayla, would you like to say something?"

Though her insides quivered with nerves, she moved up to the microphone. Back at her apartment, she'd planned out what to say, but now standing here in front of thousands of people, including Angelo, the words totally escaped her.

She swallowed hard and relied on her gut. "I want to say a huge thank-you to everyone who helped with this event. Those people who helped with the planning and the organizing, please stand." Afraid to start naming names and forgetting someone, she stuck with generalities. "This was most definitely a group effort, and what a fabulous group. So please give them a round of applause."

She handed the microphone back to Mr. Wilson before she herself started clapping. Her gaze moved back to the last place she'd seen Angelo, but he was no longer there. She searched the immediate area but saw no sign of him. Her heart sank.

And then a familiar voice came across the speaker system. "Kayla, I know I say everything wrong when it comes to you. But I want you to know that I think you are the most amazing woman I've ever met."

Just then Angelo stepped on the stage and approached her. Her heart pounded in her chest. He stopped in front of her.

"What are you doing?" Heat flamed in her cheeks.

"Kayla, you've opened my eyes and my heart to the way

life can be if I let down my guard." He took her hand in his and gave it a squeeze. "I couldn't imagine doing that with anyone but you."

Kayla's eyes grew misty. It was a good thing that Angelo was holding her hand or she might have fallen over, because everything from her neck down felt like gelatin.

He handed the microphone back to Mr. Wilson as the band started to play. "Can I have this dance?"

He wanted to dance right here? Right now? In front of everyone?

Surely this all had to be a dream. If so, what did it matter if she accepted? She nodded and he pulled her into his arms as the band played a romantic ballad.

Angelo stared deeply into her eyes. "I never thought it was possible for me to feel this way, but I love you."

A tear of joy splashed on her cheek, a trait she inherited from her mother. "I love you, too."

"Does that mean I can rip up your resignation?"

"You still want me?"

"Always and forever."

EPILOGUE

Three months later...

"DO YOU HAVE time for a new account?"

Kayla turned from her computer monitor to face Angelo. Was he serious? It was hard to tell as he was smiling at her. Ever since the charity concert, Angelo had been a different man in the office. He'd let his guard down and put on a friendly face, but one thing that hadn't changed was that he still expected perfection—or as close to it as anyone could get with their work.

"I don't know. Since we succeeded with the royal pitch, we've been flooded with new accounts. It really put Amatucci & Associates heads and shoulders above the competition."

"Yes, it did. And I couldn't have done it without you."

She knew that praise from Angelo didn't come willy-nilly. He truly had to mean it or he wouldn't say anything. "Thank you. But you were the driving force behind it."

"How about we just settle for 'you and I make a great team'?" He approached her and held out his hand to her.

She placed her hand in his, all the while wondering what he was up to. He pulled her gently to her feet, and then his hands wrapped around her waist. What in the world was up with him? He never acted this way at the office —ever.

"About this account—" he stared deep into her eyes, making her heart flutter "—if you decide to take it, it'll be all yours."

The breath hitched in her throat. Was he saying what she thought he was saying? "It'll be my first solo account?"

He smiled and nodded. "I thought that might get your attention."

As much as she wanted to spread her wings, she also didn't want to mess up. "Are you really sure that you want to give me so much responsibility?"

"I'm quite confident that you'll handle it perfectly. You are amazingly talented in so many ways." His eyes lit up, letting her know that his thoughts had momentarily strayed to more intimate territory.

She lightly swiped at his arm. "We aren't supposed to talk about those things at the office. What if someone overheard?"

"Then they'd know that I'm crazy about you."

She couldn't hold back a smile as she shook her head in disbelief at this side of Angelo, which had been lurking just beneath the surface for so long. "Now tell me more about this account. I'm dying to hear all about it before I make up my mind."

"It's a wedding."

"Are you serious?" He nodded and she rushed on. "I don't know. Don't you remember all of the headaches we had with the royal wedding? I couldn't imagine having a nervous bride lurking over my shoulder. I don't think I'd be good at mollifying a bridezilla."

"I don't think you give yourself enough credit. Look at how you handled me and opened my eyes to a thing or two."

"I know. Talk about a lot of hard work to get past your stiff, cold shell—"

"Hey!" His mouth formed a frown, but his eyes twinkled, letting her know that he was playing with her. "There's no need to throw insults."

"I wasn't. I was just stating the obvious." She grinned at him, letting him know that she was playing, too. "We could take an office poll and see which boss they like best—pre-Italy Mr. Amatucci or post-Italy?"

"I think we'll pass on that idea. Besides, you're going

to be too busy for such things now that you have this very special account."

"Special, huh? How special are we talking?"

Angelo reached into his pocket and pulled out a box. He dropped down to one knee. "Kayla, I love you. Will you be my bride?"

With tears of joy in her eyes, she nodded vigorously. "Yes. Yes, I will. I love you, too."

* * * * *